Pete Georgiady's

WOOD SHAFTED GOLF CLUB VALUE GUIDE

7th Edition

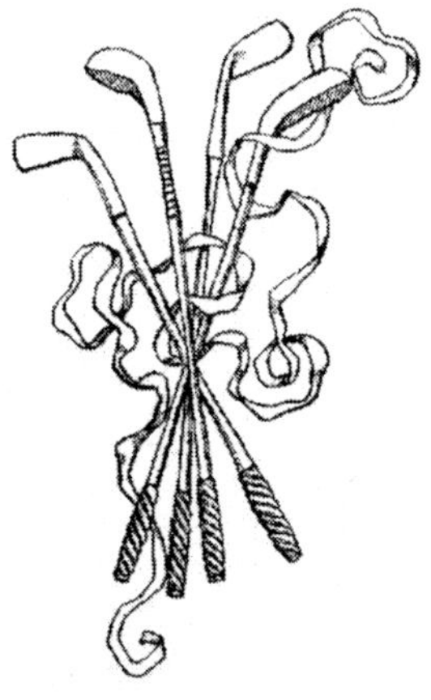

AIRLIE HALL PRESS
KERNERSVILLE
NORTH CAROLINA

2009

Seventh Edition
First Printing

ISBN 1-886752-25-7

Layout by AHP Services
Manufactured in the United States of America
Printed by Battleground Printing and Publishing Company

Published and distributed by:

AIRLIE HALL PRESS
PO Box 981
Kernersville, NC 27285-0981
airliehall@earthlink.net

Cover line art work:
Urquhart Patent adjustable club
computer rendered by master draftsman
Curt Fredrixon, Midlothian, Illinois
Background: Clan Urquhart tartan

To my wife Kay, son Bryan
and to the memory of Doug Glassey,
the old Dundonian
who first pointed me in this direction

Special thanks to ***Rand Jerris, Nancy Stulak, Bruce McBride*** *and the staff of the library and museum of the United States Golf Associationin Far Hills, New Jersey whose cooperation and support is so greatly appreciated;*

to ***Roger Hill*** *and* ***Ralph Livingston III*** *of Grand Rapids, Michigan whose photographic assistance has been invaluable over many years;*

and to the large number of golf collecting friends who helped in many different ways: ***Dan Bagdade, Gene Boldon, Brendan Casey, Andrew Crewe, Dick Durran, Chuck Furjanic, John Gates, Bob Georgiade, Bryan Georgiady, Max Hill, Tom Irving, Tom Johnson, Patty Moran, Chuck McMullin, Bill Nelson, L.R. Rhett, John Roth, John Sherwood, Tom Stewart (of Dayton), Allen Wallach, Gary Wyckoff*** *as well as CAD cover art director* ***Curt Fredrixon****.*

Other books for golf collectors available from

AIRLIE HALL PRESS

Collecting Antique Golf Clubs

Compendium of British Club Makers

North American Club Makers

North American Club and Course Index

Views and Reviews: Golf Clubs in the Trade Press

Cleek Marks and Trademarks on Antique Golf Clubs

The Airlie Hall Club Maker Series:

George Nicoll of Leven

Auchterlonie Hand-Made Clubs

For further information, contact:

AIRLIE HALL PRESS
PO Box 981
Kernersville, NC 27285-0981
(336) 996-7836
airliehall@earthlink.net

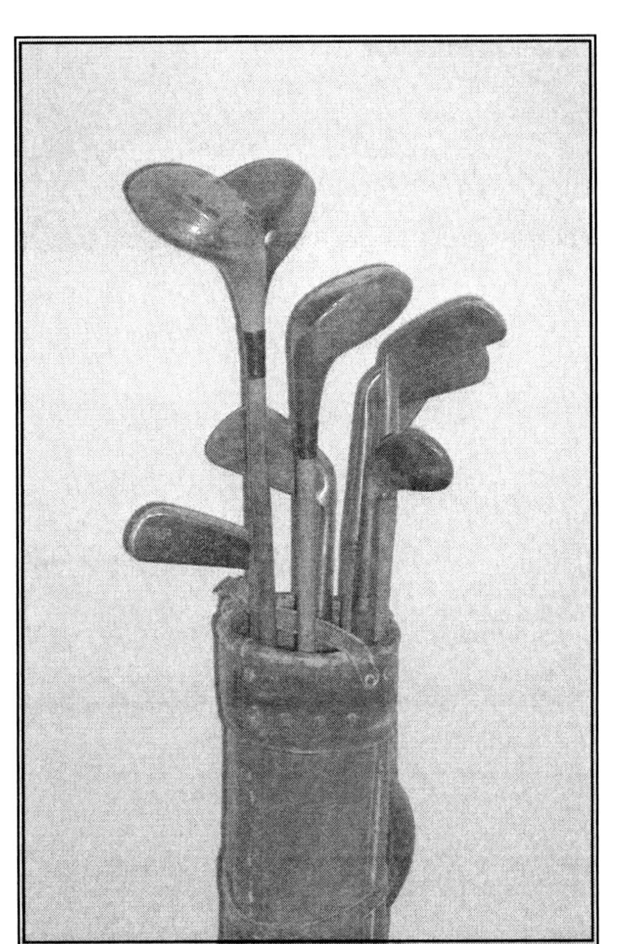

INTRODUCTION

The Philosophy Behind the Value Guide:

"Value," not necessarily "Price"

To make this guide book meaningful, one must understand the concept of **VALUE VERSUS PRICE**. Simply, price is what you pay and value is what the item is worth in relative terms. Those last few words are very important because value is truly relative depending on the individual's point of view.

For collectors of golf clubs, the range of relativity is still broad owing to individual criteria like specialty interests, re-marketablilty, degree of knowledge and amount of discretionary income. In more meaningful terms, there are serious and casual buyers, pure collectors and dealers, affluent and budget minded spenders and to each permutation club values may differ significantly.

The most important idea is that in golf clubs, like many other types of collectibles, there exist many different levels of market. At the economy end are flea markets, garage and estate sales and cleaning out grandma's attic. Expectations here are that things will not cost very much. The other end of the spectrum might include auction sales, dealer catalogs and upscale antique shows where a more knowledgeable, discerning buying public is usually in attendance. Values there are reflected in higher prices.

Today's antique golf club market includes flea markets, collectors' "swap" meetings, public auctions and dealer sales each of which has its own level of value expectations and subsequent prices. Nothing is precise and at any one of these market institutions one can easily over pay just as one can find bargains. Merging the individual characteristics of each buyer with the array of different market place opportunities creates a very complex economic network, one which would be virtually impossible to document with any authority.

Understanding that, the philosophy of this book is elementary. It is to provide a relative market value rather than give a price expectation for a given club at one or more of the various market levels. The relative market value used here is deemed to be somewhere in the middle of the road; greater than a garage sale value but less than a what might be expected in a transaction at the upper end. The relativity issues are to understand which clubs are in $50 tier, the $250 range or the $2,000 neighborhood as well as realizing that a $50 club might only cost $25 at an outdoor market but might sell for $75 among knowledgeable collectors. There are also clubs so populous in their numbers that established collectors rarely are interested. They may sell readily to novice collectors but almost never to experienced collectors--any price. Let this book be your guide, not your absolute price list.

Variance in Highly Valued Clubs

Another rule to observe is that as the relative value of clubs increase, the variance in their actual selling price broadens. Periodically we see a given club sell for one price one day and for another price, drastically different, a day, a month or a year later. Scarcity of supply causes a perception of greater value but greater price often causes a significantly smaller number of potential buyers. The smaller the available supply is, the far less *predictable* price realized will be.

For that reason, more caution should be exercised in transactions involving clubs of greater value. Within this guide, clubs in the upper price range are valued conservatively or a value spread is provided. Again, the real principle is to understand what clubs belong in the upper value bracket and to become more educated as to their standing in the market and their collector value.

Condition as a Function of Value

More than any other principle, condition plays a role in determining the price of an old golf club. An important premise of clubs listed in this guide is that they are in **"very good"** condition, not damaged, distressed, restored or mint. This takes into consideration that golf clubs were meant to be used with a certain amount of force, in outdoor conditions and that wood shafted clubs are at a minimum 70 years old if not older.

Clubs should look old and used but not damaged or abused. The worst case of condition is a club that is damaged and not fully restorable. Clubs with irreparable damage should be avoided and only retained to fill an important void in a collection. A club needing restoration, which can be spruced up without major repair work, is a better club to acquire. Clubs existing today in "as found" condition that need little repair and usually just a light cleaning are very desirable and the closest match to the values provided here.

Those rare exceptions, clubs in excellent or hardly used condition, are few and far between. They generally deserve some degree of upward valuation.

Similarly, overzealous restoration of an antique golf club can render it as worthless as one that has been damaged through abuse. The most often followed philosophy on restoration is to leave the club as closely as possible to its original state. Dirt and rust should be carefully removed, original grips and whipping should be stabilized or, if missing, carefully replaced.

Other Characteristics and Their Affect on Value

There are several other attributes that may or may not alter value. In some cases these are purely of subjective value to the individual collector.

For instance, most collectors are right-handed and tend to avoid collecting left-handed clubs. Some feel they are worth something less than their right-handed club counterparts. Yet there are left-handed collectors that prize the much rarer left-handed clubs and assiduously seek them out.

Some collectors feel that a lady's club holds a lesser value than the corresponding man's model. Just as in the above example, there are lady collectors to whom lady's clubs are very important. In my opinion, the value behind the club is the absolute terms of what it represents and by whom it was made. Theoretically, a man's club and the similar lady's from the same maker should have the same intrinsic value but the perception of the individual buyer also plays an important role, regardless of the validity of accepted valuation rationale.

The vast majority of wood shafted clubs were produced with shafts of hickory grown in America. Every once in a while, a club turns up with a shaft made from another species of wood. Exotic wood shafts made from greenheart, lemonheart, purpleheart, danga wood, lancewood, beef wood, texa ash and bamboo commanded a slight premium for clubs when they were made a century ago. Similarly, they should be viewed as slightly more valuable today.

There are some other variables such as the style and condition of grip and relative straightness of shaft that play a minor part in valuation but in general terms they are not big issues.

The Importance of a Matched Set of Clubs

Since the 1930s, manufacturers have produced product that has given we contemporary golfers a 'set of clubs,' matched set, mentality. The opposite was true a century ago when clubs were purchased one at a time without regard to how they related to the others in the bag. Matched sets were an innovation available only during the last ten years of the wood shafted era (roughly 1925-35). Related or matched sets marked the industry's turn toward more "manufactured" goods and away from the hand made, individualistic quality of older clubs.

In several places in this guide, the existence of certain club models available to collectors as matched sets is shown. In a few cases, values are given for matched sets of clubs. It should be strongly noted that a "set" of clubs could have been between 6 and 11 in number so collectors should know what they are buying. The historical significance of sets is not great and they do not occupy as important a position in golf collecting as do some other classes of clubs. A full set does make for an impressive display, though, and as collectors move into the 21st century interest in and the value of full sets is rising.

Associating Values

Millions of wood shafted clubs were produced from 1850 to 1935. The former year marks the advent of the guttie ball which made the sport more affordable and induced more people to play; the latter year being roughly the year that steel shafted clubs finally won out over wood shafts, once and for all and most manufacturers ceased to offer them for sale. The sheer number of clubs in existence, the individualistic, hand-crafted nature of the product and a shortage of space prevent every club ever made from being listed in this guide. We are trying to cover as many bases as possible without reaching a level of detail so confusing the average collector becomes frustrated.
Associating value from a club listed in this guide to another similar club not listed serves to expand the range of club values for the collector. If you have a *mid iron* in a certain model or by a certain maker and there is only a *mashie* of similar form listed, it's fair to say that those two clubs are closely associated and will probably hold similar values.

There are always exceptions to everything but some good

rules of thumb to understand are:

- A putter is generally worth more than comparable iron clubs (mid iron, mashie, etc.) of the same age, series or set;

- The same is true for wood clubs; woods are usually worth more than irons of the same age, series or set. They are less common;

- Within a group of irons, specialty irons like jiggers, sammies and spade mashies are typically more scarce and worth more than mid irons and mashies;

- Smooth face irons are generally worth more than those with line or dot scored faces;

- Splice head woods are older and more scarce than comparable socket head woods.

Use these generally observed conventions when extrapolating a value to a club which is not listed but where a similar counterpart may be shown.

HOW TO READ THE ENTRIES

Maker Name, Company or 'Brand Name'

[Location city of Company or shop followed by misc. notes]

Anderson, James*

[Anstruther s; often referred to as the "original" cleek and iron maker...]

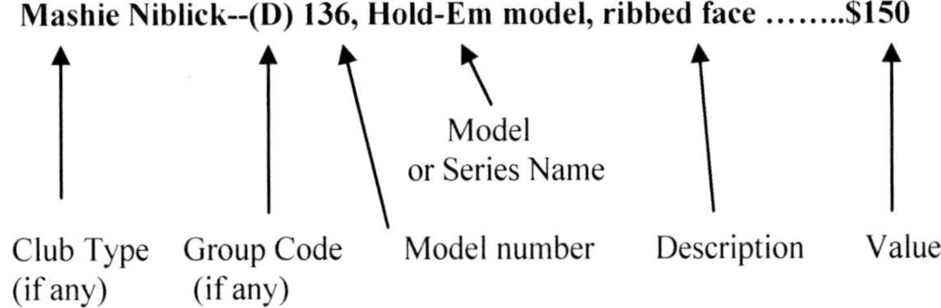

* an asterisk behind maker name indicates a profile of this maker is included in the ***Compendium of British Club Makers***

\+ a plus sign behind maker name indicates a profile of this maker is included in the book ***North American Club Makers***

Group Code: Certain clubs have one salient characteristic that categorizes them into a commonality group. The groups used are:

(A) Aluminum headed clubs, drivers, fairway clubs and putters

(B) Clubs awarded a British patent or design registration

(D) Deep Groove clubs, most of which were also patented

(L) Long nose style clubs including many 19th century woods and certain aluminum head replicas

(S) Semi-long nose style clubs including many 19th century woods and aluminum head replicas

(U) Clubs awarded a United States patent or design registration.

Note: Clubs patented in both the US and Britain are designated by (B) or (U), whichever best reflects the nationality of the patentee or manufacturer

Club makers who have worked in several cities or locations will usually have the primary venue of their work listed followed with *"et.al."* More complete lists of their working locations can be found in the books Compendium of British Club Makers and North American Club Makers.

Club types within maker which have no other delimiter of age or style are group-sorted in the following manner:

Woods--Drivers first followed by Brassies, Spoons, other clubs and 19th century wood putters.

Iron clubs--Listed individually by club type or grouped as **"Iron clubs," Named Irons, Numbered Irons** and **Sets** where the value between types is fairly consistent, followed by

Putters. The category 'Iron clubs' refers to clubs from driving iron to niblick.

Location listings: The city (cities) or club (clubs) where the maker worked is followed by a country code:

e	England
s	Scotland
w	Wales
i	Ireland

American cities are followed by their two letter state Post Office abbreviation (NY, PA, MA)

Canadian cities are followed by a three letter province abbreviation (ONT)

Select cities which need no further definition are followed by no code (London, St. Andrews, New York)

Use of bold italic indicates a photo of the club is shown on that page or an adjacent page. In a few instances, like the waterfall iron on page 269, two diverse makers can make use of the same photo, in this case Spalding and Wright & Ditson listed on page 319.

Model or series name: There is no absolute division between these two terms as they relate to golf clubs but I have observed a general differentiation. Model is normally used where the name is applied to one particular club or pattern, like a singular (Schenectady) putter or (Cran) cleek, or a small group of similar clubs, like Gibson's Genii irons. Series is used when a name is applied across a broad range of clubs or within the context of a set, like Spalding's Kro-Flite irons.

Named Irons: gives a general value for most common irons with names like mid iron, mashie or niblick.

Numbered Irons: gives a value for clubs with numbers (4-iron or 6-iron, etc.). A 4-iron may be listed but values are similar for other numbers within the set or series

Iron clubs: can mean any metal headed club with the characteristics within the model/series listed

CM: when used in the description field means Cleek Mark. A true cleek mark was only found on iron headed clubs but in the context of this guide CM refers to any cleek mark, brand mark, model mark, maker's mark or trade mark found on a wood or iron headed club.

Explanation of Terminology

Listed here are most of the terms used in the club descriptions in this guide. Some are contemporary with the clubs themselves while others are names current collectors have chosen to use.

Complete golf club collecting terminology is contained in ***Collecting Antique Golf Clubs***, an excellent accompaniment to this book.

WOOD HEADED CLUBS

Backweight--Most wood clubs have a lead weight nested in the back of the club. Some later models featured backweights of other materials fixed with screws.

Bulldog head--A design like the **Short** or **Compact** head but with a slight thickening of the toe. It was found mostly in brassies and spoons.

Long nose--Most wood headed clubs made prior to 1890 fit into this category as well as a few made after 1890. They are characterized by long thin heads and always **spliced** to the shaft. They may also be called **Long Headed**. In the guide these clubs are designated with (L).

Semi-long nose--Around the time of the invention of the bulger, shorter headed woods became more fashionable for play. One style, the Bulger head tended to be shorter and broader while the type we call **Transitional** today was narrower, more of a shortened **Long Nose** head. These two forms were also **spliced** to the shaft though after the turn of the century semi-long nose style putters were made with **Socket** heads. In the guide these clubs are designated with (S).

Short head or Compact head--As clubs became more modern wood heads became less long. Many were made very small and can be called short to differentiate them from the more elongated heads popular around 1900.

Socket head--Supplanting the use of the splice head was

the practice of socketing where a tapered hole was drilled into the neck of the wood head and end of the round shaft inserted and glued.

Splice head--The original method of joining the wood head
to the shaft was to plane a side of each flat, glue the two together and wrap with Whipping. This method continued into the first decade of the 20th century.

Stripe top--Popular in the late teens and through the 1920s,
the crown of the club was given a two-tone stain or paint treatment with a contrasting colored stripe. The maker's name was generally stamped in the stripe.

FACINGS FOR WOOD HEADED CLUBS

Fancy Face--In the 1920s, multi-part fiber faces were made in geometric designs or with images inlaid (like the Spalding Kro-Flite crow).

Fiber-- Sometimes called Vulcanite, it first appeared in black and later in the 1900s was available in colors. Fiber was a man made composite of carbon and textile fibers.

Ivorine--A white plastic substance resembling ivory. Also called Ivor or Ivora. Genuine Ivory was also used in premium quality clubs though it tended to crack with use and age.

Leather--The use of the guttie ball on wooden clubs

caused damage to the club face; most 19th century clubs with face inserts used leather tacked in place with small cobbler's nails.

Metal faces included **Steel**, **Aluminum** and **Brass**

Plugs--Some Fancy Face inserts included circular fiber studs to secure them in place. Sometimes referred to as pegs. Actual wooden pegs were used on older face inserts.

IRON HEADED CLUBS

Some Common Design Styles or Characteristics of Iron Clubs

Beveled--Some of the mass on the back of the head has been removed at an angle. Most common are clubs with Beveled Heel and Toe or Beveled Top Edge.

Blade--Also called Regular in the old days, this is a simple flat bar shaped head. This term is also commonly used for the simple putter head.

Carruthers hosel--The first use of a through-bore hosel designed by Thomas Carruthers in 1890 and imitated by many other makers.

Concentric back--Also called Centraject or Concentrated, has the weight concentrated behind the sweet spot and tapering to the top edge and heel and toe.

Diamond back--A back coming to a point behind the sweetspot resembling the facets of a gemstone.

Fairlie model--This "anti-shank" patent featured the front edge of the club head set ahead of the hosel.

Flange sole--Having a flat, broadened sole for extra bottom weight.

Foulis--A style of mashie niblick with an oval head, flat sole and concave face patented by James Foulis and imitated by other makers.

Hollow back--Has weighting top and bottom or at the sides leaving the area behind the sweet spot thinnest.

Maxwell Pattern--A design incorporating holes drilled in the hosel and a flange sole.

Monel--Also called Monel metal, it is a nickel-bronze alloy which proved to be non-rustable.

Musselback--Has a weighted portion on the bottom edge of the club back emulating the shape of a type of sea shell.

Round back--A barrel shaped club back rounded top to bottom. Convex back is a similar variation.

Smith model--The other of the two major "anti-shank" patents, it featured a hosel with a large offset bend. True Smith irons also had extra heel and toe weighting in a Hollow Back design.

IRON CLUB FACE PATTERNS

Concave face--The club face is "dished" or scooped. Dash face--Similar to Line Face but using dashed or hyphenated lines instead of continuous lines.

Diamond face--A pattern of diagonal lines creating a diamond shaped design. Sometimes a dot was struck in each diamond creating a Diamond/dot face.

Dot face--Most common among old clubs was to punch dot shaped indentations in the club face to help grab the ball. Normally these dots were arranged in rows though circular and other shaped patterns also exist.

Line face--The other most common face scoring was to cut horizontal lines.

Smooth face--Until about 1900, virtually all clubs were without face scoring.

Stagdot--This name refers specifically to a pattern of alternating dots and dashes created by MacGregor and imitated by other makers.

** Many additional combinations of Dashes, Diamonds, Dots and Lines exist.

About 1915, deeply grooved club faces, designed to impart backspin to the ball, were in wide use. They were declared illegal in 1922 and not manufactured after that date. Many designs were created and the primary ones are given here. In the guide, all deep groove clubs are designated with the (D) code.

Ball face--Used primarily by Kroydon and Robert Simpson, the face scoring is in a circular "ball" shaped pattern.

Brick face--Vertical and horizontal grooves resembling brickwork.

Corrugated face--Another name for Ribbed.

Grooved face--Extra wide, deep grooves machined into the club face, usually numbering 4 to 6; another name for Slotted.

Rainbow face--Used by Wilson in its Walker Cup series, these concentric semi-circular lines resembled a rainbow.

Ribangled face--The standard Ribbed face with thinner diagonal grooves added.

Ribbed face--Wide, deep grooves, usually numbering 8 to 15 on the club face. The most commonly used deep groove pattern.

Rotary face--A variation of Waffle used by Burke.

Slotted face--Another name for Grooved.

Waffle face--Deep vertical and horizontal grooves in a grid pattern, like a waffle iron.

Waterfall face--Used by Spalding and Wright & Ditson,

the horizontal deep grooves curved downward toward the toe resembling a waterfall.

PUTTERS

Because more attention was given to putter design than all other clubs combined, many terms are used to describe putters. A few of the more prominent ones are listed here.

Bent Blade--A straight hosel with the blade bent back behind the hosel.

Bent Neck-- Like the Park model, the hosel is bent slightly backward.

Blade--The name for the simplest style of putter: a straight flat blade with no offset from the line of the shaft.

Gem--A Concentric shaped blade with the thickest portion of the blade behind the sweet spot.

Gooseneck--With greater bend than the Bent Neck.

Mallet--Usually in aluminum, this head resembles the shape of a wooden driver head.

Offset--Only a slight bend at the bottom of the hosel off setting the blade from the shaft line. Found in some later irons as well.

Park--Named for Willie Park, Jr., the originator of the bent hosel putter. Also called Bent Neck or wry neck.

Ray--A model of aluminum mallet head designed by Ted Ray for the Standard Golf Company. It featured two flat tiers on its crown.

Schenectady--Named for the city where its creator, A.F. Knight resided, this club is the original center shafted mallet putter, later copied by many companies in aluminum or wood.

Note: A more complete glossary of terminology of golf club construction, attributes, form and shape can be found in Collecting Antique Golf Clubs, Airlie Hall Press.

PRICE VS. VALUE, A LAST LOOK

A reminder once again about the difference between "values" and "prices." Some guides make a point of showing actual prices realized at auction, whether it is a live saleroom auction or an online auction like Ebay. There are two very important considerations to me made. First, auctions only reflect the interest shown by the people attending that sale, in person or online. An item may sell for one price today and a week from now may not bring an opening bid, depending on who is in attendance. So a price realized may not be truly indicative unless that same or similar items are sold in that price range on a regular basis.

Also, auctions usually charge a buyer's premium which can range from 10% of the hammer price to as high as 25%. Local sales tax may also be an issue that could add as much as 8% on top of that. A recent Sotheby sale added those fees; an item hammered down for $100 actually cost the wining bidder $135. Thus the "price" reported by the auction house and the "value" (or real cost) to the customer were different. Still further, the consignor gets less than the hammer price after seller's commission so the value to him is even further different than the buyer's value.

Similarly, items sold on the various online auction sites generally require a shipping charge of some sort. With the shipping charge added to the buyer's total and the commission and potential Paypal service charge deducted from the seller's payment, the buyer's and seller's item values are also at variance.

This guide book attempts to set down a basic value within a sensible range, where a price may vary by selling method, place--auction, flea market, online store, antique shop or collector meeting.

During the economic downturn of 2008-2009 golf club values were relatively stable. The number of transactions was down from previous years but the value of individual pieces did not change appreciably. This is due to the fact that old clubs are antiques, there is a finite number and, like most antique collectibles, they tend to appreciate in value. People may have had less disposable income to spend on their hobbies but the clubs that sold were not reduced in price.

FRANCIS OUIMET'S GOLF IRONS

Tom Stewart, the master cleek maker of St. Andrews, had scores of customers who made up the Who's Who of golf in the first third of the twentieth century. Many of those golfers had their names in autograph form stamped on their clubs. The famous amateurs were restricted from doing that lest they lose their amateur status. Two of those were Bobby Jones and Francis Ouimet.

The four irons pictured opposite were part of Ouimet's set and used by him during his stunning 1913 US Open Championship victory when he defeated Harry Vardon and Ted Ray in the play-off. Top to bottom they are his mashie niblick, mashie, mid iron and jigger. As clubs, they are fairly standard Stewart irons made around 1910.

These clubs had been privately owned for many years until they were acquired by the USGA Museum in Far Hills, New Jersey in 2006 with authenticated provenance. They are on display at the new Arnold Palmer Golf History Center at Golf House opens in autumn, 2008.

It is rare to locate the actual clubs used by early champions, especially from such an historic event . These clubs are an incredibly important part of the history of golf in America.

Used in the 1913 US Open

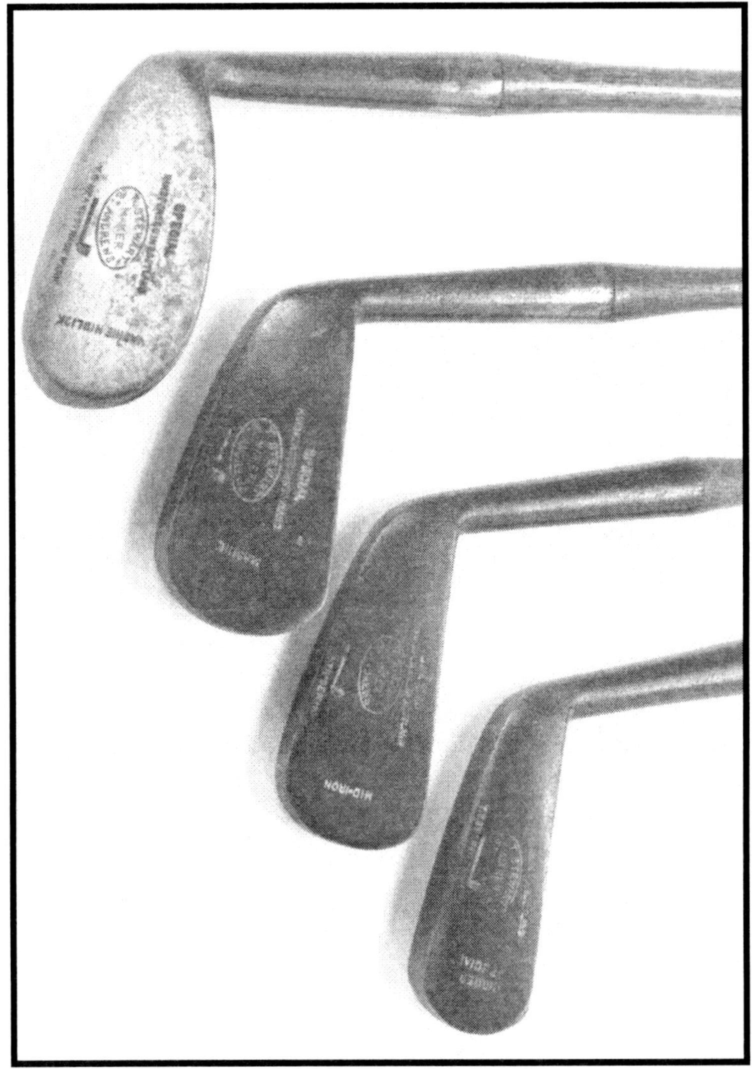

Photo courtesy of the USGA Archives

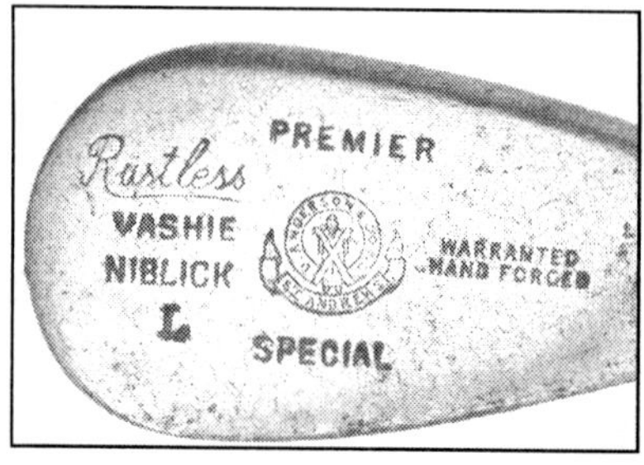

On some later clubs, D. Anderson & Sons used the image of St. Andrew as a mark.

The fox head was the mark used by W.&G. Ashford. This short blade lofter or niblick had a concave face.

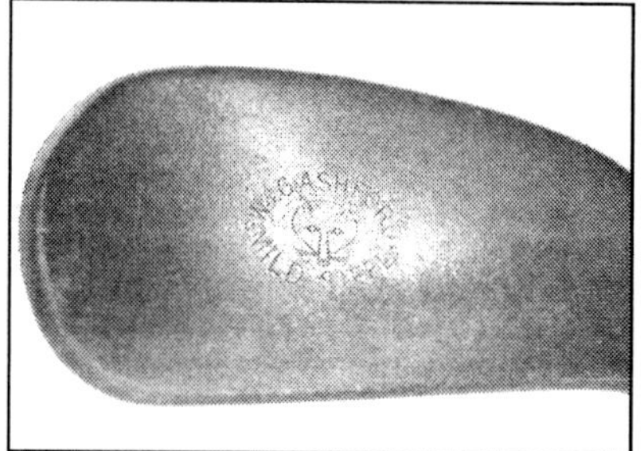

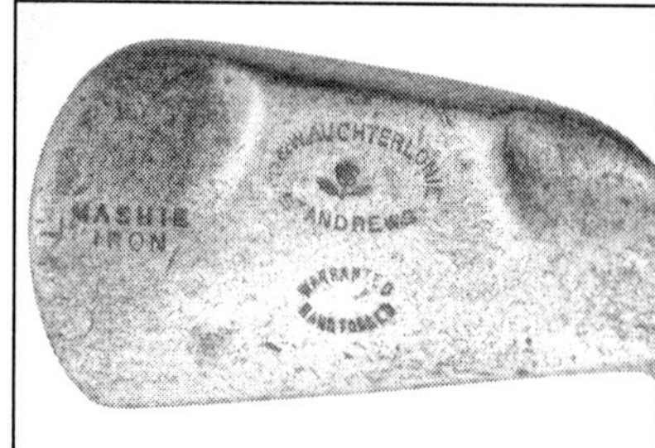

This mashie iron used the same musselback design that originated on the Auchterlonies' approaching cleek.

A

Abercrombie & Fitch

[New York department store]

Driver--(U) Master model, patent face insert with 7 ivory plugs $150
Brassie--Socket head, stripe top $50
Spoon--Socket head, face insert $65
Jigger--H1 model, round back, dot face, monogram CM $45
Mashie--Made by Kroydon $35
Mashie--Stainless, 2 AF CMs, line face $45
Mashie--Model GS3, Burke Monel $60
Mashie Iron--Monel metal, line face $50
Mashie Niblick--Line face, stainless, monogram CM $30
Mid Iron--Model WG5, marked "Burke Monel" $60
Niblick--Model J1L musselback, Monel $65
Niblick--Model NO, Monel $60
Niblick--Model WH9, Burke Monel $60
Putter--Model P1L, Monel blade by Burke $60
Putter--Model WH10, Burke Monel $60
5-Iron--Y model (youth), line face $25

'Aberdeen'

[These clubs are named Aberdeen but each was made by a different company. Cleek marks and model numbers are used to identify the respective maker]

Driver--made by B.G.I., splice head, model number on shaft $225
Driver--(U) Fork splice, made by B.G.I. $400
Mashie--Name in arc, made by MacGregor $25
Mid Iron--Line face, round back, Burke bee & flower CM $35

Abraham & Strauss

[New York department store]

Irons--Lido model, line face, stainless ....$25 each

'Acme'

Cleek--(B) 'The Acme', smooth face, Carrick cross CM $300

Adams, David

The "Gourlay Putter" was produced for Alex Aiken and featured a bent neck, notched hosel and deep faced blade.

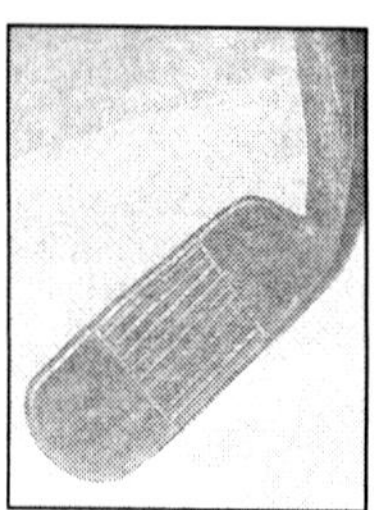

[Glasgow]
Driver--Splice head $125
Brassie--Small socket head........ $60
Lofter--Concentric back, line face $60
Mashie--Diamond back, Anderson arrow CM, line face $60
Mashie Iron--Nicoll hand CM, dot face $50
Putter--Blade $60

Adams, Jeff
Putter--(A) Coordination model, center shaft, boat shaped head with pointed back $400

'Aim Rite'
[Thomas E. Wilson Co. trade mark appearing on a majority of their clubs, often on the sweet spot of the face. "Aim Rite" clubs listed under Wilson Company, Thomas E.]
Iron clubs--Line face, "Aim Rite" in circle on face $25

Aitken, Alex*
[Gullane s]
Driver--Splice head, transitional shape........ $250
Driver--Socket head $75
Driver--Short splice head, fiber face insert $200
Brassie--(S) Splice head $500
Brassie--Bulger splice head $750
Wooden Mashie--Pear shaped splice head with dished face $400
Iron--Smooth face, shaft stamp $100
Putter--(B) Short hosel and blade with very deep face $400
Putter—(B) Notched blade at hosel, reg., # 10745, Gourlay moon/star CM $125

'Alco'

Mashie Niblick--Bronze-type metal oval head, ALCO in star shape CM, line face $75

Alexander & Company, George*
[London department store]
Mashie--Dot face, made by Forgan $30

Alexander, G.
Driver--(B) Hammer head shaped wood with 2 hitting faces $3,000

Allan, John*
[Westward Ho! e and Prestwick s]
Playclub--(L) Brown finish, thick grip, marked "J. Allan" $4,500
Long Spoon--(L) Dark colored beech head, minor worm damage . $3,500
Short Spoon--(L) Lofted face slightly damaged $4,000
Driver--(S) Transitional head, dark color $1,000
Putter--(L) Dark color $2,500
Putter--(S) Thornwood head $2,750

'Alloway'
Putter--(B) Oval head with red guttie face insert $3,500

Allday Company, P.G.*
[Birmingham e]
Putter--Northwood brand, gun metal blade, monogram CM $75
Putting Cleek--(A) Northwood brand, model A, mallet head $100
Putter--Northwood brand, Brown-Vardon type in gun metal, steel face $250
Putter--Northwood brand, later splice wood head $125
Putter--Northwood model E, wood head, lead weights $95

Allen Putter Company
Putter--(U) Adjustable, two lofts, swivel center shaft $1,500
Putter--(U) Adjustable, hosel screws to lock angle $750

Allied Golf Company
Driver--Stripe top, socket head $35

Altman, Albert J.
[London]

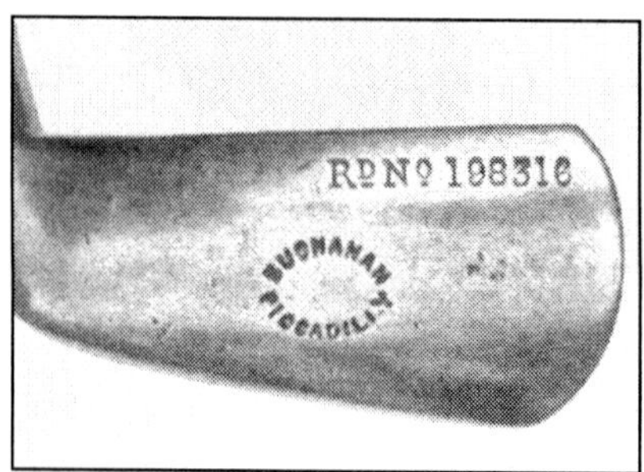

Albert Altman registered his design in 1894 for a club with a crimped hosel. It was sold through Buchanan's London store.

Lofter--(B) Smooth face, round back, crimped hosel $225

Altman & Company, B.
[New York department store]
Driver--Stripe top socket head $75
Brassie--Stripe top, 'Selected,' ivory insert $100
Mashie--Made by Everbrite, stainless, dot face $35
Mashie--Name in script, stainless, dot face $30

Ampco Metal Golf Club Company+
[Milwaukee, WI; Ampco metal is a bronze-like alloy, Dow metal is a harder version of aluminum. All Ampco irons were made from Ampco metal]
Driver--Dow metal head, Ampco face insert...................................... $175
Brassie--Dow Metal head, Ampco metal face insert $175
Jigger--Line face $80
Driving Iron--Line face, name in box $75
Mid Iron--Lie face--Marked "more yards per stroke" $75
Mashie--Line face $75
Niblick--Marked "more yards per stroke", line face $80
Putter--Thick blade $100
Set of 8 irons $750

An Company, The
Iron--Juvenile, large bee CM $40
Putter--Juvenile blade, line face, large bee CM $50

The firm of Anderson, Anderson and Anderson, India rubber merchants, sold clubs marked with this highly detailed escutcheon mark.

Anderson, Anderson & Anderson, Ltd.*
[London waterproof manufacturers and retailers also selling golf requisites]
Driver--Splice head, pear shaped head $350
Driver--Socket head, escutcheon CM $250
Driving Iron--Company escutcheon with two globes CM, also
Anderson arrow CM, smooth face $150
Mashie--Company escutcheon, line face $150
Mashie-Rustless, beveled toe, large crown CM $75
Putter--(B) J. Anderson bronze mallet, steel face, escutcheon CM .. $400
Putting Cleek--Company escutcheon & Gourlay moon/star CMs $200
Putter—Bronze mallet w/ steel face, escutcheon CM $200

Anderson & Blyth*
[St. Andrews]
Driver--Juvenile socket head $75
Driver--Socket head, white fiber insert $90
Driver--Invincible model, large socket head, fiber face insert $125
Brassie--Socket head, name in arc $80
Cleek--Stewart pipe CM, line face $50
Cleek--Short blade, dot face $50
Iron--Push model, deep face, dot face $100
Mashie--(B) Weymiss model, bi-level back $90
Putter--(S) Splice head $600
Putter--Wood splice head, fiber slip in sole $200
Putter--Wood splice head, brass face insert $250

Anderson & Gourlay*
[St. Andrews]
Approach Mashie--Sovereign series, 3-facet back, A & G CM $75
Driving Iron--Wellington model, line face $70
Mashie--Round back, dot face $65

Numbered Irons--Diamond Iron model, line face, diamond back, monogram A & G CM $65
Putter--Small iron mallet head, shaped like Ray model, A & G CM $150

Anderson, D. & W.*
[St. Andrews]
Cleek--Smooth face $250
Iron--Smooth face, name stamped in oval $250
Lofter--Smooth face $300

Anderson & Sons, D.*
[St. Andrews; David Anderson, son of "Old Da'" and younger brother of Jamie, the champion, was assisted in this business by his six sons]
Driver--Spliced-head, Texa ash shaft $350
Driver--(S) Splice head, leather insert $450
Driver--Supreme model, ivorine insert, stripe top socket head $100
Driver--Semi-circular black fiber insert in face $125
Brassie--Socket head $75
Brassie--Swilcan model, large socket head $95
Spoon—SH, marked Bulldog, semi-circle face insert $125
Cleek--Smooth face, name in oval $100
Cleek--marked "Diamond Cleek", diamond back, line face $65
Driving Iron--Dot face $50
Driving Iron--Zenith model, dash face $50
Driving Iron--Glory model, diamond back, line face $65
Jigger--Glory series, diamond back, dot face $75
Jigger--Monarch series, dot face, beveled heel and toe $75
Lofter--Single fern frond CM, smooth face $225
Mashie--(B) G.F. Smith model (anti-shank), hollow back, line face $200
Mashie--Glory series, diamond back $75
Mashie--Smooth face, tiny Millar thistle CM, compact blade $150
Mashie--Smooth face, Condie single CM $250
Mashie Niblick--Premier series, St. Andrew CM, stainless, line face... $50
Niblick--Large size, line face $60
Niblick--Medium size, dot face, diamond back $75
Niblick--Small head, smooth face $300
Putter--Bulge back, dot face $75
Putter--Excelsior model, concentric back, diamond/dot face $100

This iron from R. Anderson & Sons was one of the first of several center shaft irons made in the 1890s.

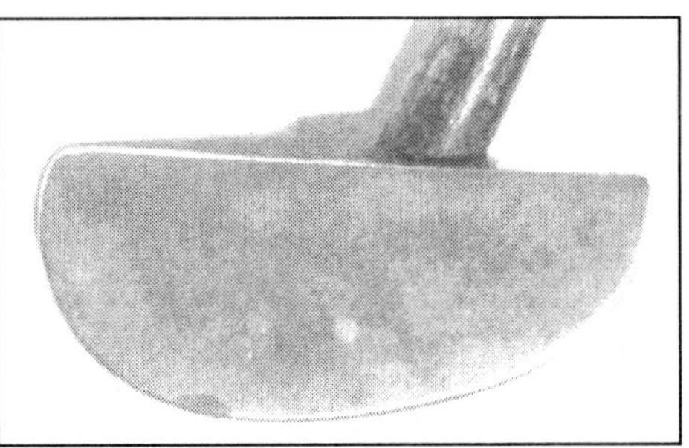

Putter--Triumph model, offset blade, peaked top edge $150
Putter--100 model, concentric shaped head $100
Putter-Glory series, diamond back $85
Putter--Iron blade ....$ 50
Putter—Ace model, blade w/ concentric back $40

Anderson & Sons, R.*
[Princes Street, Edinburgh]
Driver--(B) short head, through-bore center shaft $4,250
Driver--Socket head $125
Driver--Socket head, leather face insert $150
Driver--(A) Small head, checkered face $350
Driver—(B) Wood head with leather wrap all around *(page A)*..***$2,250***
Brassie--(A) Marked "Cleek", small head $500
Cleek--C.1895, smooth face, greenheart shaft $150
Iron--(B) Crescent shaped center shaft head $1,500
Lofter--(B) Crescent head, center shaft $2,000
Lofter--Smooth face, large head, Spalding Gold Medal $65
Mashie--Compact blade, smooth face $80
Putter--(S) Wooden socket head..250
Putter--Blade, heavy hosel 100
Putter--Gun metal blade 150

Anderson, Carl H.
[Lake Geneva, WI, et al]
Driving Iron--Super Stroke series, monel, line face $45

Anderson, David*
[Bromley & Bickley G.C. e]
Brassie--Socket head, shaft stamp $60

Anderson, Grant
Jigger-Acorn Brand, acorn CM, dot face $60

Anderson, James*
[Anstruther s; often referred to as the "original" cleek and iron maker, James began the club head forging business in 1865 and died in 1895. The firm continued into the 1930s under his son Alex. Clubs marked with the name in a 1/2" diameter circle generally date from the 19th century. The name mark in the 5/8" circle and the name mark within two concentric circles are 20th century clubs]
◇◇Smooth face irons (1/2" dia. CM unless noted)
Cleek--C.1875, long thin blade, 4 1/2" hosel with deep nicking $500
Cleek--Made for Goudie & Co., convex back, double circle CM $75
Iron--Smooth face $100
Iron--Double circle CM $75
Lofting Iron--C.1890, long blade, slightly dished face, thick hosel, dark stained shaft $400
Lofting Iron--C.1890, large F.H. Ayers markings on shaft, slightly concave $300
Mashie--Double circle CM, short blade $80
Mashie--C.1890, short head, deep face blade, heavy hosel $350
Mashie Iron--(B) Fairlie model, serial number $200
Niblick--C.1895, medium size head $150
Niblick--C.1885, small head $800
Niblick--(B) G. Lowe's patent (anti-shank), like Fairlie model, serial number, smooth face, small head $300
Niblick--Small head, smooth face, Sherardized, marked for Army & Navy Store $400
Putter--(B) Kurtos model, convex face and back $300
Putter--Deep face blade $300
Putter--C.1895, thick blade and hosel $200
Putter--Gun metal blade $225

◇◇Scored face irons showing model number where applicable
Approaching Cleek--38, musselback, dot face $60
Cleek--3, dot face $60
Cleek--4, centraject-type head $65
Cleek--127, musselback $65

The Anderson of Anstruther model 2 driving iron with round sole .

Cleek--(B) 1919, "Non Slice" model $80
Driving Iron—2, rounded sole, smooth face $65
Driving Iron--85, round sole, line face, arrow CM $65
Driving Iron--121, dot face, arrow CM $50
Jigger--88, musselback, dot face, arrow CM $60
Jigger—Very large double circle marking, Sherardized $60
Mashie iron—model 15, arrow CM $45
Mashie--Double circle & arrow CMs, line face $50
Mashie--Royal Crown brand, line face $55
Mashie--21, diamond back, arrow CM $50
Mashie--22, regular back, arrow CM $40
Mashie--24, flange sole $50
Mashie--(D) 54, arrow CM, ribbed face $125
Mashie Niblick--Magic model, oval head, line face $60
Mashie Niblick—29, flat sole, arrow CM $40
Mashie Niblick--115, Maxwell pattern $85
Mashie Niblick--(D) 136, Hold-Em model, oval shaped head, ribbed face $150
Mashie Niblick—138, oval head, arrow CM $40
Mashie Niblick--30, thick sole, dot face $60
Mid Iron--6, line face $50
Mid Iron—10, dot face, arrow CM $40
Mid Iron--Juvenile, marked B $50
Niblick--33, concave dash face, arrow CM $150
Niblick--150, large head, arrow CM, line face $80
Niblick--Vardon autograph model, medium size head, line face $125
Pitcher--41, round sole $100
Sammy--2, dot face, notched at hosel $65
Sammy--5A, round back, dot face $65
Sammy--6, thick sole $65
Sammy Iron--133, dot face $65

Putter--51, steel blade $50
Putter—63, steel blade, arrow CM $45
Putter--68, dot face, peak on top edge $100
Putter--91, iron blade, notched at hosel $100
Putter--105B, iron blade $65
Putter--151, offset blade $65
Putter--Magic model, thick sole, beveled toe, arrow CM $80
Putter--Blade with horizontal weight ridge on back $150
Putter--(B) Small gun metal mallet head, steel face insert $250
Putter--As above with wood face insert $350
Putter--(B) The Coaxer model, iron blade, bent neck, arrow CM $125
Putting Cleek--(B) Twisted neck, reg. # 277771 .... $125
Putting Cleek—(B) Regd. number 277771, gun metal** (page A)* ***$150

Anderson, James ("Jamie")*
[St. Andrews; eldest son of "Old Da'" Anderson. Three time Open Champion, worked for Robert Forgan, several other firms and in his own shop in St. Andrews 1859-1905]
Playclub--(L) C.1870, beech head, thin shaft, marked "J. Anderson" $2,500-7,000
Playclub--(L) In juvenile size $2,500
Putter--(L) C.1880 .... $3,000-4,000
Putter--(S) C.1895 .... $1,500-2,000

Anderson, Joe*
[Perth s]
Driver--Splice transitional head $300
Driver--Socket head, circle-K CM $100
Mashie--Stainless, O K Brand, dot face $50
Mid Iron--O K Brand, line face $35
Mid Iron--Smooth face, OK CM, made for Murrie & Sons $75

Joe Anderson, the prolific club maker from Perth, registered the "Quiksite" putter in the late 1920s.

This Anderson putter can be dated precisely to 1910, the year he moved to St. Louis and the year he passed away.

Putter—(B) Quiksite model with aiming notch in top edge. $80
Putter--(A B) Mallet head, offset with extreme goose neck $450
Putter—Steel blade, Stewart pipe CM $80
Putter--Vardon style, rounded top, shallow face $100
Putter--C.1910, splice wood head $250
Numbered Irons--OK Brand, stainless, line face, fancy
large OK monogram CM $40

Anderson, R.C.B.
[Saratoga Springs, NY]
Driver--Rex model, socket head $75
Spoon--Splice head, deep face, marked for Saratoga & Troy $325
Spoon--Small splice head $300
Mid Iron--Smooth face $75

Anderson, Willie
[Baltusrol, St. Louis, et al, America's first repeat Open Champion (1903-5) who later endorsed clubs made by Worthington Mfg. Co.]
Driver--Socket head, made by Worthington Mfg. Co. $200
Driver--Socket head, steel face insert (5-screw), name in oval $125
Cleek--Smooth face, marked "W. Anderson, Champion" $150
Lofter--Concentric back $150
Niblick--Smooth face, St. Louis $100
Putter--Iron blade, name in oval $90
Putter—St. Louis-St. Augustine address $125

Anderson's Rubber Company, Ltd.
Putter--LOTSIRB model in Hawkins Never Rust steel $75

Annan, C.
Driver--(B) Compressed socket head $200

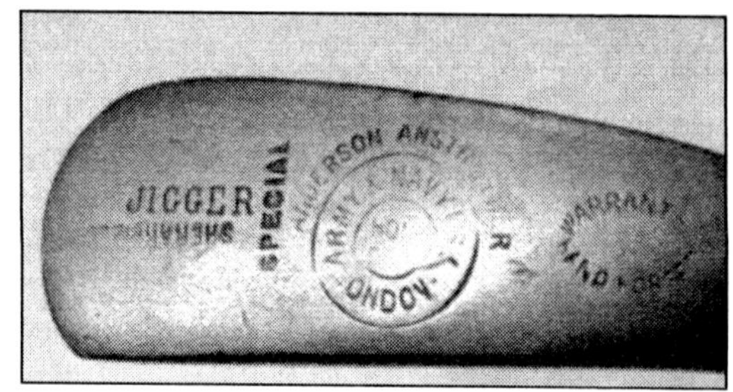

A jigger from the Army & Navy CSL store with an unusual large circular mark.

I'Anson, John
Driver--Splice head, leather face insert $300
Cleek—Monel metal with three hollow chambers in sole $1,000

'Argyle'
Brassie--Socket head $50
Iron--Smooth face, u-over-u CM $50
SET--Juvenile clubs (brassie, mid iron, mashie, putter) $150

Arlington Manufacturing Company+
[Arlington, NJ; a division of the Kempshall Rubber Company. Also see Kempshall]
Driver--Black Pyralin composition socket head $600
Putter--Semi-round, center shaft Pyralin head $400

Army & Navy Cooperative Stores, Ltd.*
[London department store making some of their own clubs]
Driver--(L) C.1890, late long nose period, beech head $2,000
Driver--Short splice head $200
Brassie--(S) Splice head, beech wood $450
Cleek--Smooth face, name in arc, "C" $150
Iron--Smooth face, marked in block letters "A & N CSL" $250
Jigger—Very large double circle Anderson marking, Sherardized $60
Mashie--Smooth face, "A & N CSL" mark $250
Mashie--Smooth face, marked "Deep Face Mashie" $175
Mashie--Line face, stainless, name in oval $50
Lofter--Smooth face, "A & N CSL" $300
Niblick--Medium size head, smooth face, "A & N CSL" $350
Niblick--Medium size head, smooth face, heavy thick blade, oval name stamp, also marked "Sherardized" $275

Niblick--Small head, smooth face, Sherardized,
Anderson small circle CM $400
Putter--(S) C.1895, wood head, shaft stamp $750
Putter--Blade, "A & N CSL" $250
Putter--Hold Fast series, iron blade $200
Putter--Hold Fast series, gun metal blade, small Anderson CM $225
Putter--(B) Anderson gun metal mallet, steel face $250

'Arrow'
[Eagrow Co. brand name]
Irons--Stainless, line face $30

'Arrowflite'
[Golf Specialty Co. brand name]
Mashie--(D) Ribbed face, stainless $100
Mashie--Stainless, line face $45

'Arrowline'
Mid Iron--Par model, line face $25

Ashford, W. & G.*
[Birmingham e]
Driver--(B) Skibbie model, combination wood &
aluminum head $3,500
Brassie--(S) Transitional beech head, one piece sewn grip,
foxhead CM $800
Cleek--Smooth face, Fore Flags CM $200
Lofter--Smooth face, sewn grip, foxhead CM, concave face $250
Mashie--Smooth face, foxhead CM, sewn grip $250
Mashie--Smooth face, foxhead CM, cork grip $400
Putter--(S) Foxhead CM, beech head, sewn grip $900
Putter--Bent blade model, foxhead CM $300
Putter--Iron blade, foxhead CM $250

Ashland Manufacturing Company+
[Chicago]
Mashie Niblick--(D) Model 9-7, ribbed face $100

ATCO
[Alex Taylor brand name; also see Taylor Co., Alex.]

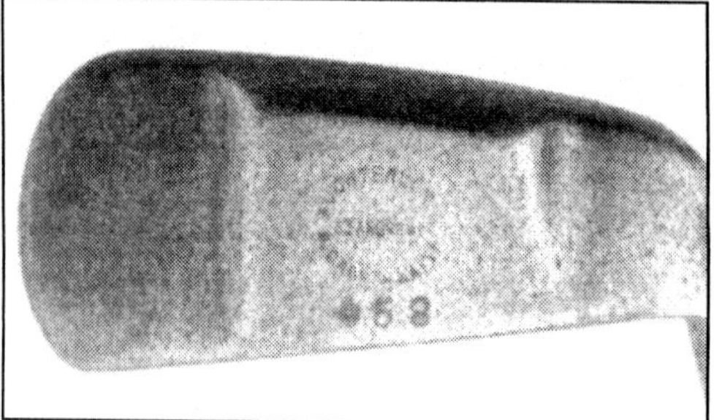

Auchterlonie & Crosthwaite registered the Approaching Cleek in 1894, the first of the musselback irons.

Mashie--Stainless, line face $25
Mashie Niblick--Dot face $35
Putter--Burke model 69 .... $75

Auchterlonie & Crosthwaite*
[St. Andrews]
Driver--(S) Boxed straight line name stamp $1,800
Brassie--Short transitional splice head $550
Approaching Cleek-(B) Registered model, musselback, SF, names in circle, registration (sequence) number $250
Iron--Center shafted, smooth face, 2 fern frond CM $2,000
Lofter--Smooth face, two fern frond CM $300
Mashie--Smooth face, oval stamp $150
Putter--Gun metal blade, boxed straight line stamp $250
Putter--Gun metal blade, straight name, 2 fern frond CM $300

Auchterlonie, D. & W.*
[St. Andrews; brothers David and Willie started this firm in 1896]
Driver--(S) Transitional beech head $500
Driver--C.1910, splice head, shaft stamp $150
Driver--Socket head, made for Alex Taylor Co., shaft stamp $60

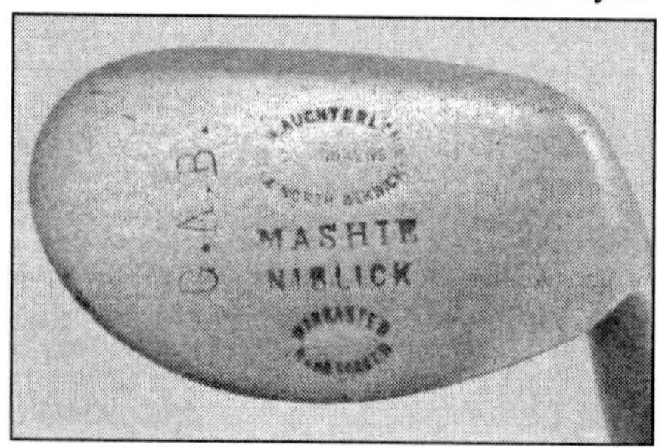

A Foulis-style mashie niblick made by D & W Auchterlonie during the period 1909-1915 when they had a shop at N. Berwick.

Laurie Auchterlonie made and sold his Professional model putter while at the Glen View club.

Driver--The Champion series, splice transitional beech head $200
Driver--Gold Medal series, socket head $75
Driver--Auchtie model, stripe top socket head $80
Driver--Dreadnought model, socket head, warship CM $150
Brassie--(S) C.1900-1910 .... $700
Brassie--Socket head, made for Wanamakers $75
Brassie--Socket head, name in oval $60
Baffing Spoon--(S) C.1896, brown head, shaft stamp $1,200
Spoon--Socket head $95
Approaching Cleek--(B) Smooth face, musselback, sequence number, names in arc, Stewart pipe CM $200
Cleek--Musselback, line face, made by Stewart, pipe CM $100
Iron--Smooth face, made by Condie, rose CM $80
Mashie Iron—Musselback, smooth face, Condie rose CM $100
Mashie--Boy's (juvenile), rose CM, dot face $60
Mashie--Dot face, small arrow in circle and Condie rose CMs $60
Mashie Niblick--Foulis style, smooth flat face $100
Niblick--Smooth face, small head, golf club CM $300
Niblick--Smooth face, medium head, arc name stamp $100
Named Irons--D & W Auchterlonie model,
Stewart pipe CM, scored face $50
Numbered Irons--Line face, Stewart pipe CM $45
Putter--(S) C.1900, transitional shaped splice head $600
Putter--C.1915, wood splice head, fiber slip in sole $125
Putter--Line face, pipe CM $50
Putter—Bronze blade, Stewart serpent CM $100
Putter--(B) The Balance model, wood head $300
Putting Cleek--(B) Chain link face markings, horizontal weight bar on back, Condie rose CM $200
[Registered Putting Cleek also found with Stewart pipe CM or Auchterlonie golf club CM]

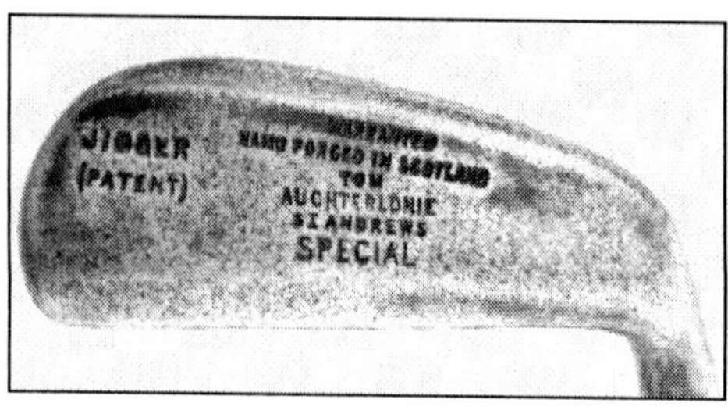

The form of this Tom Auchterlonie jigger is identical to the ITZ IT series but without the ITZ

Putting Cleek—Similar to registered model but without chain face markings, Stewart pipe CM $125
Putting Cleek--Dot face, long blade, pipe CM $60

Auchterlonie, Laurence+
[Brother of David, Willie & Tom, 1902 US Open champion, Western Open Champion; Glen View, IL; later, St. Andrews s]
Irons—Pipe Brand, marked for Glen View ....$100 each
Putter--Professional Model, topspin style blade with weighting on top edge of blade $200

Auchterlonie, Tom*
[St. Andrews]
Woods--The Ellice series, stripe top .... $75 each
Woods--Itz It Itz In series, double stripe top, name in script .... $125 each
Woods--Name stamp shaped high at ends, socket head............... $85 each
Driver—Splice head, de luxe model $175
Driving Iron--Name in circle with small arrow, Condie rose CM $60
Mashie—Maxwell pattern, drilled hosel, Condie rose CM $85
Mashie Niblick--(B) Smith model (anti-shank), pipe CM $150
Mashie Niblick--Line face, stainless, Gibson star CM $50
Jigger--(B) Itz It Itz In model $85
Jigger—(B) Patented model without ITZ IT marks $125
Push Iron—Straight line stamp, pipe CM $100
Sammy--(B) Itz It Itz In model $100
Iron clubs--Named, line face, Stewart pipe CM .... $60 each
Iron clubs--Numbered, scored face, Stewart pipe mark .... $60 each
Iron clubs—straight line name stamp (no pipe CM) .... $50 each
Iron clubs—De luxe model, Nicoll hand CM .... $60 each
Named Irons--(B) Itz It Itz In series, line face .... $75 each
Numbered Irons--Stainless, line face, straight line name stamp . $45 each
Putter--(B) Holing-Out model, prism shaped head $250

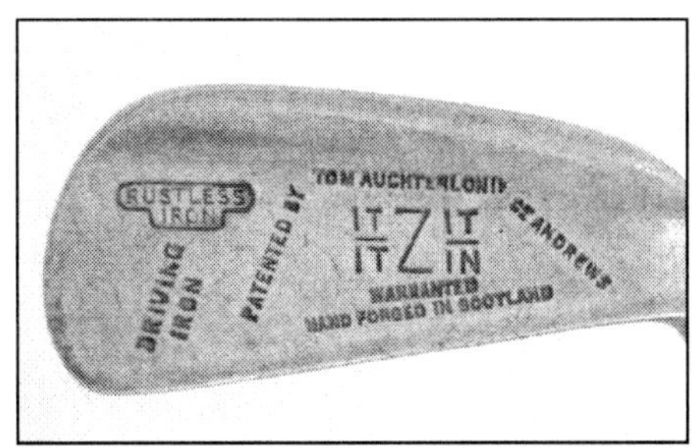

The ITZ IT series was Tom Auchterlonie's best seller and had all the attributes of a modern iron club.

Putter--(S) C. 1925, wood socket head $250
Putter--The Ellice series, iron offset blade $60
Putter--Stainless blade, straight line name stamp $50
Putter--(B) Itz It Itz In model, blade with small flange........................ $125

Auld, Robert
[Dunbar s]
Spoon--Small splice head, light color, leather face insert $150
Spoon--Socket head $95
Driving Iron--Smooth face, Stewart pipe CM $60
Putter--Iron blade, name in oval $50

Aveston, Willie*
[Cromer e]
Brassie--Transitional splice head $250

Ayers, F.H.*
[London]
Driver--(L) Dark color, leather face insert $2,000
Driver--(S) C.1890, shaft stamp $1,600
Driver--(B) Dagnall model, socket head $1,000
Driver--(B) P.A. Vaile model, gooseneck socket head $650
Driver--The Olympic model, socket head $150
Iron clubs--Smooth face, marked for Army & Navy Store (A & N CSL) or Ayres:

Cleek--Marked "C" $150
Driving Iron--Marked "D" or "DI" $150
Iron--Marked "I" $125
Mashie-Marked "M" $125
Mashie-(Boy's) Marked "BM" $200

Driving Mashie-Marked "DM" $175
Lofter-Marked "L" $175
Mashie-Marked "LM", ladies mashie $150
Niblick-Marked "N", small head $500
Putter-Marked "P", steel blade $150

Iron--(B) The P.A. Vaile model, swan neck hosel, dot face $600
Iron--A2, Harry Vardon autograph, Maltese cross CM $75
Jigger--Dot face, small Maltese cross CM $65
Mashie--Line face, small Maltese cross CM $60
Mashie Iron—G4, scalloped heel & toe, Maltese cross CM, dot face $50
Mashie Niblick—(D) Cert model, slotted face, Maltese cross CM $125
Mid Iron--The Cert model 2, square extension on sole, Maltese cross CM $200
Mid Iron--Line face, small Maltese cross CM $60
Mid Iron—Vardon autograph model, Maltese cross CM $75
Niblick--Smith-type (anti-shank) $200
Niblick--Large head, Maltese cross CM, line face $75
Sammy—Vardon autograph, Totteridge mark $75
Putter--Gun metal blade, thick hosel $175
Putter--(S) C. 1895, beech wood head, short thick shaft $800
Putter--(A B) The Cert model, square head with 4 hitting surfaces $1,200
Putter--(B) The Cert model, made from wood $2,500
Putter--(A) CSP model (early version), like Schenectady, shaft in exact center of head $325
Putter—S S model, oval head, long thin hosel $85
Putter—S24, stainless blade, Maltese cross CM $50
Putter--(A) Tru-Put model, Schenectady style, fiber face insert $250
Putter--Oak Brand, made for W.G. Oke, oak tree CM $80
Putter—Buffalo model, stainless blade, buffalo CM $50

The F.H. Ayres model S S putter had a long, pencil thin hosel.

Putter--The Facet model, bar-back weighting, maltese cross CM, name on face $125
Putter--The Hesketh model, Maltese cross CM, long hosel, name in script $125
Putter--Long, tapered hammer head, like polo mallet $500
Putter--Model S31, Staynorus stainless, name in script, Maltese cross CM $60
Putter--SX model, long blade, semi-long tear drop shaped hosel, beveled top edge $125
Putter--The Birko model, iron blade $70
Putter--The DW Grand model, top flange, script name $125
Putter--Steel blade with pointed toe $100
Irons--Delta series, round sole, line face, Cheshire autograph .... $65 each
Irons--Deltoid series, round sole, line face, Cheshire autograph ..$65 each

Ayrton, W.
Cleek--(B) Gun metal head with black gutta percha face insert, markings on hosel $3,000

Ayton, Laurie
[Chicago, IL]
Driver--Socket head, ivor insert $80
Mashie Niblick--Line face, pipe CM $55

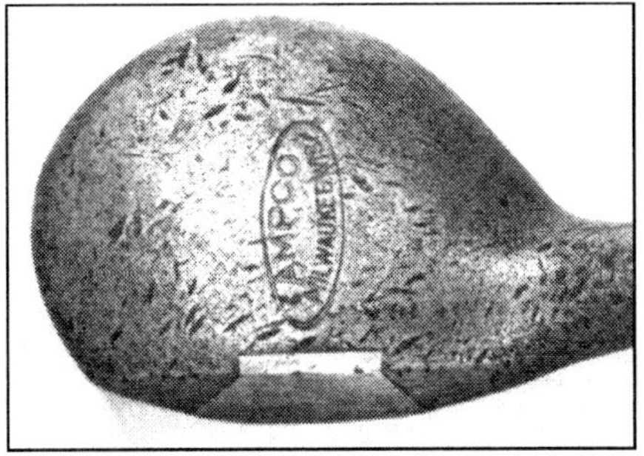

Ampco metal woods were made from a silver colored material called Dow Metal. The face insert was made of bronze colored Ampco Metal.

B

B.A.M. Company+
[Bridgeport Athletic Manufacturing Co.: the name for B.G.I. after 1905]
Driver--Socket head, light finish, oval name stamp $150
Brassie--Socket head, oval stamp $150
Spoon--Socket head, for BGI $150
Iron--smooth face, oval stamp $125

B.G.I. Company+
[Bridgeport Gun Implement Co., Bridgeport, CT; 1897-1904]
◇◇Listed by model number (stamped on shaft below grip)
41--Driver, Simpson model, socket head $150
43--Brassie, Simpson model, socket head $150
51--Driver, Chevy Chase model, socket head $125
51--Driver, Chevy Chase model, splice head $250
61--Driver, Hibbard model, splice head $225
71--Driver, Dunn model, splice head $250
73--Brassie, Dunn model, bulger face, splice head $225
81--Driver. Kilgour model, splice head $225
81--Driver, Kilgour model, socket head $125
90--Driver, standard straight face, splice head $225
91--Driver, bulger face, splice head $225
92--Brassie, straight face, splice head $225
92--Brassie, straight face, socket head $125
93--Brassie, bulger face, splice head $200
96--Putter, wood splice head $400
97--Brassie niblick, New model, splice head $500
004--Cleek, juvenile $125
006--Lofting iron, juvenile $150
009--Iron, juvenile $150
010--Putting cleek, juvenile $150
091--Driver, juvenile $250
093--Brassie, juvenile $250
101--Driving iron, J.D. Dunn model $100
102--Putting cleek, gooseneck $125
103--Driving cleek, Carruthers-type hosel $175

104--Cleek, regular hosel $100
105--Mashie, centraject model $100
106--Lofting iron $100
107--Lofting cleek (jigger), concave $150
108--Lofting mashie, Taylor model $125
109--Iron $80
110--Putting cleek $100
111--Niblick $125
112--Driving Mashie $100
113--Putter, gun metal blade $125
114--Medium mashie $80
115--Mashie, convex back $100
116--Medium mashie, deep face, Taylor model $125
117--Driving mashie $80
118--Approaching mashie, Simpson model $125
119--Putting cleek, twisted neck $125
120--Putting cleek, deep face $150
121--Mashie iron $100
122--Cleek, short blade $100
123--Light mid iron, Simpson model, line face $100
124--Mashie, Taylor model $125
391--Driver, small splice head $225
392--Brassie, Simpson model $200
500--(B) Driver, one piece, straight face $1,500-2,000
501--(B) Driver, one piece, bulger face $1,500-2,000
501--(B) Driver, one piece, lion CM, Kempshall face insert $2,250
503--(B) Brassie, one piece, bulger face $1,500-2,000
502--(B) Brassie, one piece, straight face $1,500-2,000
590--Driver, Tom Morris model, splice head $350
590--Driver, Tom Morris model, socket head $175
591--Brassie, Tom Morris Model, socket head $150

The BGI model fork splice driver has a much longer, more delicate fork splice than the earlier AH Scott club.

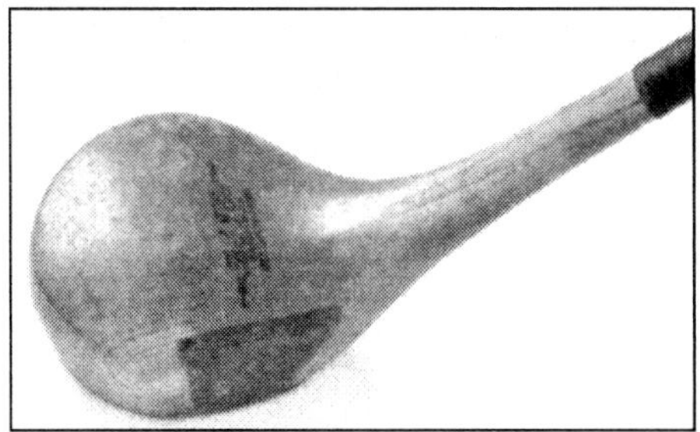

690--Driver, McEwan model, splice head $250
690--Driver, McEwan model, socket head $150
693--Driver, Dundonald model, socket head $175
694--Brassie, Moore model, splice head $200
791--Driver, Brooklawn model, splice head $175
891--Driver, St. Andrews model, splice head $175
893--Niblick Brassie, Kilgour model, splice head $500
893--Niblick Brassie, Kilgour model, socket head $250
991--Brassie, Kilgour model, deep face, splice head $250
Driver--(B) Fork splice head, leather face insert $650
Putter--(A U) Schenectady, marked in double circle
Wright & Ditson outside, BGI inside $300
Putter--(A U) Sprague model, block shaped head,
ball-in-socket adjustable hosel $1,500

B T N
[see Butchart-Nicholls]

Ball, Tom*
[Raynes Park e, et al; brother of John Ball]
Driver--(S) Beech head, name stamp in script $600

Baltimore Putter Company+
Putter--(A U) Triangular shaped adjustable head rotates for
three different lofts $2,600

'Banner'
[Brand line of the Kroydon Company]
Driver--Model 7116, circular steel face insert w/ 2 screws $100
Driving Iron--Diagonal line face, 15-degree loft $60
Driving Mashie--20 degree loft, wide line face $50
Mashie--35 degree, wide line face $45
Mashie Iron--30 degree loft, wide line face $50
Mashie Niblick--45 degree loft, wide line face $45
Mid Iron--25 degree loft, wide line face $45
Niblick--50 degree loft, vertical line face $100
Niblick--Leo Diegel series, chrome, crossed clubs CM $30
Spade Mashie--40 degree loft, wide line face $50
Putter--Pendulum style with center shaft $500

James Batley was a successful London area professional who made a fair amount of clubs for export.

Barker, H.H.
[Garden City, NY]
Driver--Socket head, white face insert fastened with 6 dowels $85

Barnes, Heffron
[New York, NY]
Putter--Adjustable, angle gauge at hosel $1,500

Barnes, Jim
[Pelham, NY, et al]
Mashie--Spalding anvil CM, line face $75
Mid Iron--Autograph series, marked Tacoma, dot face $90
Niblick--Medium round shaped head, line face $85

Barnes, N.
[Leeds e]
Mashie--The Birco series, Ayers cross CM, stainless $40

Batley, James*
[Bushey Hall e, et al]
Driver--Socket head $60
Mashie Niblick--line face, name in oval $40
Putter--Ayers Maltese cross CM, steel blade, pointed toe $100

Baugh, L.A.
[Garden City, KS]
Putter—The Silent Putting Instructor, two holes in face of blade .. $300

Baxendale & Company
[Manchester e]

Baugh: The exact purpose of the two holes is not known but they may have been strung with string for a pendulum motion.

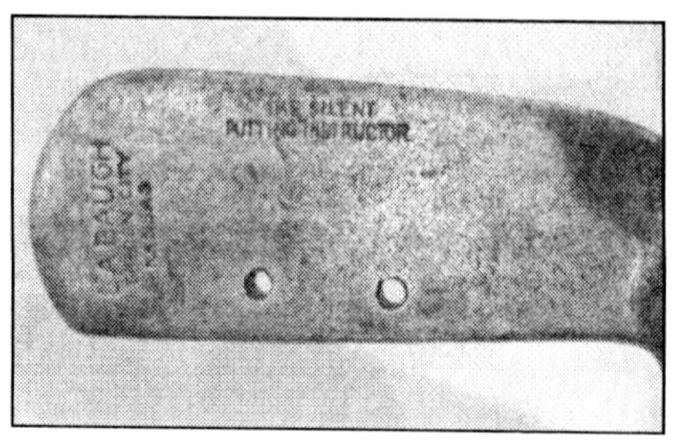

Putter—Wood mallet, socket head $175

Bayless Manufacturing Co.
[E. Hartford, CT]
Driver--(U) Stripe top socket head, laminated bamboo shaft $200
Woods--(U) Set of driver, brassie, spoon, bamboo shaft $750

Baxter, Alex+
[Chicago, et.al.]
Cleek--Dot face, PG Mfg. Anvil CM $90

'Beaumont'
Putter--(A U) Mallet head, black rubber aiming dot on crown $100

Beckley-Ralston Company, The+
Chicago]
Driver--Excelsior model socket head $90
Brassie--Jock Hutchison model, socket head $75
Chipper--Shotmaker 378 model, banana shaped head, square grip $50
Putter--No. 9, long head $50
Putter--Marked "J. Black Certified," blade $50
Putter--Solid steel rod for shaft $40

Bell, Frank
[Carnoustie]
Long Spoon--C 1875, marked "F.Bell" $4,500

Bellwood, Frank
[Garden City, Long Island, NY]

Driver--Socket head, stripe top $125
Mid Iron--Stewart pipe CM, dot face $45
Putter--Copy of wooden Travis model $250

Bembridge, A.
[Coombe Wood, London e]
Putter--(B) The Coombe model, brass blade, aiming flange $125

Bendelow, Tom
[Chicago]
Mashie Iron--Line face, signature name, Wilson large W CM..............$50

Benetfink & Company*
[London retail store]
Driver--Socket head $75
Iron--The Concentric series, dot face, diamond back $50
Mashie--Name in oval, line face $45
Putter--Offset blade $50

Beveridge, James*+
[St. Andrews, s; later Shinnecock Hills, NY]
Driver--(S) C.1895, transitional head, deep face $2,400
Brassie--Transitional splice head $400
Brassie--Socket head $200
Long Spoon--(L) C.1880, lancewood shaft $4,000
Cleek--Smooth face, marked Southampton, LI $250
Niblick--(S) Wood club with very lofted face, short head $3,000

Billet, H.N.
[Bridport e, et al]
Putter--Wood head in cylinder shape $3,500

Billings & Spencer Company+
[Hartford, CT]
Mashie--Through bore hosel, dot face $50
Niblick--Marked "Junior Champion" in script $45
Named Irons--(U) Par-A-Lel series, circular, scored face ....$125 each
Irons—Professional series, flanged sole, ...$30 each
Irons—President series ,stainless ....$30 each
Irons—Red Bird series, chromed, ...$25 each

Biltmore
Putter—Sub Sinksit model, heel & toe style in aluminum $100

'Birdie'
Putter--Thick blade $30

Bisset, Andrew*
[North Berwick s]
Brassie--Socket head $60
Iron clubs--Stewart pipe brand, scored face .... $50 each

Black, J.L.
Driving Iron--Spalding anvil CM, dot face $40

Black, Thomas
Putter--(B) Wood mallet, socket head, roller mechanism in sole ...$4,000

Blackheath Golf Company*
[London]
Jigger--Coronet series, crown CM, dash face $40
Niblick--Large head, smooth face $150
Putter—Roddy model, bronze Brown-Vardon style
with steel face insert $250
Iron clubs--Sun with rays radiating outward on face .... $60 each

Boggs, Arthur
[Cincinnati, OH]
Iron clubs--Iron Man model, stout man CM, dot face $75

Bonner, F.
[Carlisle e]
Mid Iron--The Scot series, kilted Scotsman CM $40

'Bonnie B'
Putter--Heavy blade, line face $35

Boomer, Percy H.
[St. Cloud, Paris, et al]
Jigger--Autograph series, dot face, Gibson star CM $60

James Bradbeer's Steel Face driver had three rows of steel screws set in its head in place of a face insert.

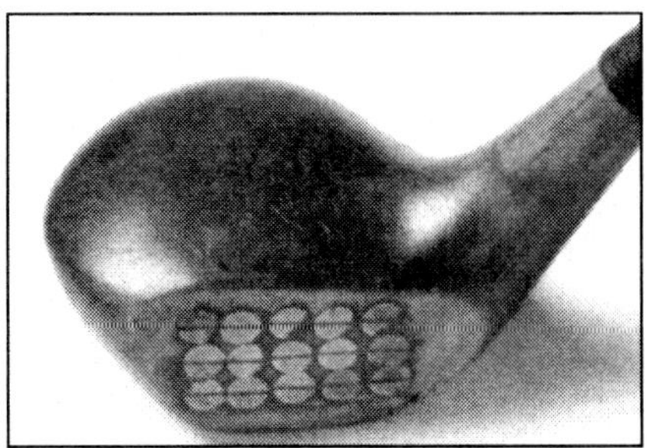

Booth, W.H.
[Beckenham, Kent e]
Cleek—long blade, smooth face $100

Bourne & Bond
[Louisville, KY]
Putter--(A) Ray-type, BB CM in double circle $75

Boyd, Tom
[Staten Island, NY]
Driving Iron--Line face, Stewart pipe CM $50
Putter--Blade, pipe CM $50

Boyden
Iron--(B) Patent fork splice in middle of wood shaft $150

Boye
Putter--(A U) Adjustable where shaft attaches to head $650

Boyle, Charles
[Havana, Cuba]
Driver--Fancy face insert $100
Spoon--Socket head, face insert $100
Niblick--Dot face, palm tree and Gibson star CMs $75
Putter--Square toe, flat sided hosel $150
Putter--(A) Mallet style head $100

Bradbeer, Charles
[Hendon e, et al]

Niblick--Junior Giant model, stainless, Goudie bear CM $800

Bradbeer, Edwin
[Cirencester e, et al]
Putter--Iron blade, smooth face $60

Bradbeer, James*
[Finchley e, Radlet e, et al]
Brassie--(B) The "Peggy" model, 20 end grain dowels set in face, socket head $300
Brassie—(B) Steel face model with screws as a face insert $350
Brassie--Socket head $90
Cleek—Bradbeer autograph, horseshoe CM $80
Iron--Top Line model, bird & bee CM, top edge extension $250
Putter--Deep face blade, 40 holes drilled through face $800
Putter--Drilled face model, holes in face $450
Putter--Own model, long stainless blade, Gibson star/G CM $100
Putter--Horseshoe shaped CM, long shallow blade $80
Numbered Irons--The Jay Bee series, bird & bee CM .... $55 each

Braddell & Sons, Thomas*
[Belfast i]
Driver--Splice head, leather face, shaft stamp $300
Driver--(A B) Leather face, horn insert, serial number marked on crown, shamrock shaft stamp $800
Brassie--(A B) As above $900
Brassie--Splice head, golden beech, leather face $300
Cleek--Smooth face, long blade, shamrock CM $300
Mashie--Smooth face, shamrock CM, shaft stamp $250
Niblick--Medium size head, smooth slightly concave face, shamrock CM $450

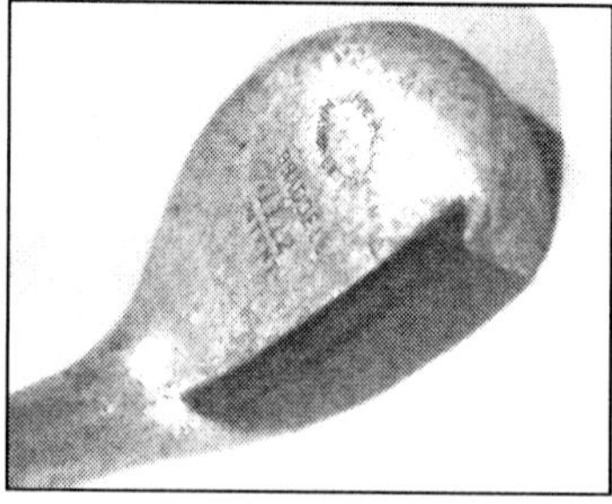

The Braddell aluminum head driver was one of the first metal woods produced in the 1890s.

Putter--Heavy iron blade, shamrock CM $250

Brady, Frank
Putter--(U) Deadly Overspin model, gun metal head,
curved face, hollow back $800

Brady, Mike
[Boston, Detroit, et.al]
Driver--Socket head, stripe top, autograph mark $75
Cleek--King series, dot face $60
Mashie--Model 6601, Monel, line face, made for Winchester $100

'Brae-Burn'
Named Irons--Line face ....$30 each

Braid & Ogilvie
Iron--Smooth face, name in arc $100

Braid, James*
[Five time Open Champion; his shop at Walton Heath, e, made a few clubs but most with his autograph were produced by William Gibson & Co.]
Driver--Splice head, marked Romford $300
Cleek--Stewart pipe CM, dot face $100
Mid Iron--Walton Heath mark in oval $50
Niblick--The "Giant" model, James Braid series,
medium size head, Gibson star CM, line face $90
Putter--Orion model, Gibson star CM, broad sole $150

Braid, W. & G.+
[New York; brothers William and George worked for Forgan before

William Braid and Dave Ogilvie partnered as club makers for a very short time in the early 1900s.

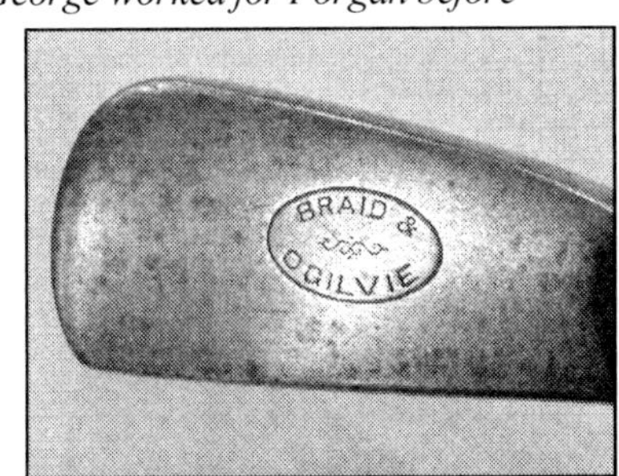

coming to America in 1898. They made clubs in the U.S. for about 10 years then moved back to Scotland]

Driver--Short splice head, line name stamp $175

Brassie--Socket head $100

Niblick--smooth face, thick sole $75

Brand, Charles*

[Carnoustie s]

Driver--Short splice head $150

Baffing Spoon--(S) C.1890, lofted face $3,000

Cleek--C.1890, smooth face, long thin blade, 4 3/4" hosel, shaft stamp $600

Cleek--Smooth face, single Condie fern CM $250

Iron--Harrower heart CM, diamond face $75

Mashie--C.1900, smooth face, deep face blade $200

Mashie--Rampant lion CM, line face $45

Niblick--C.1895, small head, thistle CM $500

Niblick--Large head, rampant lion CM, dot face $75

Putter--Standard blade, lion CM $65

Brand, Fred

[Pittsburgh, PA]

Driver-Small dark socket head $80

Brand, G.

Putter--Wood splice head with extreme gooseneck $1,800

Breare, J

Mid Iron--Line face, stainless steel $35

Breeze, G. Brodie*

[Glasgow]

Woods--Stripe top socket head, Royal Crown brand ....$75 each

Mid Iron--Royal Crown Brand, crown CM, dash face $45

Putter--Excelsior model, Royal Crown Brand, crown CM, blade $75

Putter--Royal Crown Brand, Excelsior series, iron blade $50

Brews, George

[Blackheath e]

Driver--(S) C.1885, dark stained head, shallow face $2,300
Brassie--C. 1900, splice head, lancewood shaft $300
Cleek--Short iron blade, smooth face, Condie rose CM $125
Cleek--Smooth face, Condie flower CM,
marked "Blackheath" $150
Mashie—SF, small letters in arc $125
Mashie--Stewart pipe CM, smooth face $100
Putter--(B) Trusty model, wood mallet head with large
brass backweight $175

Brewster, Francis
[London]
Driver--(B) Simplex model, centre shafted cross-head club,
boat shaped head **.. $2,200**
Spoon--(B) Simplex model, as above $2,000
Niblick--(B)Simplex model, as above $2,500
Niblick--(A B)Simplex model, in aluminum $2,500
Putter--(B)Simplex model, as above $2,000

'Briarcliff'
Putter--Blade, line face $35

Brine, J.W.
[Boston, MA sports outfitting store]
Iron clubs--Line face, company crest CM, made by Burke ....$35 each

British Golf Company, Ltd.*
[London]
Cleek--Straight line name stamp, smooth face $75
Mashie--Dot face $50
Putter--Iron blade $60
Putter--(A) Centre shaft, boat shaped duplex head $250
Putter--(A) Two-faced model, rectangular head, no hosel $300
Putter--The British model, center shafted, steel head $250
Putter--Offset blade $75

Brodie & Sons, R.*
[Anstruther s]
Iron--Stainless, triangle/BS&A CM, made for Thornton $50
Jigger--Zenith series, stainless, dot face, triangle CM $50

Clubs marked for W & D Brodie are fairly rare. The bulk of their business was to make iron heads for other makers.

Mashie--Stainless, line face, triangle/BS&A CM $50
Iron clubs--Regular steel, triangle/BS&A and Tom Morris CMs, line face, made for Tom Morris shop .... $60-100 each
Iron clubs--Stainless, triangle/BS&A and Tom Morris CMs, line face, made for Tom Morris shop .... $50-80 each
Spade Niblick--Line face, triangle CM, made for Morris shop $150
Niblick--Stainless, triangle/BS&A CM, made for Nicholson Brothers $50
Putter--Stainless, line face, triangle/BS&A CM $75

Brodie Company, W. & D.*
[Anstruther s]
Mid Iron--Dash face, stainless, initials in 4-lobes CM $60
Mashie Niblick--Bobbie model, rustless $75

Brougham, Reginald T.*
[London]
Driver--(A B) Transitional shaped head with wood block inserted in face, shamrock CM, "Clubs Are Trumps" legend $900
Brassie--(A B) As above but lofted face $1,200

Brown & Smart+
[Chicago]
Putter--Stewart pipe CM, iron blade $70

Brown, A.W.
Brassie--Bulldog socket head, fiber insert $125

Brown, Daniel*

Cleek--Smooth face, made by Stewart, pipe CM $70

Brown, David
Driver--Socket head $100
Putter--The Nipper model, made by Alex "Nipper" Campbell $90

Brown, George*
[St. Andrews]
Mid Spoon--(L) Dark head, hickory shaft, marked "G. Brown" . $15,000

Brown, Harry
Niblick--Model 17, line face, Winton diamond CM $45

Brown, J.
Putter--(S) C.1885, dark brown head $1,200

Brown, J.R.
[Montrose s; patentee of the Brown Patent Perforated Irons (i.e. "rake" iron); see J. Winton]

Brown, Jim
Iron--Smooth face $60

Brown, Melville
[Malone, Belfast i]
Driver--Bulger scare head $750

Brown, Wallace
Playclub--(L) Beech head, Forgan shaft stamp $3,000

Brown, William
[Dunksey s]
Brassie--Socket head $50

Bryant, George W.
Mashie--Stainless steel, 'Rustless' sun face CM $50

Buchanan's
[London retail store with club making facilities]
Driver--(S) Dark finish splice head $300

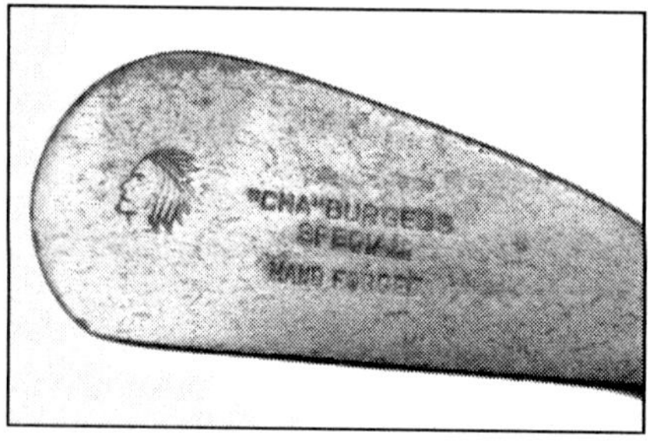

Charles "Cha" Burgess was a New England pro and club maker who gave young Francis Ouimet golf lessons.

Mashie--(B) Altman's pattern, round back, smooth face $225

'Bula'

Putter--Danga wood shaft with rib pad grip, iron blade, Gibson star CM $75

Bunker, R.A.

Putter--(A) Mallet head $60

Burgess, Charles

[Woodland, MA; many clubs marked with his nickname "Cha"]

Iron clubs--Indian head CM, scored face .... $75 each

Mashie Niblick--Marked Cha Burgess $65

Putter--Gun metal, round top $175

Burke Golf Company+

[Newark, OH; began manufacturing tennis equipment prior to entering the golf market, C.1910. They produced a large number of clubs including many prestige lines]

<><>Misc. clubs

Driver--Splice head, aluminum sole plate $125

Driver--Socket head, steel face insert with 2 screws $150

Driver—Stellite model, synthetic white face insert $200

Driver--Socket head, winged B.G. Co. CM $200

Driver--(A) End Grain model $400

Iron clubs--William Burke Leader Model in shield, stainless steel, dot face .... $35 each

Mashie--(D) Glencoe series, model 1369, ribbed face $75

Iron clubs--Long Burke series, line face, shield CM .... $40 each

Mashie--Wilson model, "Egyptian mashie" $100

The earliest brand mark used by Burke was the B.G.Co. monogram with wings, like stamped on this wood Schenectady mode. Putter.

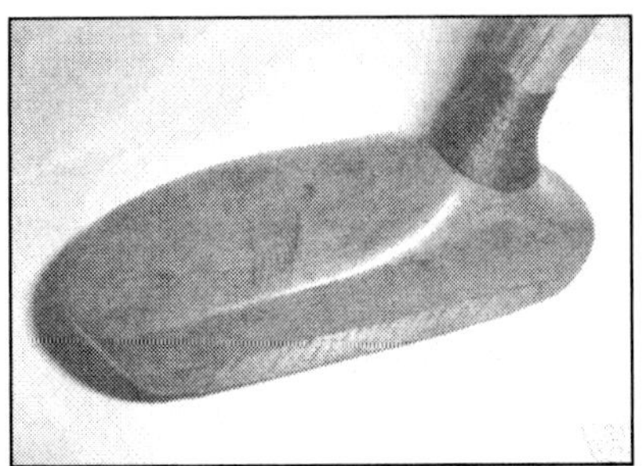

Putter--made for the Edward Tryon Company, Phila., dot face $45
Putter--(A) End Grain model, heel shafted mallet head $350
Putter--(A) End Grain model, Schenectady shaped head $400
Putter--Model 1363, Glencoe stamp, peaked top of blade $125
Putter--Brown-Vardon style steel head $200
Putter—Wood Schenectady, brass sole, Winged BGCo CM $400
Putter--Sandy Mac model, flange sole, lion CM $45
Rotary model--(D) Mashie, checkered face, Monel $300
Rotary model--(D) Mashie niblick, checkered face, Monel $300
Rotary model--(D) Mashie niblick, 'Stars and Stripes' pattern, half checkered, half slot face, Monel $450

◇◇Misc. clubs (with model number)
3--Mid Iron, thistle & scales CMs $40
4A--Jigger, Commander series $40
11--Mashie, thistle & scales CMs $40
26--Mid Iron, thistle $ scales CMs $40
36--Mashie, made for Rev-O-Noc Co. $60
BR-1--Mashie, Mike Brady model, dash face $80
BR-2--Mashie niblick, Mike Brady model, dash face $80
D5--Cleek, Hammer Forged brand, lion CM $45
D-1--Mashie niblick, Dave Ogilvie model $80
MC-1--Cleek, McLean model, dot face $80
MC-2--Niblick, McLean model $80
S-2--Mid iron, George Sargent, Monel $80
S-3--Mashie, George Sargent, Monel, line face $80
S-4--(D) Mashie niblick, Geo. Sargent, Monel, ribbed face $150
S-10--Niblick, W.C. Sherwood model, large head $80
Z-1--Mashie, slotted hosel, dot face $125

◇◇◇By model series with model number if so designated

◇◇'Bee & Flower' series irons
Named Irons--Bee & flower CMs .... $40 each

◇◇Burke Autograph series
Woods (driver, brassie, spoon)--Black fiber insert with screws, stripe top, aluminum sole plate .... $45 each

◇◇Burke Stainless series irons
Numbered Irons (1-8)--Line face, fleur-de-lis CM .... $35 each
A-Suffix Numbered Irons (3A, 4A, 7A, 8A)--Slight gooseneck, line face, fleur-de-lis CM .... $40 each
Putters (9, 10, P1, P2)--Blade .... $40 each

◇◇Burke Standard series
Driver--Plain face $40
Brassie--Plain face $40
Spoon--Plain face $45
X-1--Cleek, line face $35
X-2--Driving iron, line face $35
X-3--Mid iron, dash/line face $30
X-4--Mid iron, round back, line face $40
X-4--Mashie iron, plain back $35
X-5--Jigger, dash/line face $35
X-6--Mashie, deep face, dash/line face $35
X-7--Mid iron, diamond back, line face $45
X-7--Spade mashie, plain back $35
X-8--Mid iron, offset head $40
X-8--Mashie niblick, plain back $35
X-8A--Mashie niblick $35
X-9--Niblick, plain back $35
X-10--Putter, blade $40
X-11--Mashie, line face $30
X-17--Jigger, line face $45
X-18--Putter, blade $35
X-19--Putting cleek, blade $35
X-23--Niblick, medium head $35
X-33--Mid iron, concentric back $40

X-36--Mashie, line face $30
X-38--Mashie niblick, line face $30
X-43--Driving iron, line face $35
X-44--Cleek, round back $40
X-50--Putter, deep face $40
X-62--Mashie, deep face $40
X-64--Niblick, very deep face $40
X-68--(D) Mashie, ribbed face $75
X-69--Putter, square toe, broad sole $75
X-70--(D) Mashie niblick, ribbed face $75
X-77--Putter, round top, broad sole $75
X-78--Putter, gooseneck blade $50
X-90--Mashie, round back $40

◇◇Children's clubs

Juvenile series clubs $35-50 each
Driver
Brassie
Iron
Mashie
Putter

Junior series clubs $35-50 each
Driver
Iron
Mashie
Putter

Midget series clubs $65-90 each
Driver
Iron
Mashie
Putter

Varsity series clubs $25-30 each
Driver
Mid iron
Mashie
Putter

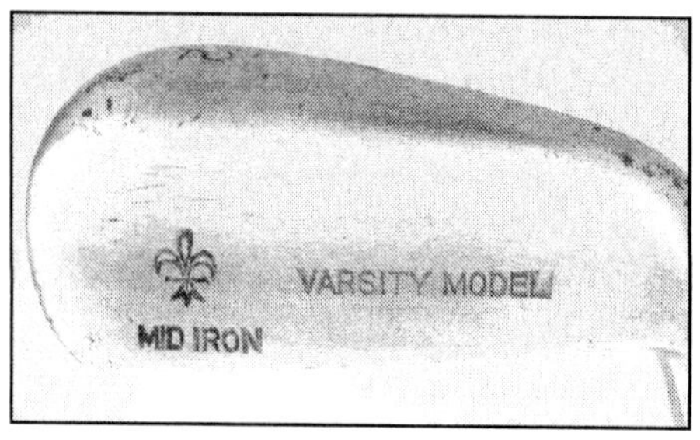

Burke's Varsity Model clubs were built for pre-teen children. They are slightly longer than the Juvenile series.

◇◇Columbia and Columbia Special Series

Driver--Plain face $40
Brassie--Plain face $40
D1--Mashie niblick, lion & crown CM $40
D1--(D) Mashie niblick, ribbed face $100
S4--(D) Mashie niblick, fibbed face $100
S8--(D) Ribbed face $100
Driving Iron--Dash face, lion & crown CM $25
Mashie--Regular head, dash face $25
Mashie--Deep face, dash face $25
Mashie--(D) Inverted waffle (deep mesh) face $150
Mashie Niblick--Dash face $25
Mashie Niblick--(D) Ribbed face $100
Mid Iron--Dash face $25
Niblick--Dash face $25
Putter--Regular blade $25
Putter--Gooseneck blade $30

◇◇Deluxe series

Woods (driver, brassie, spoon)--Black fiber insert, aluminum backweight .... $60 each

◇◇Golfrite series

Driver--Splice head, aluminum sole plate $125
Driver--Ivor face with 7 red pegs, aluminum backweight $100
Brassie--Ivor face, as above $10
Spoon--Ivor face, as above $90
GR2--Mid Iron, dot & line face $60
GR6--Mashie Niblick, dot & line face $60
Numbered Irons (1-8)--Stainless, line face, scales CM .... $30 each

Set of 8 .... $350
Numbered Irons (1-8)--Iron, line face, scales CM .... $30 each
Set of 8 .... $350

◇◇Grand Prize series
0--Cleek, narrow face, line face $50
1--Spoon, bulldog head, deep face $100
1--Cleek, line face $40
01--Cleek, Monel $50
2--Mashie, narrow face $40
3--Driving iron, long blade, line face, scales CM $45
03--Driving iron, Monel $50
4--Mid iron, round back $40
04--Mid iron, Monel $50
5--Approaching cleek, dot face $60
5--Mid iron, deep face, short blade $40
05--Mid iron, Monel $50
6--Mid iron, round sole, scales CM $45
7--Mid iron, diamond back, dash face $50
8--Mid iron, offset blade, line face, scales CM $40
9--Mashie niblick, semi-gooseneck, dash face $45
09--Mashie niblick, Monel $55
10--Driver, splice head $125
10--Mashie, offset head $40
010--Mashie, Monel $50
11--Spoon, large head $90
11--Mashie, medium blade, line face $40
011--Mashie, Monel $50
12--Brassie, splice head $125
12--Mashie, round sole, short blade $45
12--Putting cleek, blade $45
13--Jigger, musselback, scales CM $55
013--Jigger, Monel $65
14--Spoon, small bulldog shaped head, fancy face insert $95
14--Mashie, deep face, flange sole $55
014--Mashie, Monel $60
15--Mashie, half musselback, dot face $75
15--Mashie, long blade, flange sole $50
16--Driving iron, round sole, line face $45
17--Jigger, narrow face, line/dash face $50

017--Jigger, Monel $60
18--Putter, blade, line/dash face, scales CM $40
018--Putter, Monel $60
19--Putting cleek, blade, scales CM $45
20--Putter, gooseneck, scales CM $45
020--Putter, Monel $55
21--Putter, round sole, straight neck $40
22--Driver, small head, deep face $60
22--Mid iron, J.H. Taylor model, line face $60
23--Niblick, medium size head, dash face, scales CM $45
023--Niblick, Monel $55
24--Driver, Balista combination face insert $150
24--Niblick, short blade, line face $45
25--Niblick, thistle & scales CMs, flange sole, line face $60
25--Brassie, Balista combination face insert $150
25--Mashie niblick, deep face, line face $40
025--Mashie niblick, Monel $55
26--Mashie niblick, line face $40
26--Mid iron, short blade $40
026--Mid iron, Monel $50
26--Putter, flange sole $50
27--Mid iron, musselback $50
027--Mid iron, Monel $60
28--Niblick, dreadnought style large head, scales CM $50
028--Niblick, Monel $60
29--Putting cleek, musselback $60
029--Putting cleek, Monel $70
30--Driver, bulls-eye face insert $90
30--Putter, musselback, semi-gooseneck $50
030--Putter, Monel $60
31--Driving mashie, scales CM $45
32--Brassie, bulls-eye face insert $90
32--Driving mashie, round sole, short blade $50
33--Mid iron, concentric back, dash face $45
033--Mid iron, Monel $55
34--Driver, thick Ivor face insert $80
34--Mid iron, medium length blade, line face $40
35--Brassie, thick Ivor face insert $80
35--Mashie iron, heavy blade, dash face $45
36--Mashie, deep face $40

36--Putter, slight gooseneck $50
036--Mashie, Monel $50
37--Approaching cleek, scales CM $60
037--Approaching cleek, Monel $70
38--Pitcher, line face, scales CM $55
038--Pitcher, Monel $65
40--Driver, socket head, plain face $40
40--Mashie niblick, line face, scales CM $40
41--Mashie iron, short blade $50
42--Brassie, plain face $45
42--Putter, blade with point on top, scales CM $60
43-Spoon, plain face $50
43--Driving iron, long blade, deep face $40
043--Driving iron, Monel $50
45--Mid iron, concentric back, deep face $50
045--Mid iron, Monel $50
45--Wood cleek, bulls-eye face insert $200
45--Wood cleek, fiber face insert $150
46--Mashie, concentric back, scales CM $45
046--Mashie, Monel $55
51--Putter, straight neck, very deep face $55
52--Putter, flange sole, gooseneck $55
052--Putter, Monel $65
53--Mid iron, long blade, deep face, flange sole $60
053--Mid iron, Monel $70
54--Driver, Victory model $100
55--Niblick, offset head, line face $45
056--Niblick, Monel $55
56--Brassie, Victory model $100
56--Cleek, celtic shaped offset head, deep face $45
056--Cleek, Monel $55
57--Cleek, diamond back, line face, scales CM $50
59--Cleek, musselback, line face $50
62--Mashie, medium length blade, line face $40
062--Mashie, Monel $50
63--Putter, long narrow blade, slight gooseneck $50
64--Niblick, very deep face $60
66--Mashie, musselback, scales CM $55
066--Mashie, Monel $65
67--Spoon, Victory model $125

68--(D) Mashie, Shur Stop model, ribbed face $100
69--Putter, broad flange sole, square toe $75
069--Putter, Monel $85
70--Driver--plain face $45
70--(D) Mashie niblick, Shur Stop model, ribbed face $100
070--(D) Mashie niblick, Monel $110
72--Brassie, plain face $45
73--Spoon, plain face $50
73--(D) Mashie niblick, Shur Stop model, ribbed face, offset head .$100
74--(D) Mashie niblick, Shur Stop model, slotted face $100
074--(D) Mashie niblick, Monel, slotted face $120
74--Driver, fiber face insert $55
75--(D) Cleek, ribbed face $100
76--Brassie, fiber face insert $55
76--(D) Niblick, ribbed face $125
77--Putter, round top, broad sole $75
77--Spoon, fiber face insert $80
78--Putter, extreme gooseneck, scales CM $60
80--Driver, semi-bulldog head $75
82--Brassie, semi-bulldog head $75
84--Niblick, concave face, scales CM $85
085--Driving iron, bulger face, Monel $100
086--Mid iron, bulger face, Monel $100
087--Mashie, bulger face, Monel $100
088--Mashie niblick, bulger face, Monel $100
089--Putter, bulger face, Monel $125
90--Driver, long narrow head $100
90--Mashie, round back, line face $50
91--Mashie, diamond back $60
91--Putter, flange sole $75
92--Brassie, long narrow head $100
92--Putter, blade, slight gooseneck $50
140--Driver, bulls-eye face insert $90
142--Brassie, bulls-eye insert $90
144--Driver, pear shaped head, semi-bulger face $125
146--Brassie, pear shaped head, semi-bulger face $125
320--Driver, dreadnought head $90
322--Brassie, dreadnought head $90
511--Brassie, J.H. Taylor model $100
522--Spoon, J.H. Taylor model, round sole $125

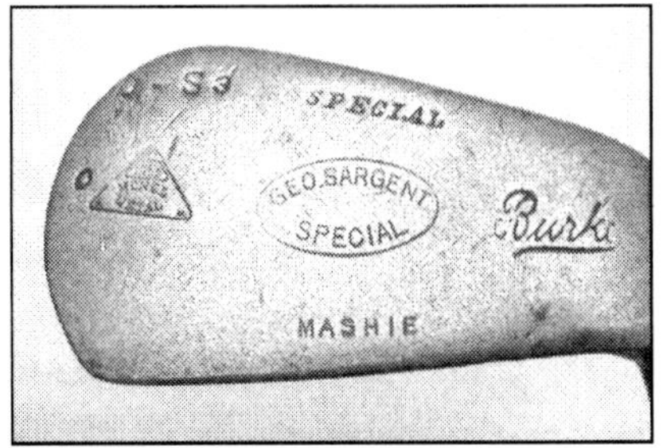

Burke capitalized on the fame of 1908 US Open Champion with a replica of his mashie, their model S3.

600--Driver, large head $80
602--Brassie, large head $80
800--Driver, bulls-eye face insert $90
802--Brassie, bulls-eye face insert $90
844--Driver, plain bluger face $45
846--Brassie, plain bulger face $45
849--Spoon, plain bulger face $50
849--Spoon, small head $75
857--Spoon, fiber face insert $80
857--Spoon, plain face $50
875--Spoon, fiber face insert, round sole $80
G-1--Putter, gun metal blade, scales CM $65
G-2--Putter, gun metal, straight neck, wide sole $75
G-3--Putter, gun metal blade, musselback, scales CM $75
G-4--Putter, gun metal blade, flange sole $75
S-1--Putter, George Sargent model, round back, steel $75
S-1--Putter, George Sargent, Monel $85
Schenectady Putter--(A) $125
Z1--(A S) Putter $125

◇◇Grand Prize series numbered irons
Numbered Irons (1-8)--Dot face, regular blade ....$35 each
A-Suffix Numbered Irons (3A, 4A, 7A, 8A)--Dot face, slight gooseneck ....$40 each
Putters (9, 10)--Blade ....$40 each
Individual Irons (21-26)--Flange sole, line face ....$40 each
Individual Irons (42-45)--Musselback, line face ....$40 each
Individual Irons (71-72)--Diamond back, line face ....$40 each

◇◇Hutchison Autograph Series

74--Driver, fiber face $100
76--Brassie, fiber face $100
77--Spoon, fiber face $125
6640--(D) Niblick, slotted face $100
6641--(D) Mashie Niblick, slotted face $100
H-1--Mid iron, Monel, flange sole, line face $75
H-2--Mid iron, Monel, plain sole, line face $60
H-3--Medium iron, Monel $75
H-4--Mashie iron, Monel $75
H-5--Mashie, line face, Monel $60
H-6--(D) Mashie, Monel, slot face $150
H-7--(D) Mashie niblick, Monel, offset head, slot face $150
H-8--(D) Niblick, Monel, slotted face $200
H-9--Putter, Monel blade $75

◇◇Lady Burke series
1--Cleek $30
2--Spoon $50
2--Driving iron, line face $35
3--Mid Iron, line face $35
4--Mashie iron, line face $35
6--Jigger, line face $40
7--Mashie, line face $35
9--Spade mashie, line face $35
10--Mashie niblick, line face $35
11--Niblick, line face $35
13--Putter, blade $35
17--Jigger $40
18--Putter $40
23--Niblick $35
25--Mashie niblick, thistle & scales CMs, dash face $45

One of the more unusual clubs from the grand Prize Grand Prize series is this model Z1 old style aluminum putter.

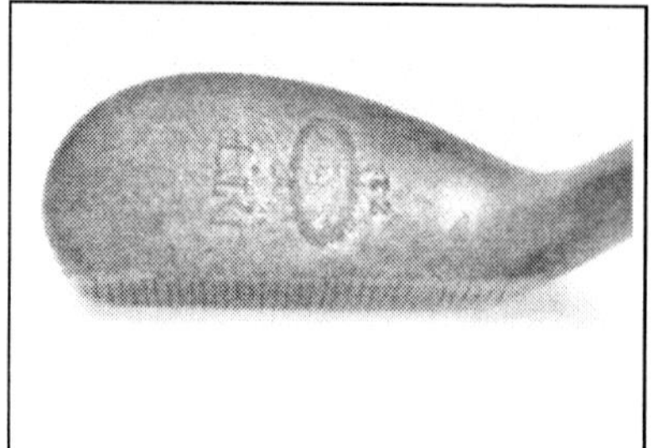

Burke Jock Hutchison
model deep groove irons

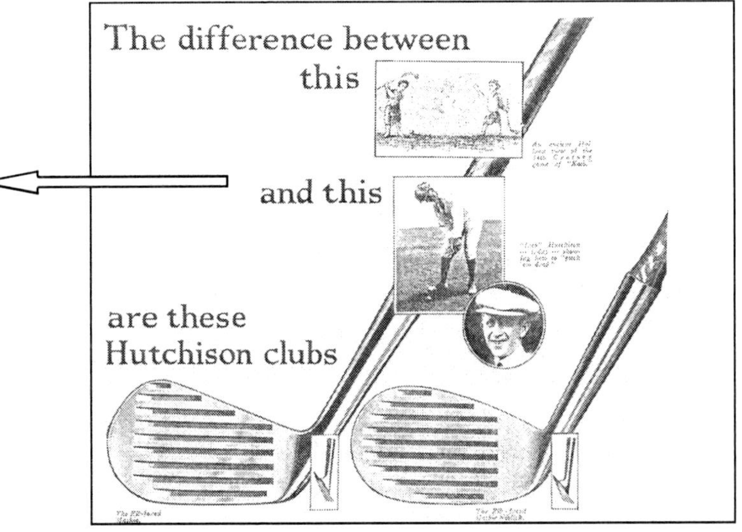

Jock Hutchison was born in St. Andrews but spent his adult life in the U.S. When he returned to St. Andrews in 1921 to win The Open Championship he was an American citizen. Jock used the Burke Grand Prize models 68 Mashie and 74 Mashie Niblick during his Open victory. After his win Burke sold those irons as Jock Hutchison autograph models H-6 and H-7.

All deeply grooved irons were banned in 1921, effective January 1, 1922.

26--Mid iron $30
40--Driver, Ivor face $75
40--Driver, plain face $40
42--Brassie, Ivor face $75
42--Brassie, plain face $40
42--Mid Iron, line face $35
43--Spoon, plain face $45
44--Mid Iron, line face $35
45--Wood cleek, fancy face $200
45--Wood cleek, fiber face $125
68--Mashie $30
69--Putter, square toe, broad sole $75
70--Mashie niblick $30
90--Mashie, round back $50
91--Putter, broad flange sole $90
92--Putter, gooseneck blade $40
G-2--Putter, gun metal $65
430--Driver $50
432--Brassie $50
800--Driver, fiber face $90
800--Driver, fancy face $90
802--Brassie, fiber face $90
802--Brassie, fancy face $90
844--Driver, plain face $40
846--Brassie, plain face $40
846—Brassie, ivorine face $80
849--Spoon, plain face $45

◇◇Parplay series woods
P40--Driver, black fiber insert with screws $45
P70--Driver, as above $45
P42--Brassie, black fiber insert, brass sole plate $45
P72--Brassie, as above $45
P43--Spoon, black fiber insert, brass sole plate $50
P73--Spoon, as above $50

◇◇Pickwick clubs
[Also see Winchester Arms Co. for additional Pickwick models]
Named/Numbered Irons--Chrome, line face,
small shamrock CM .... $30 each

◇◇Plus Four series
Woods (driver, brassie, spoon)--Red fiber face insert with screws, aluminum sole plate .... $45 each

◇◇Prestwick clubs
Woods--Socket head, plain face .... $40 each
Woods--Socket head, plain face, model number .... $60 each
Named Irons--Name in oval, scales CM, line face .... $35 each
Mashie--(D) Ribbed face $100
Putter--Like the Brown-Vardon, round hosel $100

◇◇Ranger series
Woods (driver, Brassie, spoon)--Aluminum face insert and sole plate .... $45 each

◇◇Sportsman series woods
S30--Driver, plain face, stripe top $40
S32--Brassie, as above $40
S33--Spoon, as above $45
S40--Driver, as above $40
S42--Brassie, as above $40
S43--Spoon, as above $45
S70--Driver, long head $40
S72--Brassie, as above $40
S73--Spoon, as above $45
S320--Driver, large head $40
S322--Brassie, as above $40
S323--Spoon, as above $45

◇◇Ted Ray Autograph Series

The Gene Sarazen series was one of the premium lines of Burke clubs, made after Burke got the rights to use Monel metal in 1920.

852--Driver, bulger face $125
854--Brassie, bulger face $125
R-1--Mashie, Monel, dash face $75
R-2--Cleek, Monel, dash face $75
R-3--Mongrel iron, Monel $100
R-5--Mongrel mashie, Monel $100
R-6--Mid iron, Monel, line/dash face $75
R-7--Mashie, Monel $75
R-8--Pitcher, Monel $90
R-9--Jigger, Monel $90

◇◇Gene Sarazen Autograph Series
GS 1—Driving iron, Monel head, line face $80
GS6--Putter, Monel blade, 7" hosel $175

◇◇Harry Vardon Autograph Series
[Some Burke Vardon series irons also appear with model numbers beginning with A instead of V. Those marked A are the first series and carry the same relative values as the later V series.]
830--Driver, splice head $250
832--Brassie, splice head $250
840--Driver, Ivor face $150
842--Brassie, Ivor face $150
842--Brassie, plain face $125
844--Driver, bulger face $125
846--Brassie, bulger face, fiber face $125
846--Brassie, plain $125
857--Spoon, fiber face $175
857--Spoon, no insert $175
V-1--Cleek, line face $100
V-2--Driving iron $100

The Burke Vardon series model numbers begin with the letter V and were made in Monel Metal.

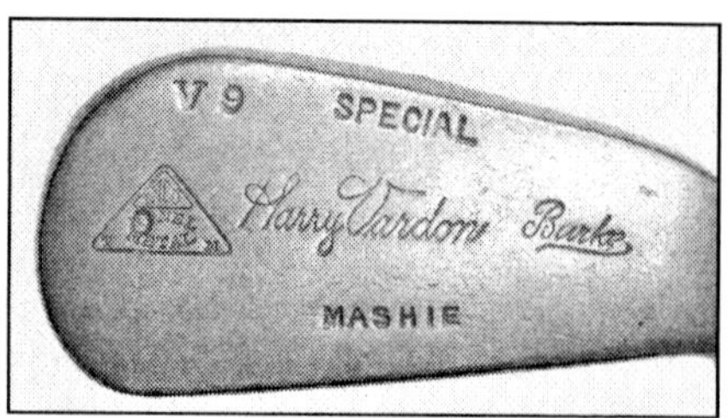

V-2--Driving iron, Monel $125
V-3--Mongrel iron $200
V-3--Mongrel iron, Monel $225
V-4--Mid iron $100
V-4--Mid iron, Monel $125
V-5--Mid iron $100
V-6--Mongrel mashie $200
V-6--Mongrel mashie, Monel $225
V-7--Jigger $125
V-7--Jigger, musselback, Monel $150
V-8--Approach mashie $150
V-8--Approach mashie, Vardon, Monel $175
V-9--Mashie, Vardon autograph $100
V-9--Mashie, Vardon autograph, Monel $125
V-10--Mashie niblick, Vardon autograph $100
V-10--Mashie niblick, Vardon, Monel $125
V-11--Mashie niblick, Vardon autograph $100
V-12--Niblick, Vardon autograph $100
V-12--Niblick, Vardon, Monel $125
V-13-Putter, Vardon autograph $90

◇◇Walter Hagen series irons
Mashie Iron--Monel, Hagen autograph, line face $100
Mashie Niblick--Monel, autograph, dot face $100

◇◇Zenith series
Woods (driver, Brassie, spoon)--Stripe top,
plain face, aluminum backweight ....$40 each

Burr-Key Bilt+
[R.H. Buhrke Co., Chicago]
Driver--Majestic series, socket head $40
Driver--(U) Ritewood series, multi-part face insert $125
Brassie--Regal series, ivorine face insert, 5 black dowels $80
Brassie--Regal series, red face insert $75
Driving Iron--Classic series, brass disc in face $75
Mashie--(D) Baxpin model, ribbed face $100
Iron clubs--Mohawk series, dot face ....$30 each
Iron clubs--Princess Pat series, line face ....$35 each
Iron clubs--Burr-Key Built series, dot face ....$30 each

Iron clubs--Majestic series, line face .... $30 each
Iron clubs--Stylist series, dot face, stainless .... $30 each
Iron clubs--RHB Monogram series, stainless $40each
Iron clubs--Medalist series, stainless, line face .... $35 each
Iron clubs--Andy Robertson series .... $40 each
Spade Mashie Niblick--Andy Robertson series $45
Spade Mashie Niblick--Classic series, brass disc in face $85
Putter--Finalist, blade $30
Putter--Majestic, blade $30
Putter--Mohawk series, regular blade $30
Putter--Rambler series, thick blade $30
Putter--Speedway series, chrome, blade $30
Putter--Stylist series, blade, chromed head $30
Named Irons--Classic Series, brass disc in face .... $60 each

Bussey, George G.*
[London sports outfitter; patented a two-piece iron head with blade braised to a hosel for improved quality]
Driver--Transitional splice head $500
Brassie--Splice transitional beech head, one piece sewn grip $500
Cleek--(B) Short smooth face blade, marked
"Patent Steel Socket", one piece sewn grip $250
Iron—(B) Usual Bussey markings but with "New Metal" for
rustless material $400
Iron--(B) Patent steel hosel, "Patent Perfection Handle"
marked on sewn grip $275
Iron--(B) Marked as above, smooth face, sewn 1-piece grip...............$200
Lofting Iron--(B) Long blade, smooth face,
sewn one piece grip $250
Mashie--(B) Smooth face compact blade, wide toe $200
Putter--(B) Gun metal blade, steel hosel, sewn 1-piece grip................$350
Putter--(B) Iron blade, marked "Thistle", sewn 1-piece grip $250
Putter--(B) Thistle series, steel socket model $200

Busson, J.H.
[Formby e]
Driver--Autograph model, socket head $50
Brassie--Autograph model, stripe top $50
Putter--XLALL model, iron blade, square socket $200

Butchart, C.S.*+

[Worked at several locations in Britain and Ireland; moved to America in about 1918 where he served as professional to the Westchester Country Club, NY and was a principal in the Butchart-Nicholls Company]

Driver--C.1920 Butchart Bilt series, late splice head with aluminum insert $250
Driver--Genuine Butchart model, split bamboo/hickory laminated shaft $200
Driver--Butchart Bilt model, stripe top, fiber insert $75
Jigger—Model 2, line face $50
Mid Iron—Autograph model, Westchester address $65
Niblick--Ayers CM, Autograph series own model $70
Iron clubs--Autograph series, Stewart pipe CM, l ine face .... $60 each

Butchart-Nicholls Company+

[Glenbrook, CT]

Driver--(U) Model 120, laminated bamboo & hickory shaft $175
Driver--(U) Model 110 socket head, laminated bamboo shaft $150
Spoon--(U) Model 112 socket head, laminated bamboo shaft $175
Spoon—(U) Model 122, socket head, laminated bamboo shaft $175
Mashie Iron--4, dot face, stainless steel, shore bird CM $45
Mid Iron--(U) BTN model, laminated shaft $100
Niblick--11, laminated bamboo & hickory shaft $100
Niblick--(U) Model 11, bamboo shaft $75
Putter--(U) 12, laminated bamboo & hickory shaft $125
Putter--(U) BTN model, laminated shaft $150
Numbered Irons--(U) Bamboo shaft .... $65 each
Set--(U) Bamboo shaft, irons 1-11, putter 12 .... $1,000

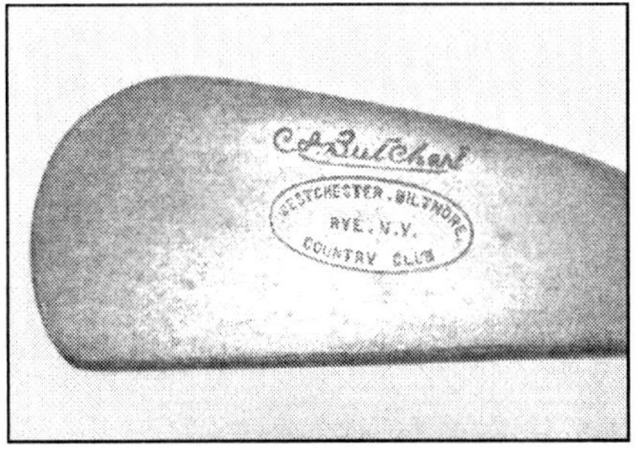

Cuthbert Strachan Butchart was highly successful in Britain before moving to the USA. Most of his clubs carried his autograph.

C

Cafferty, Peter*
[Edinburgh]
Spade Mashie—Deep face, dot fsce, H&B Mitre CM $65
Putter--Top Spin model, stainless, negative loft $200

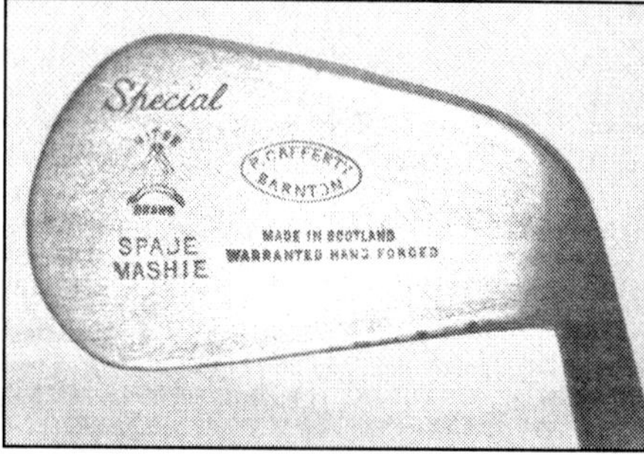

Peter Cafferty was professional and club maker to the Edinburgh Burgess Golf Club for twenty years.

Caird, Adam
[Tynedale e]
Driving Iron--Diamond back, name in circle, diamond/dot face $60

'Caledonia'
[MacGregor store brand]
Driving Iron--Name stamp in arc, dot face $30

Callan Brothers*
[London]
Iron clubs-Leaf brand, 3-leaf CM, stainless .... $60 each
Putter--Leaf brand, 3-leaf CM, stainless $75

Callaway, Christopher
[Haslar & Gosport e; later Europe and U.S.]
Named Irons--Pipe brand, name in oval .... $50 each
Putter--(S) Splice head $400

Campbell, Alex+

Willie Campbell was the first top-class Scottish professional to emigrate to America. He made clubs in Boston until his untimely death in 1900.

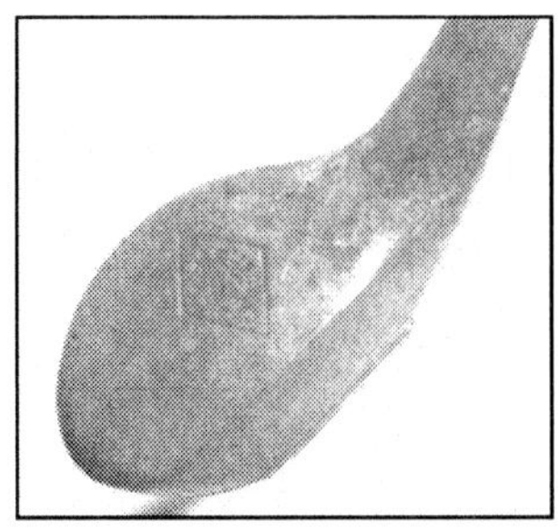

[Boston, MA, Cincinnati & Dayton, OH]
Driver--Socket head, stripe top $100
Iron--Smooth face, Stewart pipe CM $75
Mashie--Stainless, line face $50
Named Irons--Alex Campbell irons, Stewart pipe CM,
scored face .... $60 each
Jigger--The Nipper model $80
Putter--The Nipper model $85

Campbell, Jamie
Mid Iron--Smooth face $100

Campbell, Matt
[Boston]
Mid Iron--Lined face, Burke scales CM $60

Campbell, Willie*+
[Bridge o' Weir s & Boston, MA]
Driver--Socket head, name in diamond $175
Driver--Splice head, shaft stamp $250
Brassie--Socket head, Boston address $150
Iron clubs--Marked "I.J.S.G. Co." in double oval ....$100 each
Mashie--Smooth face, name in diamond $75
Mid Iron--Marked "Wm. Campbell, Boston" in
semi-circle stamp, smooth face $125
Putter--Gun metal blade, oval name stamp $100
Putter--Gun metal blade, name in arc, "Franklin Park" $250

Campbell, W.W. (William W.)
[Colorado Springs, CO]

Woods--Socket head .... $85 each
Mashie--Smooth face, Spalding 2 roses CM $50
Jigger--Rampant lion CM $50

Cann & Taylor*+

[Founded, Winchester e, most clubs produced at Richmond, Surrey e and two US sites; a partnership of Open Champion J.H. Taylor and club designer George Cann]

◇◇Early clubs

Driver--(S) Splice head, marked "Cann & Taylor" in block letters ...$300
Driver--Small splice head in oak wood $400
Brassie--(S) Short, bulldog shaped head with long splice $175
Spoon--Short splice head $225
Iron--Smooth face, marked for Winchester (England) $250
Lofter--Smooth face, marked Winchester and Wimbledon $200
Mashie--Smooth face, marked Richmond and Pittsburgh $200
Mashie--(B) Smooth face, marked "Winchester & Richmond and Deal Beach, USA" $275
Putter--Gun metal blade, marked "Winchester & Richmond and Deal Beach, USA" $150
Putter--Gun metal blade, stamped for Asbury Park $200

◇◇Clubs with J.H. Taylor Autograph CM

Driver--Autograph CM on head with Williams & Cie. oval import mark $125
Driver--Stripe top socket head, shaft stamp $90
Driver--Confidus model $100
Brassie--Stripe top socket head, shaft stamp for Williams & Cie. , Paris $100
Spoon--(B) Cynosure series, stripe top socket head $125
Spoon--Confidus model $125

J.H. Taylor won the 1894 Open demonstrating approaching with the newly developed mashie. With this fame, he began marketing "Taylors Mashie."

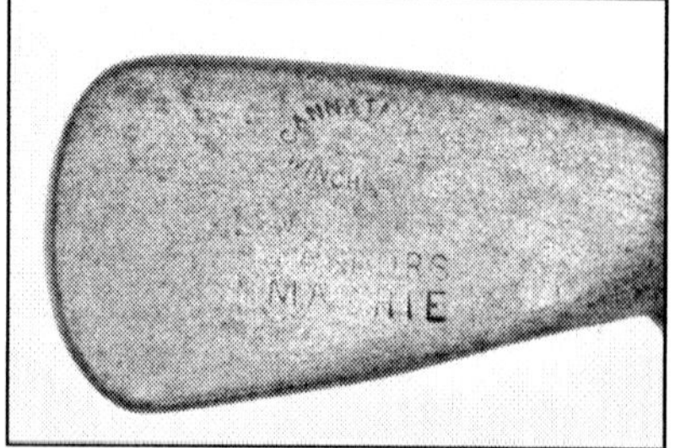

Cleek--Smooth face $80
Lofter--Smooth face, long blade $100
Mashie--Smooth face $80
Mashie--Smooth face, heavy blade, "Taylors Mashie" $125
Mashie--Line face, autograph CM & registration number $50
Mashie--(B) Mule's Patent spring face $500
Mashie--Fliweel model, flywheel CM, dot face $50
Mashie--Quickstop model, oval head, dash/dot face $75
Mashie Iron--Line face, short blade with deep face $90
Mashie Iron--Smooth face, short blade with deep face $100
Mashie Niblick--Dot face, autograph CM with registration number .$50
Mid Iron--Mascot model, greyhound CM. line face $70
Iron clubs--Cynosure series, line face ....$50 each
Mid Iron--Smooth face $80
Niblick--Smooth face, small heavy head $350
Putter--Bent blade style, marked "Taylor's Putter" $150
Putter--Fliweel series, gem style $100
Putter--Model V-15 blade, Vardon autograph, Fliweel CM $125
Putter--(B) Billiard Cushion model, top edge of face raised $300
Putter--(A B) Mallet head, negative loft,
Taylor autograph w/ registration number $250

Cannon, William Kempton

[Cambridge e]

Mashie--Flange sole, line face, cannon CM $75
Mashie—(B) Pointed toe, line face, Winton diamond CM $150
Lofter--(B) Pointed toe, line face $150

Carew

Iron clubs-Name in oval with arrowheads $75

Carrick, F. & A.*

[Musselburgh s; iron tool manufacturers, used a small cross cleek mark, C. 1860-1904]

Cleek--Circa 1875, long face, 4 ½-5" hosel, straight
line name stamp, cross cleek mark $650
Cleek--(B) 'The Acme', smooth face, Carrick cross CM $350
Cleek--Circa 1890, long face, 4 1/2" hosel, name stamp in arc,
cross cleek mark $400
Cleek--Circa 1900, shorter face, 4" hosel $300

Iron--Circa 1875, 4 3/4" hosel, straight line name stamp $750
Iron--Circa 1885, 4 1/2" hosel, no name stamp, cross CM $350
Lofter--Circa 1880, long blade, not concave, 4 1/2" hosel, straight line name stamp $400
Mashie--C.1880-85, straight name stamp $400
Mashie--Circa 1885-90, name stamp in arc, medium length blade with deep face $300
Mashie--c.1890, short blade, wide toe, marked for J.H. Hutchison $500
Niblick--Circa 1875, small almost circular head, thick heavy hosel, marked only "Carrick" $1,500-2,500
Niblick--Circa 1880, smooth face, round head marked with Carrick cross CM *(page 339)*.. ***$1,200-1,500***

Carruthers, John
[London]
Putter--(A B) Mallet head with hooked face $1,200

Carruthers, Thomas*
[Edinburgh; inventor of the short hosel, through-bore iron club]
Brassie—Sylviac wood sockethead $400
Cleek--(B) Smooth face, short blade, short hosel drilled through, Carruthers name in oval stamp $300
Iron--Smooth face, hosel ***not*** drilled $200
Mashie--(B) Smooth face, regular length hosel drilled through $250
Niblick--(B) Smooth face, regular length hosel drilled through $250
Putter--(B) Smooth convex face, short hosel drilled through $300

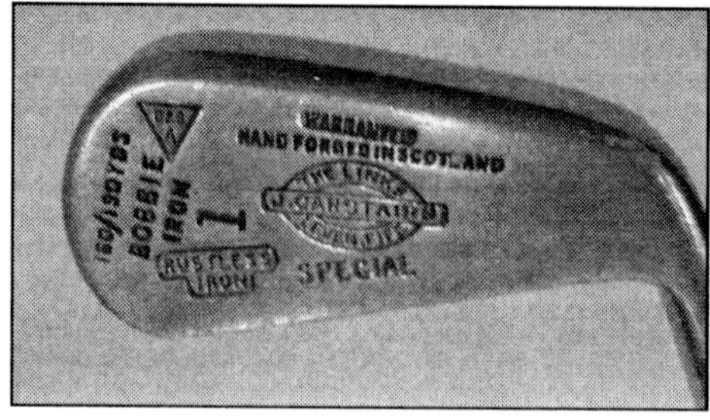

The Carstairs firm produced clubs in the 1920s with heads forged by Brodie & Son.

Carstairs, J.

[Leven s]
Driver—Stripe top socket head, ivorine fancy face $75
Irons—Numbered, with Brodie B&SA triangle CM $45

Carter, George*
[Guildford e]
Driver--Socket head, straight line name stamp $75
Mid Iron—Stewart serpent CM, dot face $75
Mashie--Signature marking, line face $75
Iron clubs—Stewart pipe CM, Curtis autograph ....$75 each

Cassidy, J.L.*
[Aldburgh e, et al]
Driver--Starbeck model, socket head $95
Putter--(A B) The Vee model, mallet head, V-shaped
aiming bar on top $125

Catlin, A.
[Barnet e, et al]
Driver--Socket head $60

Clubs fitted with the patented Cawseygrip (teardrop shaped) carried this cleek mark on the club head.

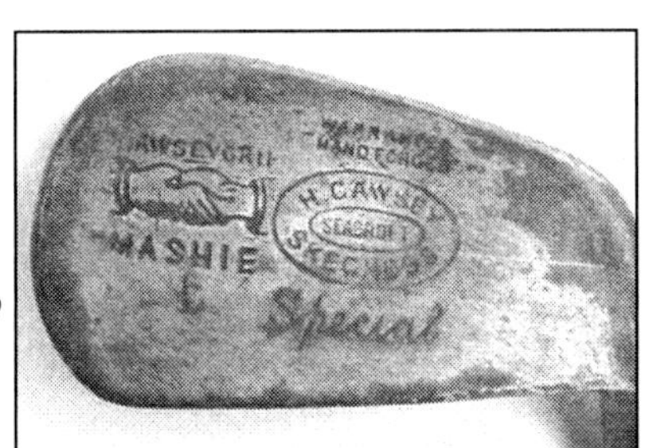

Cawsey, Harry*
[Skegness e, et al]
Driver--(B) Angsol model, beveled sole socket head $250
Brassie--(B) Picmup model, socket head, round sole $150
Brassie--(B) Spli-Sok model, combination
splice/socket joint $350
Spoon--(B) Angsol model, H-shaped sole plate $250
Mashie--Cawseygrip model $125
Spade Mashie--Line face, Stewart pipe CM $60

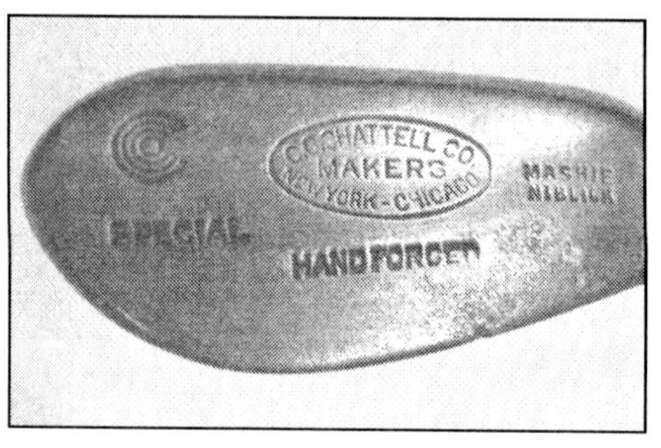

A Foulis-style mashie niblick with flat sole and the concentric C cleek mark.

Niblick--Cawseygrip model, 2 hands CM $100
Putter--Tramline model, wood mallet head, brass sole $125
Putter--Cawseygrip model, 2 hands CM, square handle $175

Chambers, F.
Driver--C.1905, splice head $150
Driver--Socket head $50

Chambers, J.
Putter--(S) Beech head with pointed toe, shaft stamp $400

'Champion'
Putter--Cross in shield CM $45

Chattell Company, C.C.+
[Chicago]
Driver—Socket head, crown marked Special with CCC logo centered on C in special $65
Iron--Juvenile, CCC CM $50
Iron—Marked for Jackson Park Golf Shop $200
Mashie--Stainless (nickel) steel, musselback, dash face $75
Mashie Niblick--stainless, CCC CM $50
Mashie Niblick--Foulis model, smooth concave face, CCC CM ... $250
Spade Mashie--CCC CM, dot face $40
Putter--Blade, CCC CM $60

Chestney, Harry*
[London]
Spoon--small socket head $70

Chicago Golf Company
[Chicago]
Iron clubs-Line face, large shamrock CM ....$35 each

Chicago Golf Shop+
[Chicago, IL]
Approach Cleek--Model 19, Celtic series musselback,
Forgan crown CM $75

Churchill, James
[Quincy, MA]
Mashie--(U) Rectangular cut out in sole, dot face $300

'Clan'
[in bell CM, see F.A.O. Schwarz]

'Clan'
[find more Clan clubs in the Spalding listings]
Cleek--Smooth face $250
Cleek--Smooth face, juvenile, stamped shaft $200

The Clan Golf Company made their own clubs for several years before procuring from other makers like William Gibson.

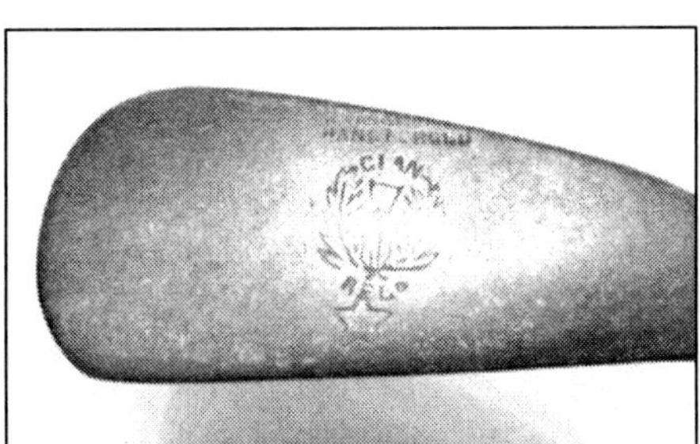

Clan Golf Company*
[London]
Driver--(S) Transitional shaped head, original black
paint finish, large thistle CM $850
Brassie--Light colored head, large thistle CM $600
Cleek--Smooth face, thistle CM $300
Iron--Smooth face, long blade with deep face, large thistle CM $400
Lofter—Smooth face, Clan CM and Gibson star CM $225

Mashie--Smooth face, compact blade, large thistle CM $300
Niblick—Old style round head, large thistle CM stamped horizontally to fit it on the club head, smooth face $500
Putter--"Made by Spence & Gourlay for Frank Bryan, Clan London", club pip CM $60

Clark, A.
Mashie--Smooth face, Millar small thistle CM $150

Clark, D.W.
[Lansdowne, PA]
Putter--Shield CM $50
Putter--Name in small oval $60

Clark, J. & D.*
[Musselburgh s]
Driver--Transitional shaped short splice head, bulger face $450
Driver--Splice head, marked for Tryon, Philadelphia $250
Brassie--(B) Compressed splice short head $350
Cleek--Smooth face, short round back blade, name in small oval $150
Cleek--Smooth face, Carrick cross CM $250
Lofter--Smooth slightly concave face, ash shaft $350
Mashie--Smooth face, compact blade $200
Mashie--C. 1900, dot face $100
Niblick--Small head, long hosel, smooth face $800
Putter--(S) Dark stained wood head $900
Putter--Bent blade style $275
Putter--Blade, name in oval $80
Wooden Niblick--Splice head, bulger face, brass sole plate $450

A mammoth or giant niblick from J.P. Cochrane was about the size of a pie pan.

Clark, Peter
Mashie Niblick--Diamond face $60

Clark, Tom
[Kansas City, MO]
Mashie--Flange sole, name in script, unusual diamond cartouche design on face $200

'Climax Fife'
Putter--Crown CM, made by Wm. Gibson $40

Clucas, J.
[Bridlington e, et al]
Putter--Iron blade $40

Clydesdale Rubber Company*
[Glasgow]
Lofter--Smooth face, straight line name stamp $100
Mashie--Smooth face, Nicoll small hand CM $200

Cobb, R.T.
Brassie--(L) C.1890, long wide head $600

Coburn, George*
[West Bromwich e, et al]
Brassie--Socket head $60
Niblick--Line face, medium size head $40

Cochrane & Company, J.P.*
[Edinburgh; headed by James Pringle Cochrane who had formerly worked for the S.G.C.M. Co. Originally a major factor for golf balls they became a large iron club manufacturer as well, using two CMs, a knight in armor and a bowline knot]
Driver--(U) The Everlasting Model, combination wood in steel casing $1,250
Driver--Walter Hagen autograph model, large socket head $150
Driver--Socket head, marked "J.P. Cochrane & Co." $80
Brassie--Walter Hagen autograph model, socket head $125
Brassie-Joe Kirkwood autograph series, face insert $125
Cleek--Juvenile (marked "B"), smooth face, knight CM $95

Driving Mashie—(B) Harrower patent, knight CM $50
Mashie Niblick--(B) XL Model, thin sole, thick top edge $250
Mashie--"Challenger Rustless Metal" on face $80
Mashie Niblick--Extra large oval head (like giant niblick), knot mark, line face $2,000
Mid Iron--Deep face, knight CM, made for T & G McKenzie $60
Niblick--Small head, smooth face, marked J.P. Cochrane $400
Niblick--Mammoth model, huge face, knot CM $1,200-2,000
Niblick--Mammoth model, "Junior" giant niblick $800
Pitcher--(D) Dedli model, grooved face, knight CM $150
Putter--(B) The Mac model, thick, short blade, knot CM $100
Putter--The Nigger model, long thin blade and hosel $350
Putter--The Nigger model, deep face iron blade $350
Putter--UOT model, cut out section at toe $600
Putter--Blade, Clyde Alloy stainless $60
Putter--(U) Travers model, rectangular wood head, centre shaft $600
Putter--P model, Walter Hagen series autograph, knot CM, stainless blade $100
Putter--Model Z, flat side on hosel, broad flange sole, knight CM $90
Putting Cleek--JPC model, JPC monogram CM $75
Putter--Holem model, musselback, knight CM $85
Putter--Model 28, Walter Hagen autograph, knot CM, stainless blade $90
Putter--(A) Mallet head, knight CM $125
Putter--Q model, bent neck, Challenger rustless iron $75
Putter—XXX model, like Orion with broad sole/flange $100
Numbered irons--Walter Hagen autograph model, rustless, knot CM $75each
Numbered irons-Repeter series .... $60 each

Cogswell & Harribone
[London & Feltham e]
Driver--Dint patent with C&H CM on silver sole plate $400
Putter--Gun metal gem-style, large C&H CM and Halley swords CM $150

Collins, William+
[Ryton-on-Tyne e and Staten Island, NY]
Spoon--Socket head, marked for Tenafly, NJ shop $125

Iron--Smooth face, marked Fox Hills $150
Jigger—(D) D-1, Spalding with Willie Collins autograph $120
Mashie--Smooth face $75
Niblick--"The Willie Collins," by Spalding $75

Willie Colllins' family was prominent in golf in Northern England in the late 19th century. It later played a significant role in NY area golf.

Collis, Harry
[Homewood, IL]
Lofter-Concave face, long thin blade, rounded sole $100

Columbia Special
[see Burke]

'Comet Brand'
[see Craigie, J. & W.]

Compston, Archie
[Manchester e, et al]
Driver--Socket head, stripe top $45
Numbered Irons--Own model, made by A. Patrick ....$45 each
Numbered Irons--Champion autograph series by
Thos. E. Wilson ....$60 each

Condie, Robert*
[St. Andrews]
Cleek--Smooth face, rose CM $85
Cleek--Smooth face, short 2 1/2" hosel, rose CM $140
Iron--Black gutta percha insert in face of blade
(imitating Nicoll patent), C.1900 .... $2,500
Mashie--Smooth face, name in oval, rose CM, Slazenger
name in oval $100

Mashie--Smooth face, Condie single fern CM $225
Mashie--Dot face, rose CM $60
Mashie--Boy's size, dot face, early rose CM $60
Mid Iron--Dot face, Tom Morris model, rose mark $85
Lofter—Smooth face, single fern CM $200
Lofter--Smooth face, long blade, small rose CM $125
Niblick--Smooth face, small head, rose CM $300
Niblick--Medium head, smooth face, rose CM $100
Niblick--Large head, dash face, rose CM $65
Putter--Gun metal blade, rose CM $65
Putter--Excelsior model, iron blade, rose C $65

Named Irons-Smooth face, rose CM ....$50-75 each
Named Irons-Line or dot face, rose CM ....$45-60 each

Connellan & Campbell+
[Boston, MA]
Driving Iron--Smooth face, Stewart pipe CM $100

Connellan Brothers
[Boston, MA]
Mid Iron--Smooth face, St. Andrew Golf Co. stag head CM $80
Iron--Smooth face, marked Connellan Selected in oval
with scrollwork design $60

Connelly, H.E.
Putter--Vimbo model, wood socket head, brass sole $250

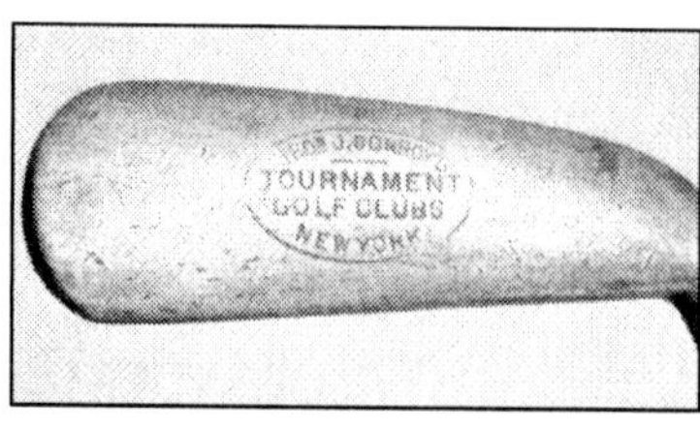

Thomas J. Conroy was a New York sporting goods house known for their fishing equipment. They offered a broad range of house brand golf implements in the early 1900s.

Conroy, Thomas J.+
[New York]
Driver--Splice head, brown color $150

Cleek--Smooth face, name in crest $75
Cleek— "Tournament Golf Clubs" in oval $100
Mashie Niblick--Smooth face, name in arc $100

Corey & Savage+
[Schenectady, NY]
Putter--(A) Center shaft, RL boat shaped head $300

'Corona'
Niblick--Line face $25

Cosby, E.
Woods--Socket head, braided whipping at socket and grip ends, made by Wm. Gibson, hand holding arrows CM ....$200 each
Mashie Niblick--(D) The Dead'un, rows of holes drilled through face $650
Named Irons--Braided whipping, hand/arrows CM ....$125 each

Cowan Golf Company*
[Sunderland e]
Brassie--(A S) Mills-style fairway club, cross hatch face $250
Putter--(A) Model F, Rodwell-type, arrow aiming line $175

Cowan & Clasper Ltd.
[Sunderland e]
Putter--(A) Model 322, mallet head $150

Cox & Sons
[Southampton e]
Mashie Niblick--Dot face, Gourlay moon/star CM $45

Craigie, J. & W.*
[Montrose s; originally timber merchants, the Craigie brothers produced quality wood and iron clubs around the turn of the century]
Driver--Splice head, black color, straight line name $400
Brassie--Socket head, straight line name stamp $175
Brassie--Comet Brand, small head, comet CM in oval mark $150
Wood Cleek--Socket head, face insert $225
Mashie--Line face, rifle mark $80
Mashie—Condie rose CM, smooth face $80

Mid Iron--Smooth face, rifle CM, shaft stamp $100
Lofter--Smooth face, long blade, rifle CM $225
Lofter--Smooth face, short blade, rifle CM $100
Niblick--Smooth face, small head, rifle CM $400
Niblick--Line face, large head, rifle CM, oval name stamp $100
Niblick—Smooth face, tiny Gibson star CM $150
Putter--Comet Brand, iron blade, comet CM, line face $75
Putter—Gun metal blade, tiny Gibson star CM $150
Putter—Gun metal blade, rifle CM $100

Crawford McGregor & Canby Company+
[Dayton, OH; see MacGregor]

Crawford-Bartlett Company
[Chicago]
Mashie--Child's club for game of Lawn Golf, W in diamond CM $50

Crighton, J. & R.*
[Carnoustie s]
Cleek--Dot face, heart CM $75
Iron--Line face, heart CM $75
Mashie--Dreadnought model, dot face $75
Mashie Niblick--Oval shaped head, line face, heart CM $80
Niblick--Large head, dot face $75
Putter--Heart CM, iron blade $80
Putter--Steel mallet head, heart CM $250

Croke, Jack
[Oak Park, IL]
Driver--Socket head, name in script $75
Niblick--Dot face, heavy head, S&G club pip CM $60

Crook, Henry
[Leigh-on-Sea e]
Iron--Line face, blacksmith's forge CM $60
Irons—Line face, Spalding anvil CM ....$35 each

Crosthwaite, Andrew W.*
[St. Andrews]
Putter---(S) Marked "Crosthwaite" $850

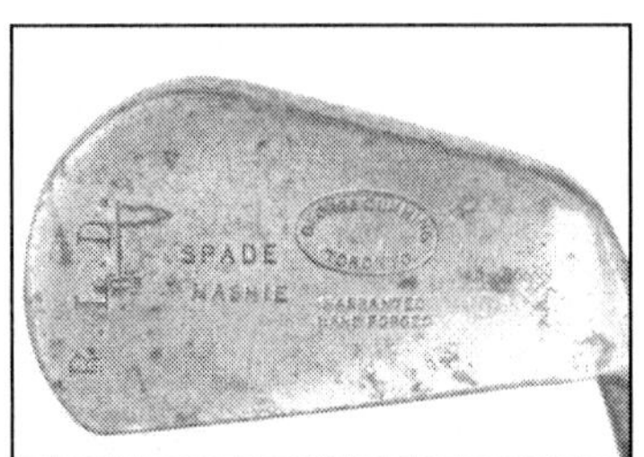

George Cumming was professional to the Toronto Golf Club for many years and a participant in several early US Open Championships.

Crosthwaite & Lorimer*
[St. Andrews]
Brassie--(S) Transitional shaped head $450
Iron---Smooth face, heavy blade $200
Putter—Carbon composite head, lead edge strip $400

Crowley, James
[Glasgow]
Playclub--Beech head $1,500
Iron clubs--Nicoll Indicator series,
Crowley name in oval .... $50 each
Putter---Gun metal head, three legged Manx figure CM $100

Crowley, R.
Playclub--(S) Beech head, bulger shape $1,200

'Crusader'
Putter--9, shield CM $40

Cumming, George+
[Toronto, ONT]
Driver--Large socket head $100
Mashie--Dot face blade $65
Mashie Niblick--(D) Corrugated face, Spalding roses CM $125
Spade Mashie--Dash face, Forgan flagstick CM $75

Cunningham, William*
[Edinburgh]
Driver--Dreadnought-style large socket head $85
Brassie--Stripe top, socket head $60
Brassie--Gullen model, socket head $75

Iron clubs--Stewart pipe brand .... $60 each

Cupples Golf Company+
[St. Louis, MO]
Iron clubs--Rhino series, rhinoceros CM, dot face .... $45 each
Iron clubs--Pro series, target CM .... $35 each

Currie, J.D.
Driver--Socket head, juvenile $50

Currie, T.
Brassie--Short splice head $175

Currie, William
Driver--(S) Beech head $350
Driver--(B) Bronze head with red gutta percha or rubber
covering all the face $5,000

Curtis, H.L.*
[Bournemouth e]
Driver--Socket head $75
Driving Mashie--Autograph model $75
Mashie--Line face, oval name stamp $45
Mashie--X35, dot ball face, autograph CM $75
Sammy--Autograph CM, round back, dot face $75
Niblick--(B) Smith model (anti-shank), smooth face $175
Putter--Wood centre shaft head, brass sole $300

Cuthbert, G.
[Carnoustie]
Iron clubs--"Caddie" Brand .... $40 each

Cuthbert, J.
[Stanmore e, et al]
Driving Iron--Dot face $35
Putting Cleek--Three crowns CM, made by Premier Golf Co. $85

'Cutlas'
Putter--(A) Mallet head $75

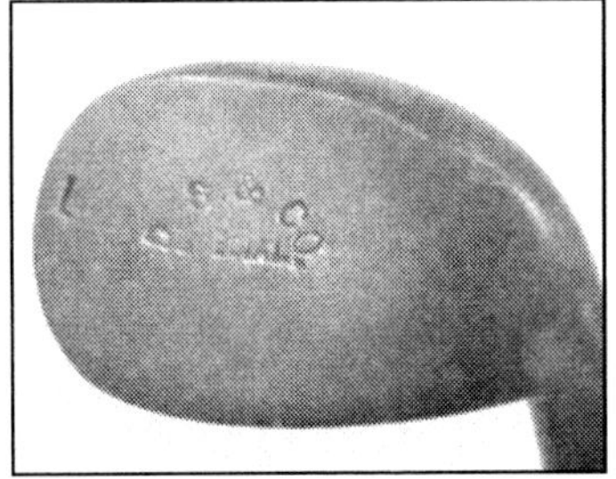

Dame, Stoddard & Co. was an early seller of golf clubs in America. This ladies niblick is a scarce 19th century American club.

D

D.S. & Company+
[Dame. Stoddard & Co., Boston, MA]
Mid Iron--Trimount series, smooth face, knurled hosel $100
Mashie--Smooth face, D.S & Co. $60
Niblick—Small heavy head, smooth face $350
Putter--Iron blade, dot face $50
Putter--Gun metal blade $125

D.S. & K.+
[Dame, Stoddard & Kendall, Boston, MA]
Driver--Socket head $55

Dagnall, George*
[Sevenoaks e, et al]
Driver--(B) Socket head, The Dagnall $250

This Bobby model putter from George Dagnall was prism shaped and made by F.H. Ayres.

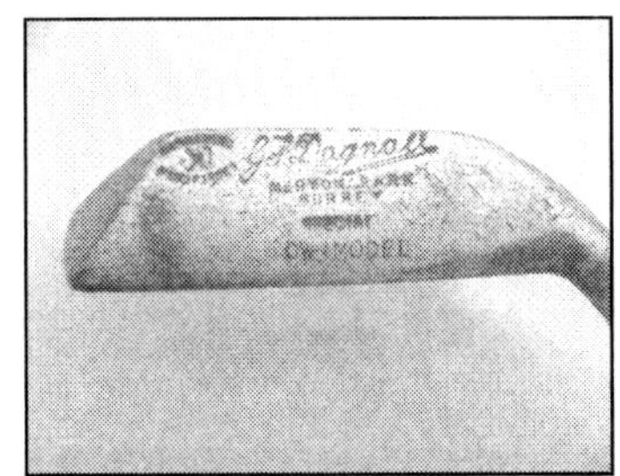

Mashie--(D) "Handy Andy Kutspin Highball Iron",
large dot/dash face $600
Mashie Niblick--(D) Handy Andy Kutspin model,
brick face with deep circle punches $400
Putter--Bobby model, low profile dot face, sloped back $125

Dailey, Allan
Driver--Stripe top socket head $50

Dalgleish, J.
[Kansas City, MO]
Driver--Splice head $150
Putter--Blade, Spalding anvil CM $55
Putter--Missouri Topspin model, top flange $250
Putter--Old Elm Special model, offset blade $60

Dalrymple, Sir Walter H.*
[Famous amateur golfer and club patentee; clubs made by R. Forgan, J.H. Hutchison and other makers]
Duplex Club--(A B) Cylindrical aluminum hammer
shaped head with two hitting surfaces, shaft stamp $2,000
Duplex Club--(B) Brass cylindrical hammer head, one surface
used for chipping and one for putting, marked
by J.H. Hutchison $4,800

'Daniel'
Putter--(A B) Rectangular head with adjustable weights in toe $2,500

Dargo, J.H.*
[Edinburgh]
Driver--Socket head $50
Mashie--Line face, oval stamp, Gibson star CM $40
Mid Iron--Line face, oval stamp, shaft stamp $35

Dargie, Bert
[Biltmore Forest, NC]
Irons—Blue Diamond brand, line face .... $30 each

Davega+
[New York City sporting goods house]

Driver--Metropolitan series, socket head $35
Brassie--Wicklow series, stripe top $40
Driving Iron--Gairlock series X2, line face $30
Iron--Gairlock series, X-88, Burke bee/flower CM $35
Mashie--(D) Baxpin model 2A, ribbed face $85
Putter--Tommy Armour model $50
Putter, Wicklow series, blade, line face $35
Putter--Gairlock series, blade $35
Irons--Cameo series ....$30 each
Irons--Gairlock series ....$30 each
Irons--Imperial series, stainless, line face, heart CM ....$30 each
Irons--La Salle Club series, star & crescent CM ....$30 each
Irons--Lassie, dash face ....$30 each
Irons--Metropolitan series, dot face, chromed ....$30 each
Irons--Wicklow series, star CM, chrome ....$30 each
Numbered Irons--Tommy Armour model ....$40 each

Davey, Ashley*
[Margate e, et al]
Cleek--Smooth face, Stewart serpent CM $100
Mashie--Line face, Stewart pipe CM $50
Mashie--Excelsior series, A.H. Scott lion CM, dot face $60
Niblick--Gun metal head with large extension at top,
smooth face, two surface face (concave) $2,250
Putter--Gun metal blade, oval name stamp $80

Davidson, C.*
[Musselburgh s]
Deep Face Mashie--Line face, three crowns CM $60

Davidson, Robert*
[Montrose s]
Playclub--(L) Long head, whippy shaft $6,000-9,000
Baffing Spoon--(L) Lofted face, name stamped in script $6,500
Driving Putter--(L) Straight face, thick neck, dark stained head ... $8,000

Davidson, W.*
[Musselburgh s]
Driver--Splice head, name in block letters $250

Davis, Willie F.+
[William H. Vanderbilt brought this young Scotsman to the U.S. to serve as the first professional to the Newport, RI Golf Club, later at Shinnecock Hills. During the 1880s Davis worked in Canada]
Playclub--(L) Marked 'W. Davis', C.1890 Montreal $8,000
Driver—Short splice head, honey colored stain (page A) $300
Brassie--(S) Beech head, marked 'Thornton' $750
Brassie--Splice head $300
Cleek--Smooth face, name stamp from Newport $200
Putter--Iron blade, Willie Wilson 'St. Andrew' CM $200

Day, Arthur
[Ganton e, et al]
Mashie Niblick--Eeze series, line face $50

Dayton Art Metal Co.
[Dayton, OH]
Putter--Birdie model, flying bird CM $50

Dayton's
[Minneapolis, MN department store]
Putter--Interlachen series, flange sole,
Burke lion & crown CMs $75

De La Torre, A.
Mashie--Line face, made by Stewart, pipe CM $45

'De Luxe'
Putter--Maxwell pattern, kangaroo & kiwi CMs,
made in Australia $50

Willie Davis was one of the earliest club makers in North America He played in the first four US Opens representing the Newport GC.

Dean, H.E.
Mashie--Stewart pipe CM $45

Dean, R.M.
Cleek--Smooth face, juvenile, shaft stamp, dark stained shaft $125

'Dedli'
Putter--(U) Blade with large cylindrical weight chamber
on top edge, Marsh patent $2,500

'Demon, The'
[name also used by Slazenger]
Iron--Made by Fred Blaisdell, smooth face small 6-point
asterisk CM $100

Denholm, Andrew*
[Brighton e]
Driver--Transitional splice head $350
Driver--Splice head, thick scare, leather face insert $200
Driver--Socket head $50

Derby, Jack
[Meridian, MS]
Putter—All Square model, long thin hosel, made by Jack White $80

Des Jardins, A.
[Montreal, QUE]
Driver--Laval model, stripe top $60

Dewar, Hugh
[Troon s]
Mashie Niblick--A9, triangle CM, line face $50

Dewsbury & Son, Jos.
Numbered Irons--Dewralex series, rustless dot face ....$40 each

Diamond Manufacturing Company+
[St. Louis, MO]
Mashie--M-31, name in double diamond, dash/dot face $60

J. & A. Dickson was one of Edinburgh's finest club making firms until they closed their doors in 1908.

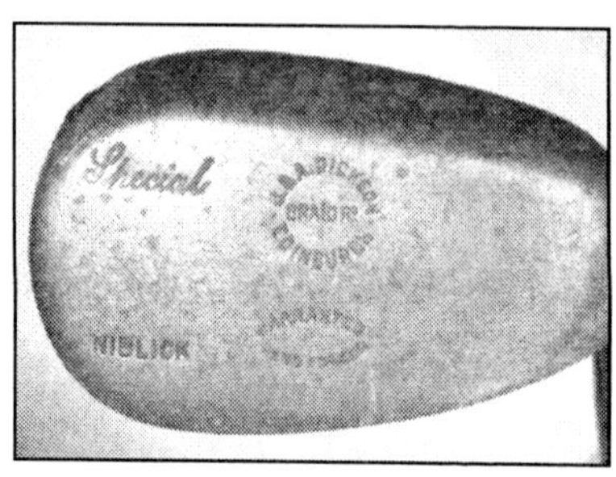

'Diamond State Brand'
Mashie--(D) Marked for Wilfred Reid, corrugated face $100

Dickinson, M.
Brassie--Splice head, hickory shaft $300

Dickson, J. & A.*
[Edinburgh]
Brassie--Short splice head $225
Spoon--Short splice head $250
Cleek--Smooth face, short blade, Braid Rd. address $100
Iron--(B) Simplex model, two-tine hosel,
like short Seely Patent $1,500
Jigger--Dot punch face $50
Mashie--Convex face, calfskin grip $400
Mashie--Deep face, X face, Gibson star CM $75
Niblick--C.1895, small head, smooth face $400
Niblick—Smooth face, larger 20th century head $80
Putter--Gun metal blade $150
Putter--Iron blade, bent hosel, small Gibson star CM $150

Dint Patent Golf Company, Ltd.
[Malvern Link e]
Woods (driver, brassie, spoon)--"The Dint", socket head,
German silver sole & face plates $400

Doerr
[Made by Laclede Brass Works, St. Louis, MO; also see Laclede]
Putter--(U) Doerr Topem model, stainless, top flange $150
Putter--(U) Doerr Topem model, phosphor bronze,
negative loft, bottom flange, deeply scored line face $300

Doleman, Frank*
[Edinburgh]
Driver--Splice transitional head, dark stain on head & shaft $450
Brassie--(S) Transitional splice head $650
Iron--Smooth face, straight line name stamp $125
Mashie--Smooth face, Gibson star CM $100
Putter--(S) C.1895, beech head, heavily leaded $650

Donald & Son, J.
[Weston-Super-Mare e]
Mashie--Dot face, swan CM $60

Donaldson Manufacturing Company, Ltd., J.*
[Glasgow]
Driver--(B) Rangefinder-Rapier series, Duralwood socket head $100
Driver--Rangefinder-Rapier series, socket head $75
Woods (dr br sp)--(B) Rangefinder series, double stripe top, splice head ....$125 each
Iron--Birdie model, bird CM, stainless, line face $60
Iron--Skelpie model, pointed toe, line face $70
Iron--Speug model, round sole, dot face $80
Iron clubs--Rangefinder series, line face, circular CM ....$50 each
Mid Iron--Rapier series, dot face $45
Niblick--Power 80 model, Rangefinder series, large head sand iron $200
Putter--Bunny model, stainless mallet head, brass face plug, bunny CM $175
Putter--Rangefinder series, blade, dot face $60

Donaldson, J.A.
[Glenview, Chicago]
Mongrel Mashie--Stewart pipe CM, line face $80

Donaldson, J.T.
[Glasgow]
Putter--Shallow face, round back $75
Numbered Irons--Dot face $30

Doughty, George
[*Margate; Surbiton e]*
Mashie—The Doughty model, low profile blade,
Regd. number, sun CM $85

Dow, Robert*
[Montrose s]
Driver--C.1900 Transitional splice head $500
Driver--Short splice head $300

Draper-Maynard Company+
[Plymouth, NH sporting goods firm]
Driver--Socket head, Ideal model $75
Brassie--The Lucky Dog Kind series, dog CM $75
Mashie--(D) Lucky Dog series, corrugated face $125
Mashie--Lucky Dog series, dot face, stainless, dog CM $40
Niblick--Bulls Eye model, dot face, dog in circle on face $85
Putter—Bulls Eye model, steel blade $60
Spade mashie--Doggie series, dog CM, dot face $40
Named Irons--Ideal series, stainless, dot face .... $35 each
Numbered Irons--Kingswood series, dog CM, dot face, chrome $40 each

Dubow, J.A.
Putter--Silver Cup model, offset blade $30

'Duncan Twin'
Putter--(B) Adjustable head combination putter/chipper $1,400

Duncan, George*
[Hanger Hill, Ealing e, et al]
Driver--Dreadnought type socket head $100
Driver—Akros model, thick ivorine face insert *(page A)***.......... *$120***
Brassie--Ivorine insert, socket head $85
Brassie--(U) Duncan model by Spalding, one piece sole
plate backweight $100
Cleek--Curious model $150
Named Irons--Akros model, George Duncan autograph,
Gibson star CM .... $75 each

Duncan, William

Brassie--Greenock model, socket head $60

Dunlop, A
Putter--Shoor Flite series, gem-type $75

Dunn Brothers*
[Mitcham, London; brothers John D. and Gourlay Dunn]
Driver--(B) Unbreakable compressed splice head $450
Mashie Iron--Smooth face, plume of feathers CM $300

Dunn, John Duncan
[Nephew of Willie Dunn, Jr.; headed B.G.I. and British Golf Company]
Brassie--Splice head, fiber insert $275
Brassie--Splice head, olde English lettering, small crown CM,
fiber insert $200
Lofter--Marked "British Made", made by British Golf Co. $85
Mashie Niblick--Stainless, Morehead ship's wheel CM,
dash face $50
Mid Iron--Ionic series, 2 crowns CM $50
Niblick--Smooth face, maltese cross in circle CM, "British Made" $100
Approach Putter—Musselback, ship's wheel CM, dot face $60

Dunn, Seymour+
[Nephew of Willie Dunn, Jr. for whom he worked; later to his own shop in Lake Placid, NY]
Brassie--Model 72C, splice head, crown CM $175
Iron clubs--"Vi et Arte" model, crown CM ....$80 each
Pitcher-"Viet et Arte" model 102 .... $100
Mashie Niblick--Smith model anti-shank, crown CM with
legend "Vi et Arte" $200

Dunn, Thomas*
[Son of old Willie Dunn; worked at Wimbledon, North Berwick, Bournemouth and London]
Playclub--(L) Circa 1880, black stained head $2,500-5,000
Brassie--(S) C.1890, beech head, shaft stamp $1,450
Brassie--Transitional head $550
Mid Spoon--(L) Late long nose $2,700
Short Spoon--(L) Circa 1880, leather face insert $3,200
Spoon--Transitional head, calfskin grip $1,200

Baffing Spoon--(L) Circa 1880, beech head $5,500
Iron--Smooth face, straight name stamp $350
Lofter--Smooth concave face, long blade $600

Dunn, William (Sr.)*
[Blackheath e & Musselburgh s]
Long Spoon--(L) Very long head, stained dark, ash shaft ..$6,000-8,000
Mid Spoon--Medium stain, fruitwood head $6,000-8,000
Putter--Hook face, long thin head $5,000-8,000

Dunn, William (Jr.)*+
[Ardsley Casino, NY and NYC; made clubs with his brother Tom in England until 1894 when he emigrated to America. Had his own business but also managed the B.G.I. and MacGregor golf works in the late 1890s]
Driver--(B) One piece, shaft stamp
"Dunn & Son, Bournemouth" $2,400
Driver--Short splice head, NY markings, dark color $550
Driver--(U) Indestructable (sic) model, combination
aluminum and wood head $1,500
Driver--Splice head, "Unbreakable" $150
Driver--Model 20 splice head, MacGregor shaft $250
Driver--Splice head, child's size $300
Brassie--Splice head with bulger face $400
Brassie--Short splice head in persimmon $300
Brassie--Splice head, marked "Dunn Selected" $250
Brassie--Splice head marked "Dunn Selected" $275
Brassie--(U) Convex sole model, socket head, leather face $300
Chipper--(A U) Oval hammer shaped head with two hitting
surfaces, center shaft $1,500
Cleek--Head forged by Williams with "W" mark on hosel,
MacGregor shaft stamp $300

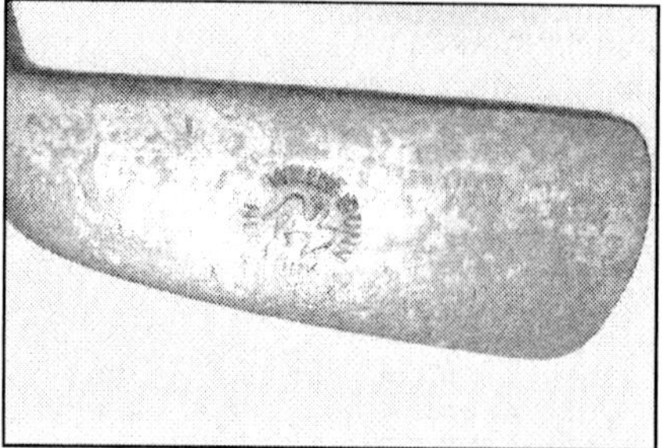

A very few clubs made by Willie Dunn's New York shop bore the eagle cleek mark like this cleek.

Cleek—Eagle CM, smooth face $200
Iron--Smooth face, "Dunn Selected" in script $175
Iron--Smooth face, "Dunn Selected" in block letters $150
Iron--Smooth face, short blade, Dunn-MacGregor
'bowtie' CM $275
Iron--Smooth face, marked New York in arc,
MacGregor shaft, I on hosel $200
Mashie--Smooth face, "Dunn Selected" in script $175
Lofter--Smooth face, name in block letters $175
Niblick--Smooth face, small head, marked "Ardsley",
small eagle CM $800
Putter--(U) 'Rotary model' two flange gunmetal head $850
Putter--Park-style bent neck blade, "Dunn Selected" in script $200
Putter--Gun metal blade, Condie rose CM,
marked Ardsley, NY $200
Putter--(A S U) Topspin-type, negative loft face $400

'Durexo'
Driver--Socket head, made by Alex Patrick $75

Duthie, Alex
[Several locations in Canada]
Heavy Iron--Dot face, Gibson star CM $70
Light Iron--Dot face $60
Medium Iron--Dot face $60

Dwight, J.H.+
Dwight Directional Clubs
[Des Moines, IA]
Driver--(U) Directional model, conic shaped head with
brass backweight $2,000-4,000
Mashie--(U) Directional model, boat shaped head,
centre shaft, dot face $1,800-3,000
Niblick--(U) Directional model, well-lofted boat shaped head,
centre shaft, dot face $2,500-3,500
Putter--Dwight Directional series, center shaft, dot face $2,000-3,000

→

Continued next page

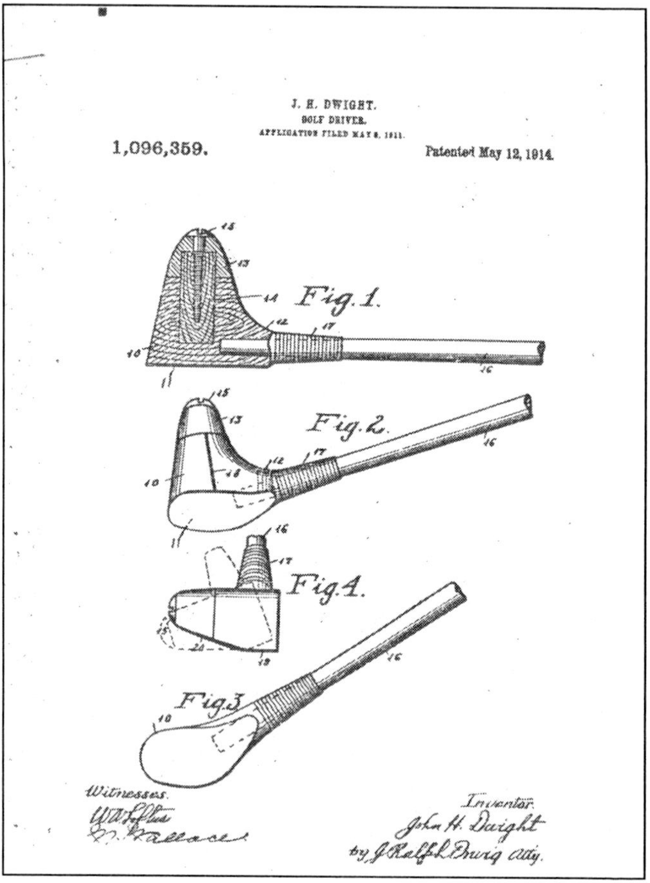

J. H. DWIGHT.
GOLF DRIVER.
APPLICATION FILED MAY 8, 1911.

1,096,359. Patented May 12, 1914.

Fig. 1.

Fig. 2.

Fig. 4.

Fig. 3.

Witnesses:
W. A. Pfleus
M. Wallace

Inventor:
John H. Dwight
by J. Ralph L. Erwig Atty.

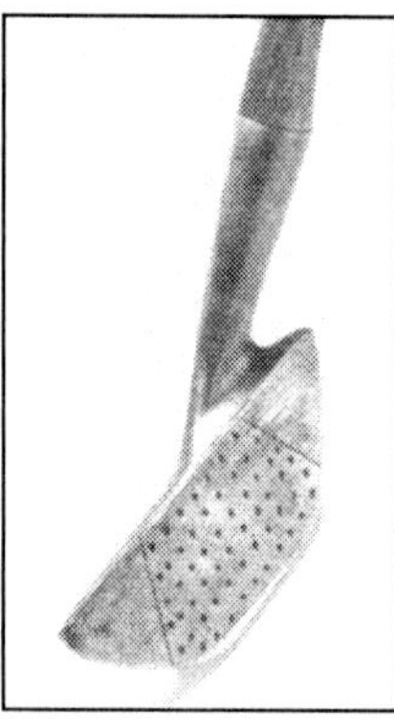

John H. Dwight's "Directional" clubs were center shafted which prompted one critic, at the time they were introduced, to call the unusual looking implements "Dutch hoes."

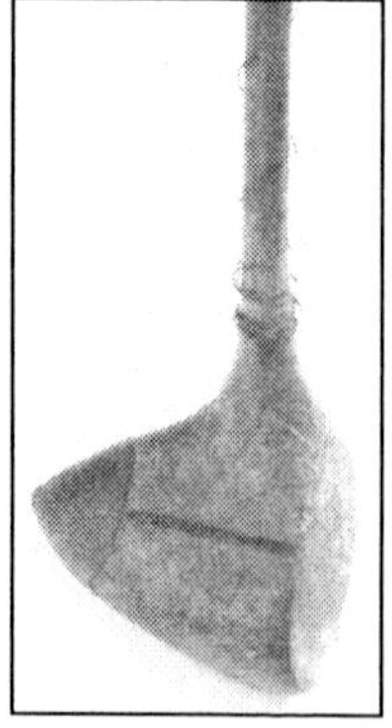

E

Eagen, Peter
[Princeton, NJ]
Brassie--Name in script, socket head $60

'Eager Special'
Putter--Offset blade $40

Eagrow Company+
[Milwaukee, WI]
Named Irons--Arrow model, stainless, line face ....$35 each

'Edco'
[Ernest Derrick Company, London]
Niblick--Dash face, triangle CM $45
Putter--Gun metal blade, triangle CM $65

Edgar, J.
[Settle e, et al]
Putter--100 model, gem style, flower CM $100

'Edgemont'
[MacGregor economy series; see MacGregor]

'Edinboro'
[made by B.G.I.]
Driver--Splice head $150
Cleek--Smooth face $125
Mashie--Smooth face $95
Mashie—Deep face, smooth face $100
Putter--Gun metal blade $150

'Elm Ridge'
Mid Iron--Chrome, line face $20

Edinburgh Club

The Edinboro brand was a line of clubs made by Bridgeport Gun Implement Co.

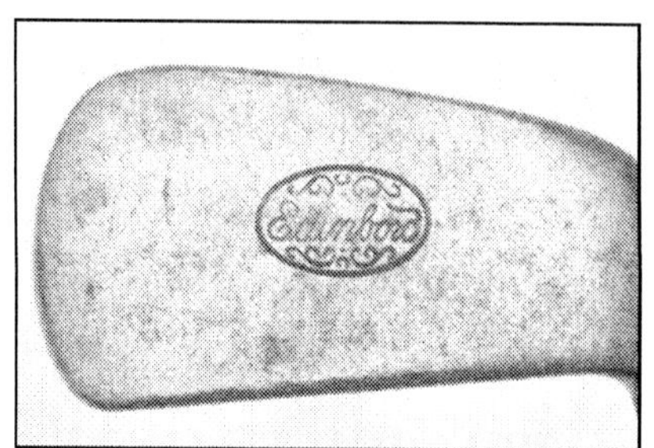

Mashie--Smooth face $60

Elvery's
[London, Dublin, Cork i retailer]
Putter--Star Maxwell model, Maxwell pattern, Gibson star CM $75
Putter--Vardon style, shallow face, curved top $150

'Emperor' Brand
Putter--Mallet shaped wood socket head, swan neck bent hosel, marked for Slazenger on toe $650
Putter--As above, unmarked $450

'Esto Perpetua'
Putter--Gun metal blade $60

'Eureka'
Driver--Made by Frank Johnson, socket head $125

'Everbrite'+
[Baltimore, MD; made by Curtis Bay Copper & Iron Works]
Mashie--High nickel content stainless, dot face $60
Mashie—Bakspin, wide groove spacing, diamond in sweetspot $75
Mashie Niblick--Dot face $60
Putter--(A) Schenectady-type, Everbrite mark on sole $250
Putting Cleek—Diamondback, nickel alloy steel $65

F

Fair, The

[Chicago department store]

Driver--Socket head, Waverly Horton autograph $85

'Fairfield'

[B.G.I. economy brand line of clubs, made from selected "seconds"]

<><>Listed by model number (stamped on shaft below grip)

004--Cleek, smooth face, juvenile $100
006--Lofting iron, smooth face, juvenile $100
009--Iron, smooth face, juvenile $100
010--Putting cleek, juvenile $100
012--Driving mashie, smooth face, juvenile $100
091--Driver, splice head, juvenile $200
093--Brassie, splice head, juvenile $200
201--Driving Iron $75
202--Gooseneck putting cleek $125
203--Driving cleek $75
204--Cleek $65
205--Centraject mashie $100
206--Lofting iron $75
207--Concave lofting cleek (jigger) $150
208--Lofting mashie $100
209--Iron $65
210--Putting cleek $100
211--Niblick, thick sole $125
212--Driving mashie $100
214--Medium mashie $75
215--Mashie, convex back $100
216--Medium mashie, deep face $100
217--Driving mashie, long blade $100
218--Approaching mashie $100
219--Putting cleek, twist neck $100
220--Putting cleek, deep face $125

221--Mashie iron $100
222--Cleek, short blade $100
290--Driver, straight face, splice head $250
223--Light mid iron $100
224--Mashie, J.H. Taylor pattern $125
291--Driver, bulger face, splice head $250
292--Brassie, straight face, splice head $225
293--Brassie, bulger face, splice head $225

'Fairview'
[House brand for The Fair department store, Chicago, IL, later by Lowe & Campbell]
Iron clubs--Smooth face (Fair Store) .... $75 each
Iron clubs--Scored face, Aim Rite clubs by Wilson
for Lowe & Campbell .... $30 each

Fairway , The
Driver—Decal on crown, "This is a first class club," socket head,
"Driver" cast into sole plate $80

Faith Manufacturing Company+
[Chicago]
Named/Numbered Irons--Big Ball series, chromed head,
line face, ball CM .... $25 each
Numbered Irons--Superflight series, chromed head,
dot face .... $25 each

Far & Sure Golf Company*
[Edinburgh]
Driver--(S) Short narrow splice head $750
Brassie--(S) Transitional splice head $600
Iron--Smooth face, straight line name stamp $250
Putter--(S) Transitional wood splice head $900

Feltham & Company*
[London]
Brassie--Splice head, bulger shape $250
Mashie--Smooth face $80
Niblick--Smooth face, small head $400

A.H. Fenn began his career as a successful amateur golfer but eventually became a professional working in Massachusetts and Florida.

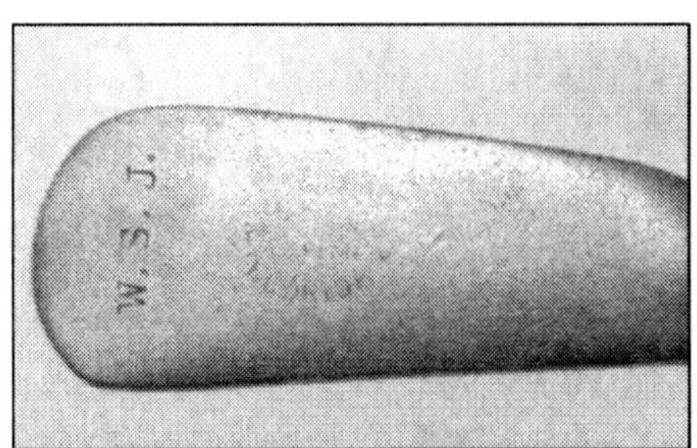

Fenn, A.H.+
[Poland Spring, ME, et al]
Driver--Short splice head $200
Driver--Socket head $80
Iron—Smooth face, marked for Palm Beach, Florida $150
Mashie--Line face, Spalding Gold Medal series $75

Fergie, William*
[Edinburgh]
Driver--Short splice head $200
Brassie--(S) Transitional splice head $450
Lofter--Smooth face, oval stamp $200
Putter--(S) Splice head $600
Putter--Wood socket head, fiber face $250

Ferguson, J. (Jacky)
[Musselburgh s; brother of Robert]
Driver--Short splice head $175

Ferguson, Robert*
[Musselburgh s, Open Champion]
Putter--(S) Dark head $2,500-3,500

Fernie & Ross
[St. Andrews]
Cleek--Ross's Own Model, Carruthers hosel, dot face $95
Niblick--Eden series, hand holding wreath CM, line face $75

Fernie, George
[Troon s, et al]

Spoon--(S) Brass sole plate, transitional head $750

Fernie, Harry
[Gosforth e]
Driver--Name in script, socket head $80

Fernie, John
[Barnet e, et al]
Numbered Irons--Par series, stainless, dot face .... $30 each

Fernie, Tom R.
[Royal Lytham e]
Driver--Socket head $100
Baffy--(B) "Wooden mashie", socket head $300
Cleek--RTJ model, Fernie autograph, Stewart pipe CM $125
Iron clubs--Stewart pipe model, autograph .... $80 each
Iron clubs--Stewart pipe model, name in oval stamp .... $70 each
Iron clubs--Line face, sword and crest CMs .... $75 each

Fernie, Willie*
[Troon s, et al]
Driver--Transitional shape splice head, leather insert $300
Driver--Splice head, oval stamp $200
Driver—Super oversize socket head $300
Brassie--Short splice head $150
Cleek--Smooth face, pipe CM $100
Putter--Steel blade, oval stamp $100
Putter--Bent hosel with steel blade ahead of shaft $400

'Field'
[Marshall Field Company, Chicago]
Mashie--Juvenile, name in shield $30
Mid Iron--Junior model, straight line name stamp $25

Fife Golf Company
[Kinghorn, Fife s; produced by William Gibson]
Iron clubs--Castle CM, line face .... $40 each
Putter--Gun metal blade, castle CM $75

Finnigan's*
[Liverpool department store]
Brassie--Socket head, oval shaft $150

Fitzjohn Brothers+
[New York]
Cleek—Spalding 2 rose CM $100
Mashie--Smooth face, name in double oval $75

Fitzjohn, Ed
[Oneita NY, Albany, NY et.al.]
Mid-iron--(U) Leitch patent (Spalding) with raised ridge on center of back, dash face $150
Putter--Adjustable, shaft bolted to center back of blade $2,500
Putter--(U) Center shaft attached to back of blade, shaped like an inverted question mark $3,500

Fitzjohn, Val
Driver--Short splice head $200

Fletcher, W.
[Luton e, et al]
Driver--Gravitum model, socket head $80
Brassie--Hornby model, ivorine face insert $90
Putter--Iron blade, dot face $40

Flood, Val
[New York]
Driver--Splice head, name in circle, eagle head CM $350
Brassie--Splice head, full sole plate $150
Brassie--Socket head, name in signature $100

The three Fitzjohn brothers, Ed, Fred and Val, worked together and individually throughout their careers.

Jigger--Dot face $90
Mashie--Spalding rose CMs, dot face $50

Forgan, Andrew*
[Glasgow s; younger brother of Robert Forgan]
Playclub--(L) Dark head $2,500
Driver--Splice head, tree CM $350
Driver--(S) Splice head, tree CM $600
Brassie--Splice head, tree CM $350
Lofter--Smooth face, long blade, long hosel $300
Mashie--Smooth face, compact blade, tree CM $150
Niblick—Small head, smooth face, tree CM $300
Niblick--Smooth face very small head, made by James Anderson ... $450
Putter--Gun metal blade, tree CM $200
Putter--(S) Light color splice head $650

Forgan & Son, Robert*
[St. Andrews; Robert Forgan grew from Hugh Philp's assistant to be principal of the largest and best known club making firm in the world. Appointed club maker to H.R.H. The Prince of Wales in 1863, early Forgan clubs are marked with the prince's symbol of a plume of three feathers. When the prince became King Edward VII in 1901, Forgan began using the crown mark.

Because of the firm's large output during the long nose and semi-long nose periods, the Forgan name is most often found on old wooden clubs. For that reason ranges of prices are given to accommodate differences in style, age and condition]

<><>Early clubs with Prince of Wales plume mark
Playclub--(L) C.1880, long head, plume over warrant CM $7,000
Playclub--(L) C.1870-1880, long head $3,500-5,500
Spoon--(L) As above $3,500-5,500
Baffy--(L) As above $4,000-6,500
Putter--(L) As above $2,500-5,500
Cleek--Smooth face, 4 1/2" hosel $250-500
Iron--As above $250-500
Lofter--As above $250-500
Niblick--As above, small head $300-500

◇◇1890s clubs with Prince of Wales plume mark

Playclub--(L) 1880-1900 vintage $1,000-2,500

Playclub-(L) Child's club circa 1890, no bone or lead $900

Spoon--(L) As above $1,000-2,500

Baffy--(L) As above $1,000-3,000

Putter--(L) As above $800-2,500

Cleek--Smooth facc, 4" hosel $150-300

Iron--As above $150-300

Mashie--As above $150-300

Niblick--As above, small head $200-500

Niblick--As above, medium head $150-300

Putter--As above, steel blade $100-300

Putter--As above, gun metal blade $100-300

Driver--(B) Fork splice joint $350

Driver--(S) C.1890-1900, shorter transitional shaped head $300-800

Driver--(S) Red fiber face insert $500-800

Brassie--(S) As above $500-800

Fairway club-(A B) Cylindrical head with striking .... surface on each end (Dalrymple patent) $2,000

Lofter--(B) Fairlie model (anti-shank), smooth face, plume CM $400

Lofter--Smooth face, compact blade $150-300

Lofter--Smooth face, long blade $150-300

Mashie--As above $100-200

Putter--(S) As above $200-800

◇◇◇20th century clubs

Driver--Swilken model A, large socket head, face insert $60

Driver--(B) Forganite model, socket head $150

Driver--Dreadnought model, oversize socket head $100

Driver--Socket head, Andrew Kirkaldy autograph $100

Driver--Maxmi model, 4-screw ivor face insert, rounded sole $125

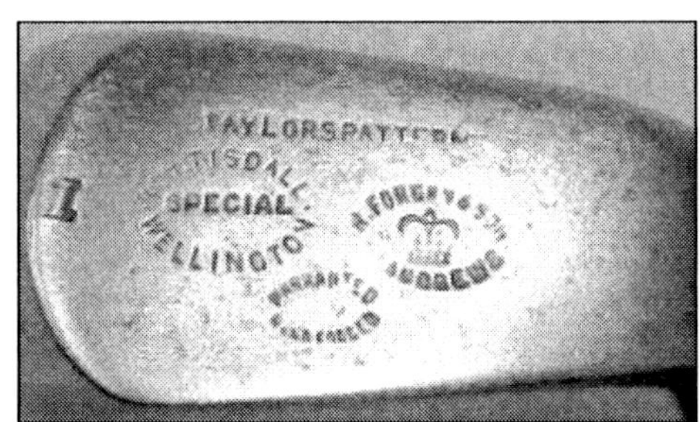

This is Robert Forgan's version of Taylor's Mashie, made after he adopted the crown mark in 1901. *(also see p.81)*

Brassie--(B) Angle Shaft model, oval shaft $175
Brassie--(B) Forganite model, socket head $150
Brassie--Dreadnought Junior model, socket head $100
Spoon--Bulldog model, ivor insert $125
Cleek—A. Kirkaldy autograph model $75
Putter--(A B Maxmi model, sounded sole $150
Putter--(A) Maxmo model, mallet head $80
Putter--(B) Maxmo model, wood mallet, 2 metal
sole plates $175
Putter--The Tolley model, wood socket head $200
Putter--The Tolley model, socket head in Forganite $250
Putter--(B) The Whee model, combination wood & metal shaft $600
Putter--Ebony wood socket head $300
Putter--Gem style, rounded back, dot face $75
Putter--Iron blade, dot face, oval name stamp $50
Putter--(A) Kent model, mallet head $75
Putter--Marked "Putter Iron," dot face, shallow face blade,
Forgan company markings on toe of face $75
Putter-Wood socket head, bulger shape, metal sole plate $200
Putter--Model B9, boy's size, iron blade, dot face $40
Putting Cleek--Long blade & hosel, line face $75
Putter—Black Magic model $100

◇◇Celtic series
Approach Cleek--Model 19, Celtic series musselback, crown CM ... $60
Iron clubs--Celtic model, name in script, line face .... $50 each

◇◇Crown CM
Driver--Crown CM, socket head $60-125
Driver--Juvenile size, smaller head, 21" shaft
(no lead backweight) $125
Brassie--Crown CM, socket head $60-125
Cleek--Dot face, crown CM $50
Driving Iron--Dot face, crown CM $50
Driving Iron--A. Kirkaldy model, crown CM dot face $90
Iron--Line face, crown CM $40
Mashie--Simple crown CM, pipe CM, dot face $65
Mashie—Taylor's Model, smooth deep face, short blade $100
Mashie-(B) Fairlie model anti-shank, dot face, crown CM $175
Mashie Niblick--Also carries Nicoll hand CM, Zenith series $50

Niblick--Small head, crown CM $200
Niblick--Marked B (boy's), dot face, crown CM $65
Putter--Gun metal blade, crown CM $90
Putter--Steel blade, crown CM $50
Putter--Steel blade, bent hosel like Park model $90

◇◇ Flagstick CM (Spence series)
Chipper--Stroke-Saver model, P.A. Vaile swan neck, round sole $300
Cleek--Juvenile, marked B, flagstick CM $50
Mashie--Line face, flagstick CM $50
Mashie--Stopded model $60
Mashie Niblick--Line face, oval head, flagstick CM $60
Spade Mashie--Dot face, flagstick CM $65
Putter--Offset blade, flagstick CM $65
Putter—The Leslie model, sculpted back along top edge $80

◇◇Forgan name in script
Mashie Niblick--Oval head, name in script $50
Niblick--Name in script, dash face $50
Mashie--Scotia series, marked "Taylor's Pattern",
smooth face $90
Mid Iron--Clan series, line face $30

◇◇Matched sets
Crown series
Woods (driver, Brassie, spoon)-- Socket head ....$60 each
Numbered Irons (1-7)--Stainless, line face ....$30 each

Eeze Series
Numbered Irons (1-6)--Line face ....$35 each

Gold Medal series
Woods (driver, Brassie, spoon)--Stripe top, socket head ....$60 each
Numbered Irons (1-9)--Line face ....$30 each

Meteor series
Woods (driver, Brassie, spoon)--Socket head, white aiming dot $65 each

Royal series
Irons—Royal in diamond CM ....$30 each

Forrester's Concentric Patent was one of the first irons designed with back weighting behind the sweetspot.

Scotia series
Woods (driver, Brassie, spoon)--Stripe top .... $75 each
Numbered Irons--Regular or stainless .... $35 each

Forrest, Charles*
[North Berwick s, East Berkshire e]
Mashie--Albion brand, abstract thistle CM, line face $50
Lofter--Forest Clubs brand, smooth face, 'FF' CM $100

Forrest, J.
[Sheffield e]
Brassie--Splice head, ivorine insert $125

Forrester, George*
[Elie s; Forrester was acknowledged by his contemporaries as one of the most innovative club designers of his time. He patented many types of wood and iron clubs though his most important contribution was his concentric back iron]
Driver--(B) Socket head, round name stamp with patent number, shaft stamp $250
Driver--(B) As above, head made of black composite fiber $650
Brassie--(S) Bulger shaped splice head $500
Brassie--Short splice head $300
Brassie--(B) Socket head, round name stamp with patent number, shaft stamp $250
Spoon--(L) C.1885, dark finish $4,000
Cleek--(B) Bulbous toe, smooth face $600
Cleek--Smooth face $125
Cleek--(B) 1919, "Non Slice" model, Anderson arrow CM $80

Iron--(B) Round back, bulger face $350
Iron—(B) Concentric back, smooth face $150
Lofter--Smooth face, Forrester and Anderson round CMs $150
Mashie--(B) Two humps on back (Double Balance model), smooth face $400
Mashie--(B) Concentric back, round name stamp with patent number $200
Niblick--Smooth face, small head $300
Putter--Little Gem model, small gem style blade $75
Putter--(B) Top Edge model, top edge bent toward face $600
Putter--(A) Boat shaped Schenectady-type $250

Forrester, James
[Elie; son of George, James ran the branch location in London before arriving as successor to the family business in Elie]
Brassie--Stripe top socket head $75

Forth Rubber Company, Ltd.*
[Edinburgh, Glasgow, Dundee s]
Driver--(S) Splice transitional head, bulger face $400
Driver--Bulger short splice head $300
Cleek--Smooth face, name in rectangle $75
Iron--Small Nicoll hand CM, smooth face $150
Iron--Small circular name CM, smooth face $125
Mashie--Smooth face, Forth Rail Bridge CM $300
Niblick--Smooth face, medium head, name in box $125
Putter--(S) Transitional splice head, name in block letters $400

Fortnum & Mason*
[London specialty store]
Driver--Socket head, stripe top, name in script $45
Spoon--Very small socket head, name in block letters, fiber face insert $60
Mashie--Fort Mason brand, stainless, dot face $40
Niblick--Fort Mason brand, giant head, stainless, dot face $1,800

Foster Brothers*
[Ashbourne e]
Driver--Socket head, ridged sole plate $90
Driving Iron--Dot face, skeleton CM $85

Jigger--Line face, skeleton CM $100
Putter--(A B) The Bogee model, square hosel, rectangular head with broad sole $200
Putter—Steel blade, skeleton CM, hyphen face $90

Fraser, Chick

Driving Iron--Line face, Nicoll hand CM $40

Foulis, David+

Lofter--Stewart pipe CM, smooth face $75
Mashie Niblic--(D) Spalding Foulis model 3, hammer, 2 Thistle CMs, patent date, ribbed face $450
Putting Cleek--Spalding Dysart series, steel blade, name in oval $75

Robert Foulis, Jr., the 1896 US Open Champion, made this driving iron while at St. Louis Country Club

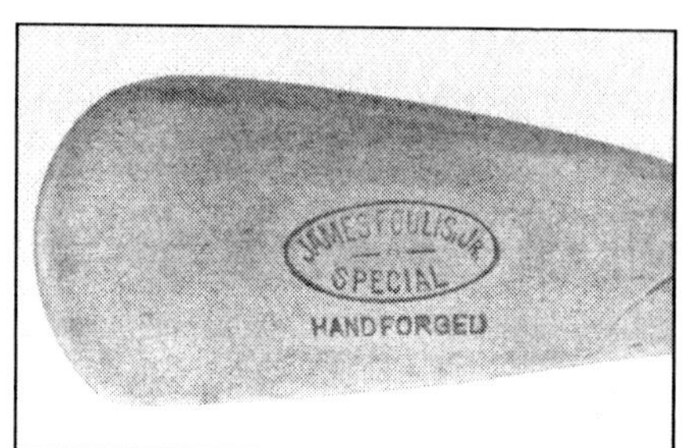

Foulis, Jr., James+

[Chicago; U.S. Open Champion 1896, inventor of the flat sole, concave face mashie niblick, which many other makers imitated]

Brassie--(S) Splice head, leather face insert $500
Cleek--Smooth face $100
Cleek--Octagon back, smooth face $400
Driving Iron—vertical and horizontal dashes on face $100
Mashie—Name in oval, MacGregor lion CM , stagdot face $100
Mashie Niblick--(U) Flat sole, concave face, star mark $250
Mashie Niblick--As above marked "Pat. Applied For" $400
Niblick--Small head, slightly concave face $500
Putter--Iron blade $200

Foulis, Robert+

[Chicago and St. Louis]

Lofting Iron--Smooth face, Stewart pipe CM $100

Fovargue, A.
Mid Iron--Concentric back, name in horseshoe $60

Fryer, James
[Edinburgh]
Driver--Made by Forrester, splice head $125

Fulford, Harry*
[Bradford e]
Sammy--Dot face $100
Iron clubs--Stewart pipe brand, scored face ....$60 each

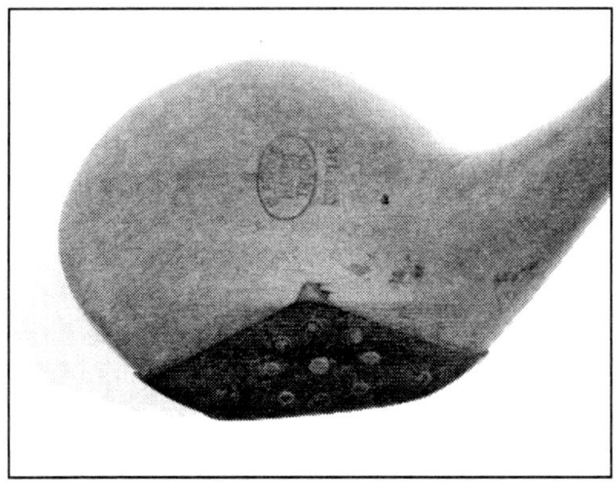

Willie Fernie, St. Andrews' own and the 1883 Open Champion, made this socket driver with 3" wide super-sized head. The club head is marked for Troon where Fernie served from 1887 to 1923.

G

Gadd, Charles*
[Roehampton e]
Putter--(A) Autograph model, mallet head, beveled top $125

Gair, Alexander*
[Edinburgh]
Cleek--Midget Marvel model, 2-sided approach club $250

Galloway, Thomas*
[Pittenweem s]
Iron clubs--Edinburgh Gold Medal stamp, dot face .... $75 each

Gamage Company, A.W.*
[London retail store]
Driver--The Gamage series, socket head $75
Driver--The Gamage series, short splice head $150
Driver--(S) Transitional splice beech head $350
Brassie--(S) Transitional splice head $350
Iron clubs-Name in oval, Spalding hammer CM .... $40 each
Iron clubs--Kromwell model, dot face .... $40 each
Mid Iron--Juvenile, marked B, by Anderson/Anstruther $50
Niblick--The Gamage series, smooth face, small head $350
Putter--(B) Duncan Twin model, adjustable
head combination putter/chipper $1,400
Putter--Bent neck, heart & arrow + lion CMs, marked "Park Putter" ..$90

Gardner, Stewart
[Garden City, NY et al]
Driver--Socket head, stripe top, red fiber insert $100
Iron clubs--Stewart pipe mark, line face .... $60 each

Gassiat, Jean*
[Biarritz, France and Baden-Baden, Germany]
Putter--Large square wood socket head, name in script $700
Putter--Large square wood head marked with reg. number $800

Putter--LCL model, name in oval $700

Gaudin, P.J.*
Driver--Socket head, stripe top $60

'Gee-Bee'
Mashie--Child's toy club, roughly cast head $20

Gibson, Charles*
[Royal North Devon Golf Club, Westward Ho! e]
Driver--(S) Bulger style splice head, leather face insert $1,500
Driver--(S) Bulger splice head, wood face insert $1,200
Driver—Socket head $80
Cleek—Stallion CM, line face $50
Brassie--Beech splice head, leather face insert $800
Spoon--The Nippy model, well lofted face, fiber insert $300
Iron--Diamond back, juvenile, dash face, stallion CM $95
Mashie Iron--Short blade, deep face, stallion CM $75
Niblick--Flange sole, dash face, stallion CM $60
Niblick--(B) Smith style anti-shank, stallion CM $200
Putter--(S)Wood splice head $450
Putter--Wood mallet, socket head $250
Putter-Gassiatt-type, large wood head $700
Putter-Winner model, rampant horse CM $75
1-Iron--Excellar series, phoenix CM, Line face $65

Gibson, Jr., C.H.*
[Oxford, later Westward Ho!; son of Charles Gibson]
Driver--Socket head $60
Niblick--Spalding hammer CM, line face $60

Charles Gibson, the long serving professional at Westward Ho!, made this cleek around 1905. His mark was the rampant Stallion.

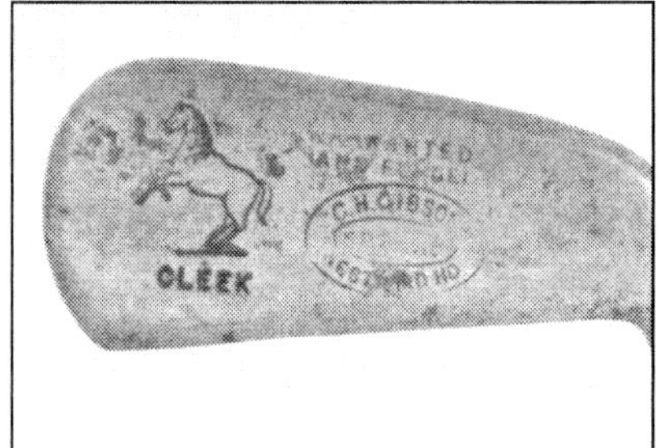

Gibson, R.J.

[Calcutta, India; son of Charles Gibson]

Mid Iron--Triplex model, Paragon series, shield with 3 Xs CM $75

1-Iron--Excellar series, phoenix CM $65

Gibson & Company, William*

[Kinghorn, Fife s. In the early part of the 20th century, William Gibson was the largest manufacturer of golf clubs in the world.]

Driver--"Gibson's of Kinghorn" in script, stripe top, socket head $75

Driver--Mignon series, bulger socket head, star CM $100

Driver--Socket head, star CM $65

Driver—George Duncan model, very small head, splice neck $150

Brassie--Stripe top, socket head, star CM $65

Brassie--Bulldog shape $125

Spoon--Short socket head, star CM $100

Baffy Spoon--Small socket head, fiber insert $125

Cleek--Smooth face, marked "Long Face Cleek", star CM $100

Cleek--Smooth face, Carruthers hosel $90

Cleek--Leather face (copied after Nicoll) $1,800

Cleek--Pixie series, offset head, dot face $90

Full Iron--Star CM, line face $45

Iron--(B) Murray model, iron head with splice joint $2,000

Iron--Carruthers hosel $100

Jigger--Shallow blade, dot face $60

Jigger--Stainless, star CM $45

Jigger--Jerko model, dot face $75

Jigger—James Braid series, autograph, star CM $75

Light Iron--Star CM, dot face $75

Mashie--Smooth face, marked for Robert Simpson, small star CM $100

Mashie--Starona series, star on face $45

The Powerful series of irons were thickest along the top edge with a very thin sole emulating a wedge.

Mashie--Stella series, model 22, diagonal bi-level back, line face $65
Mashie--King-Horn model, star in circle CM, dash face $35
Mashie--Star Maxwell model, stainless, Maxwell pattern, dot face $60
Mashie--Vardon autograph model, musselback, dash face $100
Mashie--(B) Smith model (anti-shank), concave back, star CM $175
Mashie--(B) Fairlie model (anti-shank) $150
Mashie--(D) Jerko model, corrugated face $125
Mashie--Baxpin model, diamond/dot face $60
Mashie—Wee Mashie, juvenile size Genii model $75
Mashie Iron—Deep face $60
Mashie Niblick--Akros model, George Duncan autograph, star CM .$60
Mashie Niblick--(D) Jerko model, corrugated face $125
Mashie Niblick--Baxpin model, Maxwell pattern, stainless $75
Mashie Niblick--The Skart model, line face $60
Mashie Niblick--(D) The Dead'un model, holes drilled
through face, star CM $650
Mashie Niblick--Dandy model, diamond back, dot face $85
Medium Iron--Star CM, line face $75
Medium Iron--(B) Smith model (anti-shank), smooth face $200
Mid Iron--The Horn model, hunting horn CM $45
Mid Iron--Stella model, stainless, line face $35
Mid Iron--Starona series, stainless, Maxwell pattern $60
Mid Iron--Marked Osborn's Rustless, tiny hand & heart CM $60
Niblick--Skoogee model, concave face $450
Niblick--Superior model, stainless, dash face, star CM $40
Niblick--(D) Winchester series, ribbed face, star CM $200
Niblick--The "Giant" model, James Braid series,
medium size head, star CM, line face $85
Niblick--Big Ben model, giant head $1,800
Pitcher--The Pitcher, round sole, dot face...$85
Pitcher--Model 92, shallow face, very thick sole $75

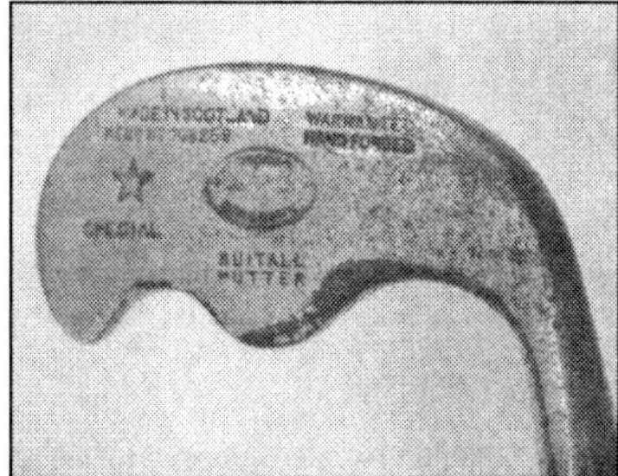

Certainly one of the most unusually shaped blade putters was Gibson's Suitall. Its rounded sole accommodated any lie angle the player desired.

Around the time Arnaud Massy won the Open, Wm. Gibson began selling a large range of autograph series clubs.

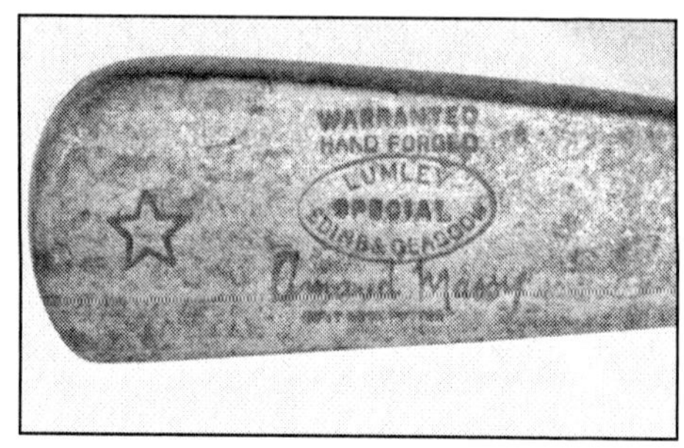

Pitcher--(D) Jerko model, ribbed face $150
Sammy--Pixie series, line face $65
Numbered Irons--Superior series, stainless, deep star CM .... $35 each
Numbered Irons—(B) Powerful series, thick top edge .... $100 each
Putter--Star Maxwell series, Maxwell pattern, extra thick flange $75
Putter—(B) Suitall, blade with wavy top edge $300
Putter--Dominie model, rounded back $125
Putter--(B) The Princeps model, top edge weighted $300
Putter--(B) Skinner model, protruding face $300
Putter--Gem style, dot face $75
Putter--Jonko model, flat sole with large hump at sweet spot $2,500
Putter--(B) Brown Vardon model, iron head $200
Putter--(B) Brown-Vardon style, Monel, star CM $200
Putter--(B) Brown Vardon model, gun metal head $275
Putter--Cara Mia model, stripe top wood mallet, socket head $175
Putter-The Skart model, shallow face, round back, same in script $100
Putter--Triple star model, stainless, offset blade $50
Putter--Marked "bent neck putter" $60
Putter--Orion model, broad flange sole, name in script $80
Putter--Kilgour Match model, blade $90
Putter--(A S) Model AA, long head $150
Putter--(A) Model BB, medium length head $100
Putter--(A) Schenectady style $175
Putter--All Square model, square hosel, offset blade $175
Putter--Bradbeer's Own, long stainless blade, star CM $100
Putter--Accurate model, iron blade, bent neck $65
Putter--Iron blade, gooseneck $65

Genii irons were a huge seller for William Gibson however the Genii putting cleek is relatively scarce.

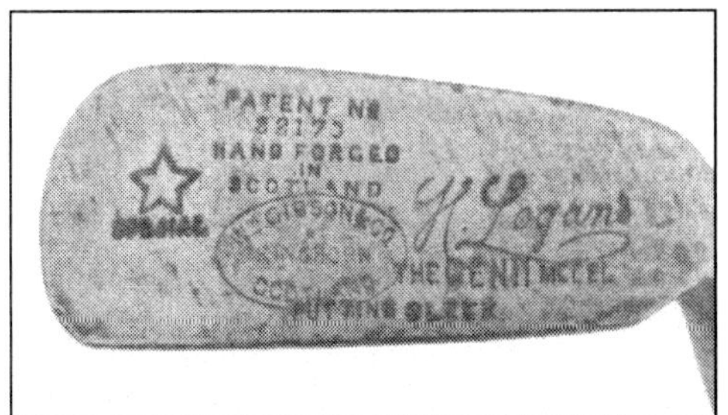

Putter--(B) Civic model, flange sole, holes drilled through face, star CM $400-600
Putter--Eskit model, offset hosel, pointed toe, square grip $125
Putter--Gleneagles model, low profile blade, grooved sole, square shaft, medium hosel $125
Putter--Varsity model, heel and toe weighting $200
Putter--Cosby series, hand holding arrows & star CMs, gooseneck hosel $125
Putter--F.G. Tait model, blade shape, star CM $80
Putting Cleek-Tait model, star CM inside double circle $80
Putting Cleek--Genii series $95
Putting Iron--Iron blade, dot face, star CM $70
Putting Iron—Gun metal blade, star CM $100

<><>Hugh Logan's Genii Model irons

Three generations of Genii irons exist, marked:
"Patent Pending" (oldest),
"Patent No. 22170" (most common), and
"Patent No. 308040" on a stainless head (most recent)

Cleek--(B) Genii model, smooth face, notched at hosel, "patent pending", star CM $150
also available in

Mashie
Mashie Cleek
Mashie Niblick
Medium Iron
Mashie Iron
Putting Cleek

Mashie--(B) Genii model, line face, patent number, star CM $60
Other Genii club types with patent number similarly valued

Mashie--(B) Genii model, line face, patent number, stainless, star CM $45
Other Genii club types in stainless similarly valued

◇◇James Braid Autograph series
Cleek--James Braid model, musselback, dot face $75
also produced as (at similar value)

- Driving Cleek (later Driving Iron)
- Medium Iron
- Light Iron
- Heavy Iron
- Niblick
- Putter
- Mashie

◇◇Arnaud Massy Autograph irons
Putter--Arnaud Massy autograph model, star CM $75
The Massy series also included these clubs (at similar value)

- Cleek
- Iron
- Mashie Niblick
- Iron (round back)
- Mashie (long face)
- Medium Iron
- Jigger
- Niblick
- Mashie (deep face)
- Putter

◇◇Selected Autograph series clubs representing various players made by William Gibson and bearing his star CM
Named Irons--George Duncan autograph, Akros series .... $60 each
Named Irons--Percy Boomer autograph series, shallow line face, star CM .... $60 each
Named Irons--A. Kirkaldy autograph series, line face .... $75 each
Named Irons--F. Cheshire autograph series, dot face .... $90 each

<><>Selected miscellaneous clubs
Mashie Niblick--(D) George Duncan autograph series 126, slotted face $125
Named Irons--George Duncan autograph series, dot face $90
Push Iron--R.H. de Montmorencie autograph series, dot face $100
Spade Mashie--George Sargent autograph series, line face, star CM ..$75

Gimbel's
[New York City department store]
Iron clubs--Gimbel name between 2 Spalding thistle CMs $40

Glasgow Golf Company*
[Charles L. Millar, proprietor]
Driver--Socket head, thistle CM $100
Iron clubs—Rustless, company name in 2 triangles .... $45 each
Putter--Blade, thistle CM, dot face $50

'Glencoe'
[Burke store brand]
Mashie--(D) Model 1369, corrugated face $75

Glover Specialty Company+
[Bridgeport, CT]
Woods--(Driver, brassie, spoon) Read Balanced model, socket head unique sole plate .... $80 each
Driver--Read-Barnes model, metal face insert $125
Putter--Read model, square wood head, heel shafted $400

'Gold Standard'
Driver--(U) Stripe top socket head, bamboo shaft, sewn grip $150

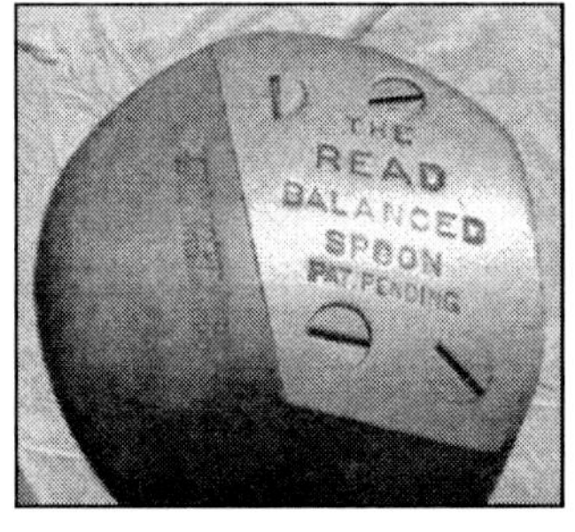

Glover's 'Read Balanced' Woods had a unique weighting system under the large sole plate.

'Golden Eagle'
[A brand from the Eagrow Company, Milwaukee, WI]
Mashie Niblick--Ampco metal blade, line face $50

Goldsmith Company+
[Cincinnati, OH]
Driver--Socket head, name in block letters $55
Mashie--Hyde Park series, line face, Maltese cross CM $35
Mid Iron--Model G, diamond back, line face $40
Mid Iron--Line face $35
Putter--Bronze alloy blade, Maltese cross CM $45
Putter--Lady Claremont series, two Maltese cross CMs $45
Putter—Lady Mac series, bronze alloy head $40
Putter-Bronze alloy, circular waffle-style face $75

Golf Company, The+
[Kansas City, MO]
Putter--The Highlander model, 2-sided, line faces $40

Golf Company, The*
[St. Andrews]
Putter--(S) Beech head, dark stain $1,000

Golf Goods Manufacturing Company+
[Binghamton, NY; around 1900 this firm was headed by Willie Tucker who produced some of his Defiance clubs here]
Driver--Socket head, stamped "G.G.M.Co." $250
Driver--Model 104, splice head $500
Cleek--Smooth face $175
Iron--Smooth face $150
Mashie--Smooth face, thick blade $200
Lofter--Smooth face, long blade $200
Niblick--Small head $800
Putting Cleek--Thick iron blade $250

Golf Shop, The
Golf Company, The
[Chicago]
Mid Iron--Name in script, dot face $30
Jigger--Anderson arrow CM, musselback, dot face $50

Jigger—4-leaf clover CM, round back $40
Mashie--(D) "Hold em" model, Anderson arrow CM,
corrugated face $150
Mashie--444 model, deep face, small shamrock CM $35
Putter--Gun metal dominie-type head $225

MacGregor had a retail shop in Chicago where they sold their own products and some imports. The four leaf clover was a MacGregor mark.

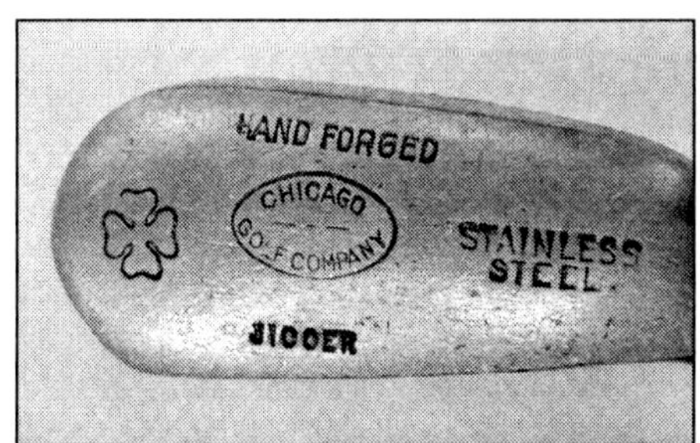

Golf Specialty Company
[Baltimore, MD]
Mashie--(D) Arroflite model, ribbed face $100

Golfers' Supply Company*
[Glasgow]
Mid Iron--Smooth face, marked 'Scotsman' $100
Putter--Iron blade, marked 'Scotsman' $125

Goodrich Sales Company+
[Chicago]
Iron--(U) Adjustable "All-One" club $2,000

Goudie & Company*
[Glasgow and Edinburgh]
Driver--(S) Transitional beech splice head $400
Cleek--Made for Goudie & Co., convex back,
Anderson double circle CM $75
Putter--(B) "Taylor's Patented Hosel", smooth face $125
Putter--Gun metal blade $100

Gouick, T.
[Dundee s]

Putter--Center shafted, pendulum style $600

Gourlay, Bert
[Glasgow]
Driver--Socket head $50

James Gourlay used several variations of the moon & star cleek mark, like this one on a short blade mashie for J. Tulloch, Glasgow.

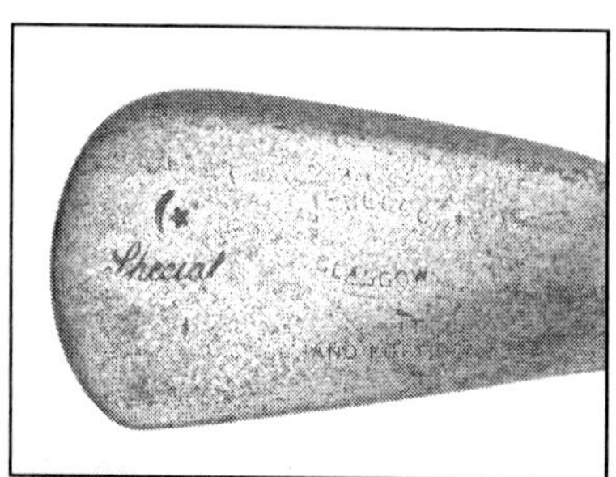

Gourlay, James*
[Carnoustie s; famous maker of iron club heads]
Cleek--Name in horseshoe CM, smooth face $75
Iron--Smooth face, crescent moon & star CM $100
Mashie—Small moon-star CM, short blade, smooth face $50
Mashie--Concentric back, diamond face, anchor CM $60
Mashie Cleek--Moon & star cleek mark, name in horseshoe $75
Mashie Niblick--Oval head, diamond/dot face $60
Mid Iron--Moon/star CM, diamond back $60
Niblick--Large head, dot face, back beveled to toe and heel $100
Sammy--Round back, round sole, moon & star CM $60
Putter--P.A. Vaile model, swan neck,
made for F.H. Ayers Co. $400
Putter--Bent neck, crescent moon & star CM $75
Putter--Beveled Edge model, radiused top edge $125
Putter--Sovereign model, floral design on face,
rounded back $100
Putter--Offset blade, musselback,
crescent moon & star CM $75
Putter-Deep face blade, crescent moon & star CM $150
Putter—Park Model (marked), bent neck, tiny moon/star CM $150

Gourlay, Walter
[St. Andrews]

Putter--Dot face, blade $45

Gourley, Thomas
Mashie--Spalding Gold Medal, marked for Marine & Field $75
Putter--Offset iron blade, marked for Baltusrol $80

Govan, James
Putter--Made by Spalding, 2 roses CM,
marked Pine Valley $100
Putter--A-1 model, blade behind hosel, gun metal,
line face $300

'Grampian Range'
[A series made by J.H. Turner; see Turner]
Woods—Mountain CM, socket head ....$200 each
Iron clubs--(B) Mountain CM, line face,
weight holes in upper edge of blade .... $150 each

'Grand Leader'
Putter--Gun metal blade $75

Grant, Frank
Driver--Model 33, deep face, socket head $50

Grant Company, W.T.
[New York]
Jigger--Chromed, curved swastika & large fleur de lis CMs $35
Iron clubs--Piccadilly series $25

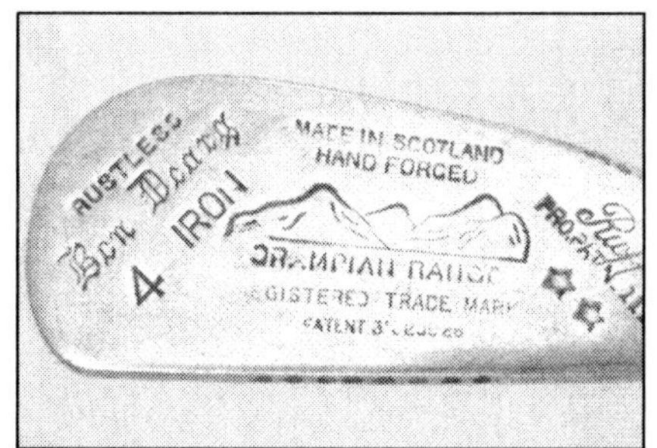

The Grampian Range series of irons had the unique feature of holes drilled in the top edge to reduce weight at the sweet spot. Each club was named for a different Scottish mountain.

John Gray was a member of Prestwick Golf Club as well as a cleek maker. He produced some of the earliest signed iron heads in the 1850s.

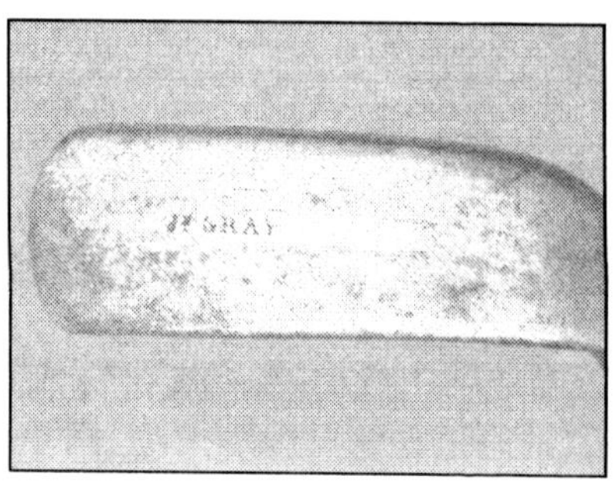

Gravitator Golf Ball Company*
[London]
Putter--(B) The Multiface model, 4 removable face inserts $4,000

Gray, A. (Andrew)*
[Carnoustie s; C.1860-68]
Cleek--Long hosel, name stamp in script $3,000
Iron--Name in large block letters, very heavy hosel $6,000
Niblick--Deep faced, short blade $7,000

Gray, Ernest*
[Littlehampton e, et al]
Driver--Splice head, light finish $150
Driver--Socket head $70

Gray & Sons, H.J.
[Cambridge e]
Cleek--Long blade, smooth face $125
Mashie--Smooth face, compact blade $100
Niblick-Mammoth style, extra large head,
Cochrane knot CM $1,200-1,500
Putter--Steel blade, name in circular CM $100

Gray, John*
[Worked in Prestwick 1852-1890 as one of the pioneer iron club makers and was one of the first to regularly stamp his name on iron clubs. First name was stamped Jn. or J.]
Cleek--Long hosel, smooth face $800-2,000
Iron--Long hosel, deep face $800-2,000
Lofter--Long hosel, long and slightly concave face $1,250-2,500

Niblick--Long thick hosel, small thick head $2,000-3,000

Great Lakes Golf Company+
[Milwaukee, WI]
Driver--Stripe top socket head $45
Driver--Glen-Eagle series, socket head $40
Iron clubs--Great Lakes name in stylized script,
swastika CM ....$45 each
Approach Putter—Ships wheel CM, musselback $60
Mid Iron--Baltic series, swastika CM, dot face $45
Mashie Iron—Model 44, swastika CM $45
Mashie—(D) Model 17, slot face $100
Niblick--Stainless, GL in circle on face $30
Niblick--Kiltie series, dot face $25
Putter--Model 10F, blade $25
Putter--New Yorker series, chrome blade $30
Numbered Irons--Lakeshore brand, Tommy Armour series,
diamond CM ....$50 each
Numbered Irons--Al Watrous Straight Eight autograph series,
line face ....$50 each
Numbered Irons--Bobby Cruikshank autograph series,
GL face mark ....$50 each
Iron Set--Bobby Cruickshank autograph series,
8 irons and putter $650

Green, W.G.
[Rumson, NJ]
Iron clubs-Line face, four-square CM (Swastika variant) ....$75 each

Grosse Ile Putter Company+
[Grosse Ile, Detroit, MI]

Clubs bearing the 'swastika' are often mistaken for German clubs. The Great Lakes Golf Co. made these clubs long before the Nazi party came to power.

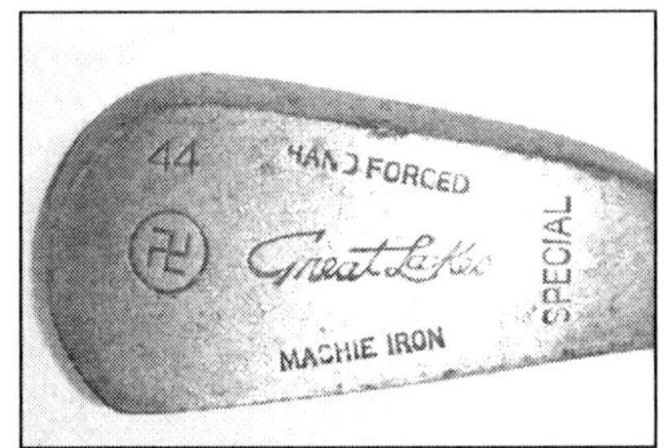

Putter--Stainless, flange sole $60

Grove & Company, George
[London]
Mid Iron--The Hawk series, stainless, flying bird CM $50

Guise, F.
Putter--Shiva, small musselback, oval steel shaft,
Winton diamond CM $125

'Gyroscope'
Mashie--(D) Diagonal grooves, circular CM $200

The Gyroscope model features diagonal deep grooves, not horizontal as in most other deep groove clubs. The small circular cleek mark belongs to an unknown maker.

H

Hackbarth, Otto+

[Primarily worked in Cincinnati, OH]

Driver--Socket head $80

Spoon--Very small splice head $400

Spoon--(U) Small socket head, 'Pat. Pending' $125

Mid iron--Stewart pipe brand, line face $50

Mashie--Made by Wilson, Hackbarth shaft stamp $50

Niblick--Smith model anti-shank model $200

Putter--(A U) "Coathanger shape," two-tined hosel, brass weight strip in sole $300-500

The Otto Hackbarth putter was made primarily in aluminum though a few were also made in bronze. (Collectors be warned, modern made copies exist)

Hagen, Walter+

[After 1926, all Hagen brand clubs were made by L.A. Young Company. Earlier clubs, like the Cochrane series, are noted otherwise. Most Hagen clubs had a small 'H' on the club face at the sweet spot]

◇◇Clubs and putters not belonging to other model sets

33-Iron--Ranger utility club $100

44-Iron--Tom Boy series, Ranger model utility club $100

66-Iron--Ranger utility club $100

Sand Iron--(U) Smooth concave face, large flange on sole $350-600

Sand Iron--The Iron Man model, large flange, flat lined face ...$150-200

Putter--Sterling silver head, hallmarked, usually with presentation inscription , made by Lambert Brothers, NY $1,000-1,500

Putter--(A) The Haig model, mallet head, regular grip $150

Putter--(A) The Haig model, mallet head, paddle handle grip $200
Putter--Lucky Len model, wood mallet head, paddle grip $250
Putter--Wood mallet Gassiat-type, Hagen name in script $400

◇◇Autograph series (see Walter Hagen Autograph series below)

◇◇Belleair series
Numbered Irons--Line face, 'H' on club face. $35each

◇◇Braeburn series
Woods (dr, br, sp)--Braeburn series, lady's weight .... $50 each

◇◇Champion series
Woods (dr, br, sp)--Plain face .... $50 each

◇◇Cochranes of Edinburgh (not L.A. Young; made in Scotland)
Numbered irons--Autograph model, rustless,
bowline knot CM .... $75 each

◇◇Crown series
Irons (1-8, putter)--Compact blades, chrome .... $40 each

◇◇Diplomat series
Woods--Socket head, stripe top .... $45 each
Numbered Irons--Stainless, dot face .... $25 each

◇◇Getaway series
Woods (driver, Brassie, spoon)--Socket head .... $40 each
Wood Set (3 clubs)--Getaway series $300
Named Irons (8)--Non-stainless, line face .... $30 each

The Hagen sterling silver presentation putter was made primarily in New York by Lambert Brothers silversmiths. Most have been inscribed as trophies, a few are still blank.

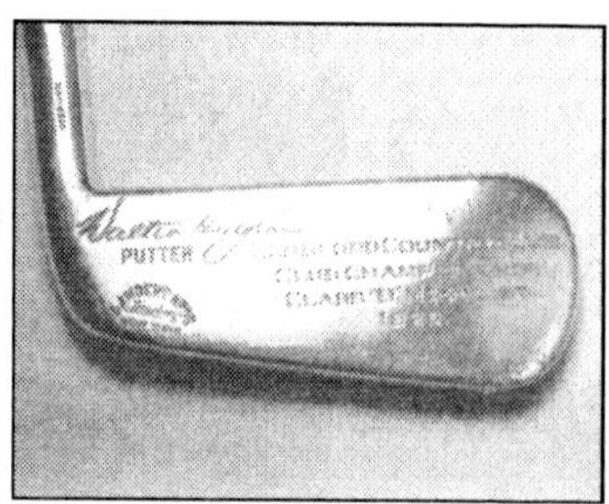

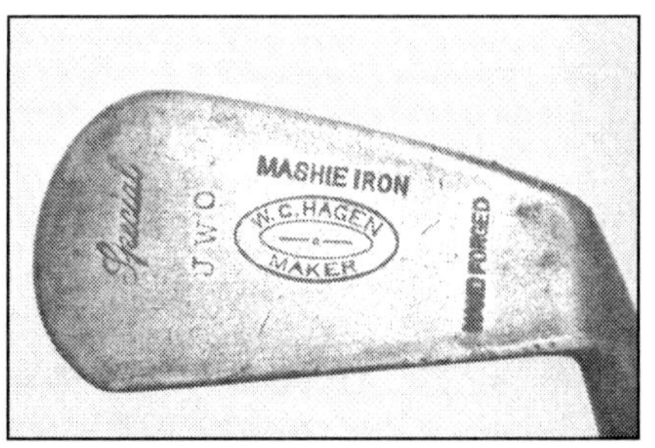

Before Walter Hagen created his large manufacturing enterprise, he produced simple clubs that resembled those from other club professionals.

◇◇Heatherdowns series (not L.A. Young)
Woods--Socket head, stripe top .... $40 each
Numbered Irons--Line face .... $30 each

◇◇International series
Numbered Irons--Stainless .... $40 each

◇◇St. James series (not L.A. Young)
Numbered Irons--Stainless .... $30 each

◇◇Staybrite series
Numbered Irons--Stainless .... $30 each

◇◇Tom Boy series
Numbered Irons--Stainless .... $30 each

◇◇Triangle series
Woods (3)--7 plug face insert .... $60 each
Woods (3)--Plain face .... $45 each
Named/Numbered Irons (8 irons & Putter)--Compact head, "Duro-Chrome" or "Stabrite", line face .... $30 each

◇◇Ultra series
Woods (dr, br, sp)--Ultra series, bull's eye insert, metal backweight .... $65 each
Numbered Irons--Stainless .... $30 each

◇◇"WH" series
Woods (3)--Socket head, plain face .... $45 each
Woods (3)--Brass face .... $75 each

Woods--Splice head, brass face .... $200 each
Numbered Irons (9)--Line face .... $30 each

◇◇Walter Hagen autograph series
Woods--Socket head, brass face insert .... $75 each
Woods--Bulls-eye insert, brass backweight .... $75 each
Numbered Irons 1-8--"DeLuxe" Registered, stainless .... $30 each

Iron Sets:	America Lady	Imperial Crown
Full 10-club set $800	Center Poise	International Tom Boy
9-club set $700	Continental	Moderne
8-club set $650	Crown T.T.	Play Boy
6-club set $500	Crown	Tom Boy
5-club set $350	Hagen Junior	Triangle
	Haig model	Trophy
	Honey Boy	Walter Hagen Autograph

Matched Set of Nine (8 irons & putter)--"Deluxe"
Registered 201, line face $850
Named/Numbered Irons 1-8--Graduated Registered,
non-stainless .... $35 each
Matched Set of Nine (8 irons & putter)--Graduated
Registered $750
Numbered Irons--"Autograph" series, line face,
stainless .... $30 each
Matched Set of Nine (8 irons & putter)--"Autograph"
series $650

The "Hagen W.S". set of driver, brassie and spoon was the last Hagen Brand set to be offered with wood shafts. It was discontinued after the 1935 season.

The Walter Hagen Autograph series became synonymous with high quality golf equipment in the 1930s.

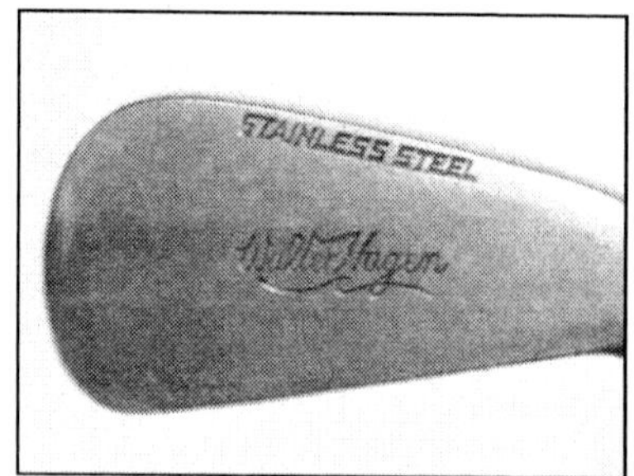

Hagen W.S. model woods, plain face .... $60 each
Set of 3 .... $300

By 1930, L.A. Young/Walter Hagen golf offered almost no wood shafted drivers though most irons were still available with wood shafts. The below list of iron club models with wood shafts had matching woods that were only offered with steel shafts.
Hagen Irons in the late 1920s and 1930s came in several set groupings. The full set included irons 1-9 plus a putter (the putter was #9, the pitching niblick was #8 and the full niblick was #10). Several shorter sets were also sold with sets varying in size almost yearly. The 9-club set was as above minus the 1-iron. The medium set came with numbers 2,4,5,7,8,9 and the small set had numbers 2,5,7,8,9. Most were sold with various types of metal shafts and were only made with hickory by special order. Hickory shafts were discontinued after 1936 though extra shafts were sold for repairs for several more years.

The Hagen Triangle was one of Hagen's many popular lines. It was made in "Stabrite" stainless steel.

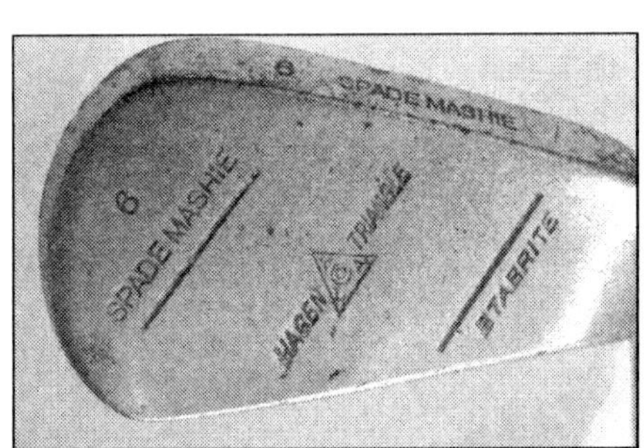

Hall, Willie
Putter--(A) The Verden model, mallet head $200

Halley & Company, J.B.*
[London]
Brassie--Autograph series, stripe top, fiber insert $100
Cleek--Maxwell pattern $50
Iron--Junior model, crossed swords CM, dot face $40
Mashie--Stainless, line face, crossed swords CM $40
Mid Iron--Dot face, H in circle CM $40
Mid Iron--Model 12, shell CM, line face $45

Mashie Niblick--Model 28, Maxwell pattern, shell CM $75
Niblick--Model 37, dreadnought, pyramid CM $75
Putter--Model 38, blade, crossed swords CM $50
Putter--Model 40, gun metal head, shallow face, pyramid CM $75
Putter--Two sided, shell CM on sole $65
Putter--Gun metal, small mallet head, shell CM $125
Putter--Pyramid model, juvenile size, gun metal blade,
pyramid CM $40
Putter--(A) Mallet head, marked J B H $100
Putter--Ideal model 42, prism shaped back $100
Putter--Holton Own Model, like MacGregor semi-putter,
shell CM $150
Putter--(B) Long Tom model, shell CM $75
Putter—Model 45, Professional, top weighted blade, shell CM $75
Putter—Model 45, Professional, top weighted blade, swords CM $75
Juvenile Set--Driver, iron, mashie, putter, iron clubs in rustless alloy with
shell CM and Ocobo brand canvas bag $300

Ham, Arthur

[Skegness e, et al]

Mashie--Pipe CM, line face $45
Niblick--Hamsole model, shallow cuts in sole $2,000
Sammy--Dot/dash face, Gourlay moon/star CM $75

Hamley's

[London toy & game store]

Irons--Juvenile, smooth face, name in block letters ,
Halley swords CM........................ $40 each

'Handkraft'

Mashie--Model A-2, chrome head, dot face $25

Hamley's is a 250-year-old toy and game store on Regents Street in London. They sold many clubs but they are all toys or juvenile.

Harders, Con

Driver-Stripe top, socket head $50
Mashie--Chrome head, line face $25
Mid Iron--Flange sole, line face $40
Mashie--Name in banner, line face $35

Hardman, Edward

Brassie--Socket head $50

Hardman & Wright+

[Belleville, NJ]

Driver--(U) Hardright brand, 'Condensite' composition head, metal neck $250

'Hardright'+

[See Hardman & Wright, above]

Hardy Brothers

[Alnwick e]

Numbered Irons--Hardy's in script, line face, bamboo shaft ...... $80 each
Numbered Irons--Palakona in script, line face, bamboo shaft .... $80 each

Harland, John

Brassie--Short socket head $100

Harris, T.

Mashie--Spalding anvil CM, line face $40

Harrison, Donald J.

[St. Louis, MO]

Irons—Wright & Ditson 'One Shot' circular dot face .... $45 each

Harrod's

[London department store]

Named Irons--Dot face, name in circular belt .... $60 each

Harrower, Thomas

[Carnoustie s]

Iron--Dot face, heart CM $60

Though this Harrison iron doesn't have any maker's mark, the circular dot punched face was used most frequently by Wright & Ditson.

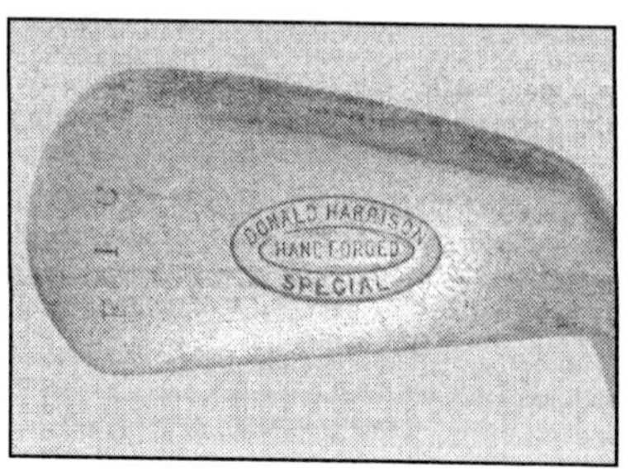

Iron clubs--Marked 'Harrower' with heart CM $75
Putter--(B) Small steel mallet shaped like Brown-Vardon with square toe, heart CM $175

Hartford, E.V.
Putter--(U) Gun metal center shafted head, aiming device on top edge $6,500

Haskins & Pulford
[Hoylake e]
Putter--Gun metal blade, Condie rose CM $100

Haskins & Sons*
[Hoylake e]
Iron--Smooth face, name in arc $80
Niblick--Stainless, dot face $40

Havers, Arthur
[Coomb Hill, London, et al]
Driver--Stripe top, socket head, name in script $50
Iron clubs--Pipe brand, line or dot face $50

'Hawco'+
[Harold A. Wilson Co., Toronto, ONT]
Driver--Large socket head $50
Iron--Made by Willie Park, smooth face $200
Iron clubs--HAWCO brand, line or dot face $45
Putter--Offset blade, name in oval $50

Hawkins
[Walsall e]
Iron Clubs—George Lowe patent anti-shank, rustless steel ...... $125 each

Haywood, Charles*
[Redditch e]
Iron Clubs--Stainless, line face, CH with spur CM $80

Hearn, J.H.
[Mitcham e, et al]
Mashie Niblick--Sun Spot brand, stainless, sun CM $40

Heather Brand
Mashie--Maxwell pattern, stainless, sprig of heather CM $40

Hemming & Son, Thomas*
[Redditch e]
Iron clubs--Smooth face, lion over long crown CM $95
Mashie--Smith-type anti-shank, smooth face oval head
lion over long crown CM $200
Mashie Niblick--Number 7, oval blade, line face,
thick sole, lion over long crown CM $150

Hemmings Golf Company*
[Redditch e]
Putter--Offset blade, lion over crown CM $150

Hendry & Bishop*
[Edinburgh]
Driver—Maltese cross on club head, ivor face insert and aiming dot ..$60
Cleek--Mitre brand, mitre CM, dot face $40
Driving Iron--Cardinal series, dot face, mitre CM $40
Iron--(B) Slog-Em model, threaded nut to tighten hosel $600
Jigger--The Master series, line face $75

The Henry "Centro" patent for woods and irons was yet another attempt at perfecting a center-shafted club that worked.

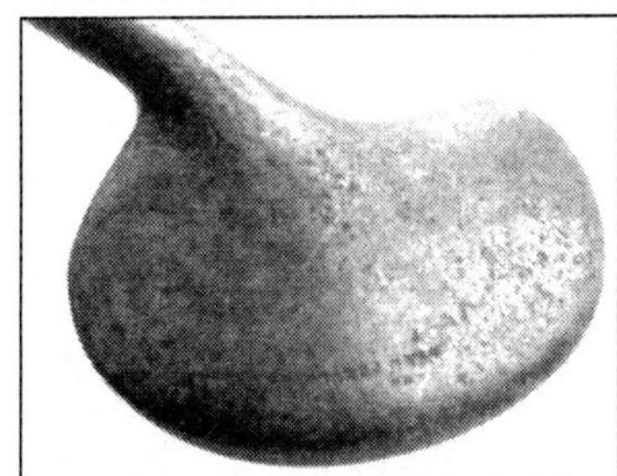

Lofter-Hiteezi model, thick top edge, thin blade, mitre CM $175
Mashie--Mitre Brand, bishop's mitre CM, line face $40
Mashie Niblick--Cardinal model, oval head, line face, mitre CM $50
Mashie Niblick--Pitch-em model, line face, mitre CM $75
Mid Iron--The Bert model, oval head $50
Niblick--Cardinal model, large head, line face, mitre CM $75
Niblick--The Master series, round back, line face, mitre CM $65
Niblick--Cardinal model, marked "Dreadnought", extra large head $150
Niblick--Cardinal model, giant head, dot face, mitre CM $1,400-1,800
Niblick--Cardinal series, Junior Giant model $1,200
Niblick--The Scottie model, dot face $60
Niblick--Archie Compston model, smooth concave face $400
Pitching Mashie--Diamond face, mitre CM $60
Sand Iron--Smooth concave face, very thick sole $350
2-Iron--Auld Reekie model, Cardinal series, dot face, mitre CM $65
Named Irons--Master series, line face $65
Numbered Irons--Cardinal series, line face, mitre CM .... $40 each
Numbered Irons-Playmore series, mitre CM .... $50 each
Putter-The Bedford, flange sole $75
Putter—The Burgess, broad flange sole $75
Putter--Offset blade, mitre CM $50
Putter--(B) Per Whit model, round blade, hollow back $400-650
Putter--Sniper model, long thin hosel and blade $250
Putter--Eagle Special, iron blade $60
Putter--Challenge model, shield with cross CM $50
Putting Cleek--Diamond back, acorn and mitre CMs $75
Putting Cleek--Long faced, dot face, mitre CM $60

'Henley'

Driver--Short splice head $150

'Henry's'

Iron-(B)Centro Machine model, center shaft, kidney shaped head $3,000

Henry, Hugh*
[Rye e]
Brassie--Socket head $60

Hepburn, James*
[Surbiton e, later Long Island, NY]
Driver--Socket head $60
Driving Mashie--Stewart pipe CM, line face $60

Herd, Alexander ("Sandy")*
[St. Andrews; Open Champion 1902]
Driver--Short splice head, leather face insert $150
Brassie--(S) Bulger splice head $400
Mashie—Stewart serpent CM, SF, marked for Huddersfield $100
Niblick--Ayers maltese cross CM, dot face $90
Push Iron--A. Herd model, Stewart pipe CM, line or dot face $100
Named Irons--A. Herd autograph model, Stewart pipe CM,
line or dot face ....$75 each
Putter--Trusty model, iron blade, Nicoll hand CM $50
Putter--(S) C.1895, splice head $600
Putter--(S) C.1910, fiber slip $200

Herd, David*
[Littlestone e; younger brother of Alex Herd]
Niblick--Smooth face, small head, Condie rose CM $200

Herd, Fred
[Chicago et al]
Driver--Small splice head $200
Iron--Dot face, Condie rose CM $75

Herd, James*
[St. Andrews]
Driver--St. Andrews model, socket head $90

Herd & Herd+
[Chicago, IL]
Driver--Champion brand, splice head $150
Driver--Socket head $75
Baffy--Long narrow socket head $150

Hillerich & Bradsby patented a cork grip in 1914 which can be found on some of their putters. The shaft bears the Kork Grip Patent information.

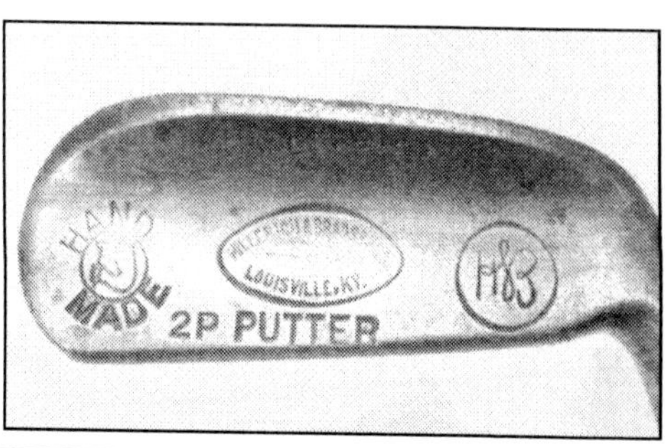

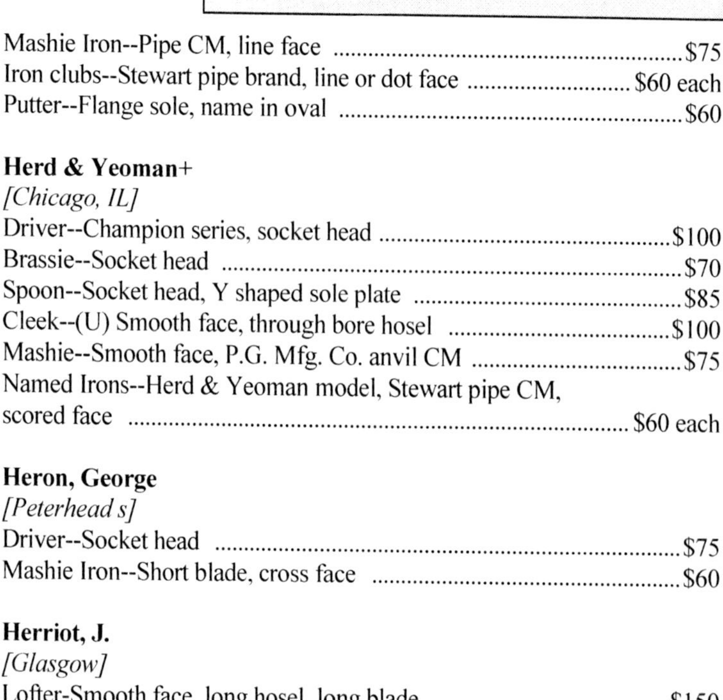

Mashie Iron--Pipe CM, line face $75
Iron clubs--Stewart pipe brand, line or dot face .... $60 each
Putter--Flange sole, name in oval $60

Herd & Yeoman+
[Chicago, IL]
Driver--Champion series, socket head $100
Brassie--Socket head $70
Spoon--Socket head, Y shaped sole plate $85
Cleek--(U) Smooth face, through bore hosel $100
Mashie--Smooth face, P.G. Mfg. Co. anvil CM $75
Named Irons--Herd & Yeoman model, Stewart pipe CM, scored face .... $60 each

Heron, George
[Peterhead s]
Driver--Socket head $75
Mashie Iron--Short blade, cross face $60

Herriot, J.
[Glasgow]
Lofter-Smooth face, long hosel, long blade $150

Hewitt, Walter

[Carnoustie s]
Iron clubs-Arrow through heart CM, dot face .... $75 each
Putter--Bent neck, heart & arrow CM $80
Putter--Bent neck, heart & arrow + lion CMs, marked "Park Putter" $90

Hiatt & Company*
[Birmingham e]
Cleek--Smooth face, 'mild steel' CM $200
Lofter--Smooth face, long blade, 'Mild steel' CM $200
Mashie--Smooth face, short blade, circular 'mild steel' CM $150

Hillerich & Bradsby Company+
[Louisville, KY; a company better known for its Louisville Slugger baseball bats]
Woods--(U) "Kork" grip model, socket head ....$125 each
Irons--(U) Any model fitted with "Kork" grip ....$75 each
Approach Iron--Model 5A1, musselback, dash/dot face $50
Approach Putter--N9, slightly lofted like jigger $100
Cleek--Model 1 DC, diamond back, arm & hammer CM $40
Driving Iron--Par X-L series, model 101, musselback, dot/dash face $50
Mashie--(D) Par X-L series, model 80, ribbed face $100
Mashie--(D) Backspin model 8BSM, ribbed face $100
Mashie--Hand Forged model, star face marks $200
Mashie--Juvenile, script H B in circle CM $30
Mid Iron--Model 80MI, dash face $40
Mid Iron--Par X-L series, line face $35
Mid Iron--(U) Par X-L series, patent "kork" grip $75
Mid Iron--Juvenile, script HB CM $30
Mashie Niblick--Model S C 1, slotted hosel, arm & hammer CM $85
Mashie Niblick--(D) Model 1 M, grooved face $125
Mashie Niblick--(D) Backspin model 1BSMN, ribbed face $100
Mashie Niblick--(D) Backspin model 3BSMN, ribbed face $100
Pitcher--Backspin model 1BSMN, stagdot face $50
Putter--(A) Par X-L series, mallet head $75
Putter--(A) Center shaft mallet head $125
Putter--N 10, shallow face blade $50
Putter—2 P, steel blade, Kork grip $75
Putter--(A) Par X-L series, Schenectady style, cork grip $200

◇◇The Kernel model

Woods--The Kernel model, socket head $50
Iron clubs--The Kernel model, line face .... $30 each
Putting Cleek--The Kernel model, iron blade $50

◇◇Stewart Maiden model
Numbered Irons--Stainless, marked "designed by Stewart Maiden" .... $40 each
Putter--# 10, stainless blade, marked "designed by Stewart Maiden" $60
Numbered Irons--Stainless, marked "designed by Stewart Maiden," fitted with B-Bow flat side shaft .... $80 each
Putter--# 10, stainless marked "designed by Stewart Maiden, fitted with B-Bow flat side shaft $100

◇◇Sets
Woods—Grand Slam series .... $80 each
Numbered Irons--Grand Slam series, hand holding cards CM .. $35 each
Numbered Irons--N-W series, line face .... $35 each
Named Irons--Hinsdale Matched Set series .... $30 each
Numbered Irons--Hinsdale Matched series, chrome .... $30 each
Woods--Invincible series, socket head .... $40 each
Numbered Irons--Invincible series, chrome duo-flange head, shield CM .... $30 each
Woods--Lo-Skore series, golfer profile CM .... $40 each
Numbered Irons--Lo-Skore series, golfer profile CM .... $25 each
Numbered Irons--Lady Lo-Skore series .... $25 each

Hills, Percy*
[Gosport e, et al]
Niblick--Large head, line face $60

The Rudder Putter, now illegal in form, is a great looking collectible that was ineffectual as a golf club in its day. Pro Tom MacNamara was a principle in the Holmac firm.

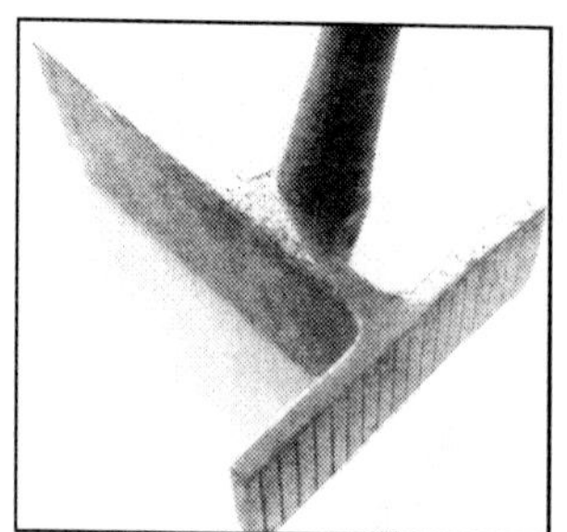

Hoare, Willie+
Iron--Smooth face, name in oval stamp $85
Mashie--Two acorns CM, line face $60
Mashie Niblick--Dot face $50
Niblick--Round head, smooth face $300

Hobens, Jack
[Englewood, NJ]
Driver--Short splice head $150
Iron clubs--Smooth face, Stewart pipe CM ....$80 each
Iron clubs--Smooth face, Spalding Golf Medal series ....$70 each
Iron clubs-Scored face, by Spalding ....$50 each

Hobley, A.J.
[Cheltenham e]
Iron clubs--Line face, bench-wheel CM $75

Holmac, Inc.+
[New York City]
Mid Iron--Model 57, swastika CM $45
Putter--(U) Rudder putter, T-shaped brass $3,250

Honeyman, Philip+
[Lenox, MA, et al]
Iron--Smooth face, line name stamp $125

Hood, Tom*
[Edinburgh, C.1880-1909]
Driver--(S) Name stamped in script, dark finish $1,800
Playclub--(L) Script stamp, dark finish $5,000
Long Spoon--(L) Script stamp, dark finish $4,500

Hood, Tom*
[Dublin i, C.1900-1920]
Mashie--Line face, Gibson star CM $60
Niblick--Line face, medium head, Stewart pipe CM $65
Putter--Combination wood head with metal
sole/gooseneck hosel $3,000

'Horn, The'

[William Gibson proprietary brand]
Iron clubss--Line face, hunting horn CM .... $50 each

Horsman, J.
[New York]
Iron clubs--Line face with Burke thistle and Horsman horseman CMs .... $50 each

Horton, Chester
[Chicago]
Brassie--Model S650, socket head $60
Spoon--Stripe top socket head $60
Iron clubs--Reaction Speed series, small eagle CM, line face .... $50 each
Iron Clubs--MacGregor model, name in oval .... $45 each
Putter--Birkwood 508, Hi Compression series, long hosel $150

Horton, Waverly+
[Chicago]
Driver--Wonder Club model, aluminum & wood combination $300
Driver--Socket head, Horton autograph, marked for The Fair $85
Mid Iron--Model 9, Burke hand CM $45
Niblick--Made by Spence & Gourlay, shaft stamped "Waverly Horton" $60
Putter--(A) Pay Me model, Schenectady style head $200

Howell, V.
Putter--(A B) The Victory, mallet $150

'Hoylake'
Jigger--Name in oval, dot face $40
Mashie Niblick--Slightly concave smooth face $80

Hub, The
[Chicago; also see Lytton]
Iron clubs--MacGregor models, scored face .... $35 each
Putter--Iron blade $40
Putting Cleek--Juvenile $50

'Hunt'+
[Shafts stamped "A.C. & P. Co. Mfgr. Westboro Mass."]
Driver--'Bead' splice head $300
Cleek--Smooth face, yellow colored non-rustable metal head $150
Driving Iron--Model 504, smooth face, wide toe,
yellow colored nonrustable metal $150
Driving Mashie--Smooth face, nonrustable metal $150
Lofter--Smooth face, nonrustable metal $150
Niblick--Small head, concave face, nonrustable metal $600
Putter--Blade, nonrustable metal $200

Hunter, C. & J.
[Prestwick s]
Putter--Iron blade, dot face $60

Hunter, Charles*
[Prestwick s]
Driver--(S) Bulger splice head $400
Playclub--(L) C. 1880, long thin head $6,500
Brassie--(S) C.1890, longish splice head, dark stain $800
Brassie--Socket head $100
Spoon--(L) C.1890, long dark head $1,600
Putter--(L) Long head $3,500

Hunter, Dave
Spoon--(U) Bap model, large head, bulger face $125

Hunter, Harry
[Deal e]
Driver--(S) Beech head $800-1,000
Brassie--Splice head, leather insert $175
Putter--Bent neck blade, Winton diamond CM $75
Putter-Hunter's model, gooseneck hosel, Winton diamond CM $100

Hunter, Maurice
[Calgary, Canada]
Iron clubs--Scored face, horsehead CM .... $50 each

Hunter, Ramsey*

[Sandwich e]
Driver--(S) Splice head, leather face insert $500-1,000
Driver--C.1910 short splice head $150
Putter-(B) Offset blade, patent #4810 .... $250
Putter--Gooseneck blade, oval name stamp $100

Hunter, Willie
[Richmond, Surrey e; Los Angeles, CA]
Driver--Short splice head $150
Iron clubs-Spalding Kro-Flite, stamped with Hunter name .... $35 each

"Huntly"
[England]
Putter--(A) Mallet head, thumb groove in grip end of shaft, made without leather wrap $100-200

Hurry, D.H.
Mashie--Smooth face, junior size $100

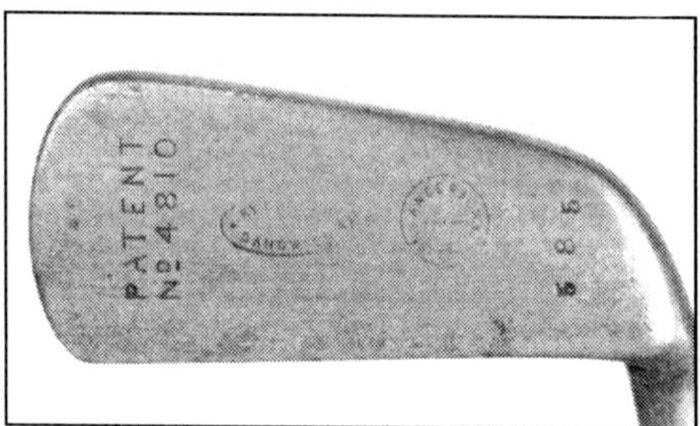

Ramsey Hunter, the Sandwich professional registered his own bent neck putter shortly after Willie Park's club realized huge commercial success.

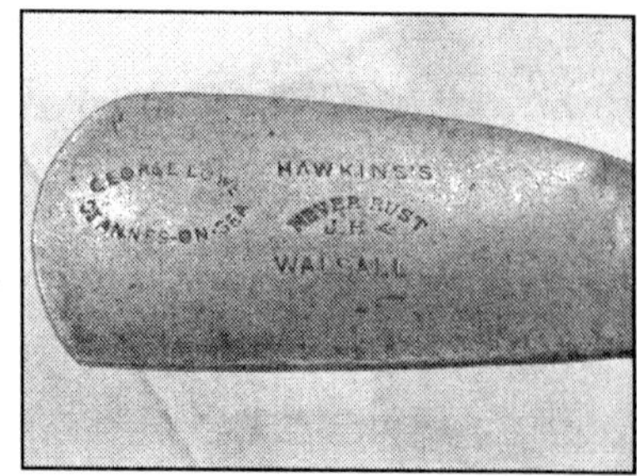

The Hawkins family metalurgists in the Midlands area. This is the George Low patent anti-shank style iron in Hawkin's 'never rust' steel.

Hurry, H.
Brassie--Broad splice head $150

Hutchings, W.
[Derbyshire e]
Brassie--Socket head $60

Hutchison, J.H.*
[North Berwick s]
Driver--(S) Light colored head, leather face insert $2,500
Driver--Compact splice head $400
Brassie--(S) C.1895, dark finish $2,000
Brassie--Socket head $250
Long spoon--(S) C.1895, narrow head $1,800
Iron--Smooth face, Carrick CM $500
Lofter--Smooth face, long blade, name in oval $250
Mashie--(B) Two level smooth face, Condie rose CM $1,200
Putter--(S) Light color $600
Putter--Gun metal blade $175
Putter--Offset blade, Pipe CM $100

Hutchison, John (Jock)
[Pittsburgh, PA and Chicago, IL; other Hutchison line clubs were sold by Burke, Wilson and Winchester]
Brassie--Socket head, marked Pittsburgh $125
Named Irons--Autograph series irons, Stewart pipe CM,
scored face .... $65 each
Iron clubs--Burke models, marked for Pittsburgh .... $55 each
Iron clubs—Burke models made for Winchester .... $100 each
Iron clubs—Autograph series made by Wilson .... $60 each

I

I.J.S.G. Company+
[see Iver Johnson Sporting Goods Co.]

'Illini'
Putter--Chrome head, long gooseneck hosel, Illinois map CM $90

Imperial Golf Company*
[Sunderland e]
Brassie--(A S) Model 1 .... $200
Mid Iron--(A S) Checkered face $200
Putter--(A S) Model 1 .... $250
Putter--(A) RM model $100
Putter--(A) The Verden, mallet shape, domed crown $200
Putter--(A) Dormie model, short mallet head $100
Putter--(A) X model, mallet, ridged crown $100
Putter--(A) Rex model mallet $100
Putter--(A) Square toe mallet, wood face insert $300

Indestro Company+
[Chicago]
Driver--Socket head, decal on shaft $25

Inglis, J.R.
[Elmsford, NY]
Putter--(A) Ray-type head, cross clubs CM $85
Putter—Blade with square weight on club back $350

'Ionic'
Driver--Name in script, socket head $30

Irving & Clark
[Sporting goods retailer, Pittsboro, MA]
Niblick--Medium head, smooth face, heard mark with legend
"In the Heart of the Berkshires" $150

Ironside, Robert
[*Australia]*
Putter—Concentrated back, R I in diamond CM $75

Isherwood, A.J.
[Warrington e]
Driver--Socket head $50

Isles, A.S.
Putter-(A) Mallet head with hole through center of club head for picking up ball $3,500-4,500

There are at least three variations of this design with differently shaped rubber gaskets for gripping the ball]

Iver Johnson Sporting Goods Company+
[Boston, MA sports outfitter]
Iron clubs--Smooth face, marked "Willie Campbell, I.J.S.G. Co." in double oval ....$100-150 each

Iver Johnson Sporting Goods Company of Boston sold Willie Campbell brand clubs, like this short head cleek, around the turn of the century.

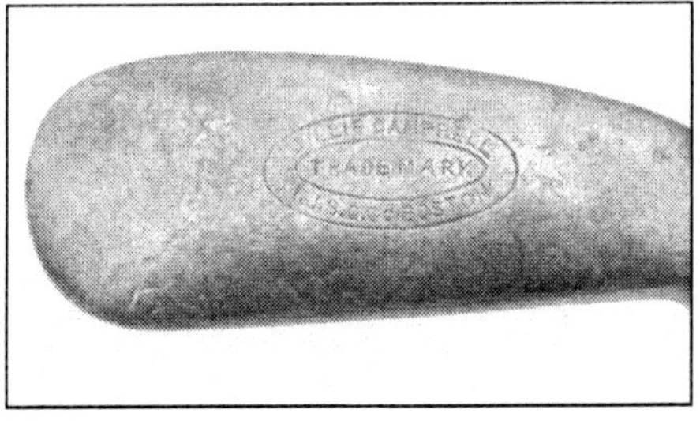

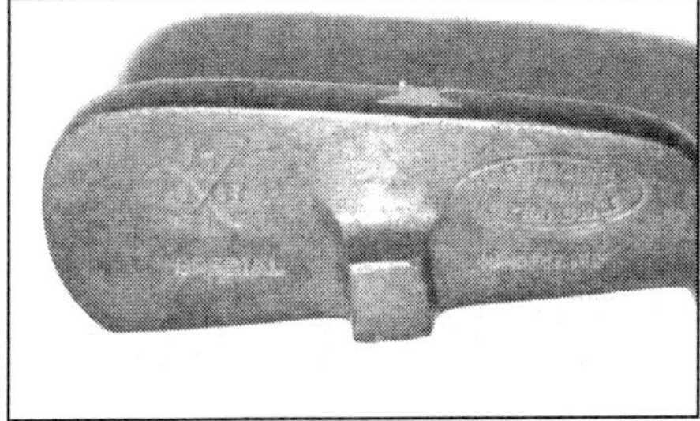

J.R. Inglis, a New York area professional made this club with the unusual combination aiming bar and back weight.

J

J.B. & Company
[Jack Burns, St. Andrews]
Iron clubs--The Falcon series, line face, falcon on hand CM ..... $60 each

Jackson, John*
[Perth s]
Playclub--(L) Ash shaft, long thin head $7,500-25,000
Short Spoon--(L) Ash shaft $10,000-30,000
Putter-(L) Brown stained head $7,500-20,000

Jacobs, Charles J.*
[Isle of Wight e]
Driver--(B) Composition splice head $550
Baffy Spoon--Socket head, fiber face insert $150

Jarvis & White
[Chicago]
Iron clubs--Line face, Burke fleur-de-lis CM $35

Jeffrey, Ben
[Worthing e]
Mid Iron--Maltese cross CM, stainless, line face $45

Johns, Charles*
[Purley e, et al]
Brassie--The Manor model, socket head $60
Cleek--Round sole, dot face $35

Johnson Company, The A.L.
[Boston, MA]
Driver--Socket head $50
Iron--Dot face $35
Mongrel Iron--Stewart pipe CM, line face $80
Niblick--Pipe CM, large head, smooth face $175

Johnson, Frank*
[London]
Driver--(B) Eureka model, full metal face $250
Iron--Smith model (anti-shank), Cygnet series 306, dot face $150
Iron clubs--Scored face with key CM $55
Mashie--6, smooth face, key CM $80
Mashie--106, Premier series, notch hosel $75
Putter--Eureka model, metal face $400
Putter--Frank model, name in script, half barrel shaped head $125

Johnson, W. Claude
Driver--(B) Round head, removable weights $2,250

Johnston, Charles
[Cranford, NJ]
Driver--Socket head, oval name stamp $45
Mashie--Model 12, Burke hand CM, diamond face $35

Johnston, T.
Playclub--(B L) Black composite head, oval name stamp $8,000
Putter--(B L) as above $9,000

Johnstone Brothers*
[Tayport s]
Iron clubs--Line face, hammer in hand CM ....$100 each
Iron clubs—Made for Tom Morris shop ....$125 each

Johnstone, R.
Driver--Splice head $150

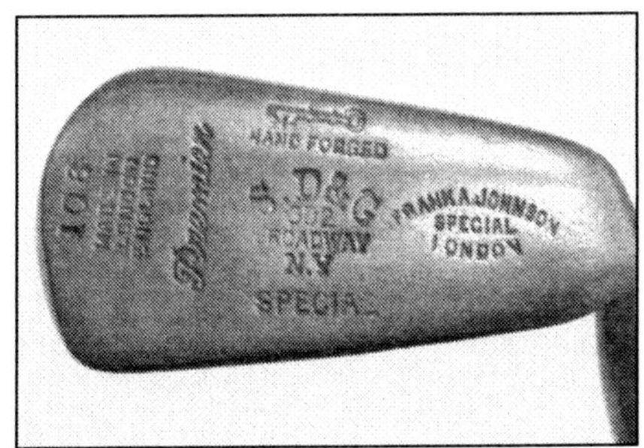

Frank Johnson, once a foreman for the Tom Morris, shop, used the key cleek mark. This iron was imported by S.D.&G.

Johnstone, R
[Seattle]
Putter--Spalding BV model, two roses CM $250

Jolly, Jack
[Newark, NJ et al]
Mashie Niblick--Foulis style with musselback $150
Putter—Wood Dunn patent mallet $300

Jones, Ernest
[Chislehurst e, et al]
Driver--Socket head 100
Iron clubs--Line face with large CM for
National Women's Golf Links .... $75 each

Jones. H.I.
[Chicago]
Mashie--Line face $25

Jones, Jr., Robert T.
[The Amateur and Open champion; he never endorsed clubs until after his retirement. Stewart's R.T.J. irons were unauthorized replicas, Spalding's were Jones's own post-retirement design]
Numbered Irons--R.T.J. series, made by Stewart ....$80-120 each
Numbered Irons--RTJ/FO series, made by Stewart ....$90-140 each
Named Irons--Robert T Jones, Jr. autograph series irons,
made by Stewart .... $300-600 each
#1 through 9-Iron--Stainless, Robert T. Jones, Jr. signature
by Spalding, dot face, registration number .... $100-300 each
Matched Set--6 or 9 Spalding clubs in sequence
with matching registration numbers .... $200-400 each
Putter--Calamity Jane model, 3 bands of whipping on
(wood) shaft, Spalding Kro-Flite CM $150-250

[The following are steel shafted clubs, usually found with a plastic coated shaft with simulated wood grain or plain yellow plastic coating. These are included because Robert T. Jones, Jr. clubs of all types are becoming more collectible daily]

Jones, Rowland*

[Wimbledon e]
Driver--Socket head $80
Iron clubs--Stewart pipe brand, scored face .... $50 each
Niblick--Medium head, smooth face, pipe CM $175
Putting Cleek--Anderson reg'd. #277771 .... $200

Jones, T.W.
[Llandudno w]
Driving Iron--Line face, anvil CM $40

K

Kay, James
[Seaton Carew e]
Driver--Socket head $75

Keffer, Karl+
[Ottawa, ONT]
Putter--(A) Mallet head $100

Kempshall Manufacturing Company*+
[Arlington, NJ & London; an automobile tire manufacturer that entered the golf business making balls and pyralin golf clubs]
Driver--(U) Socket head, made from black pyralin $700
Driver--(U) Wood socket head with pyralin marked/dated face insert $400

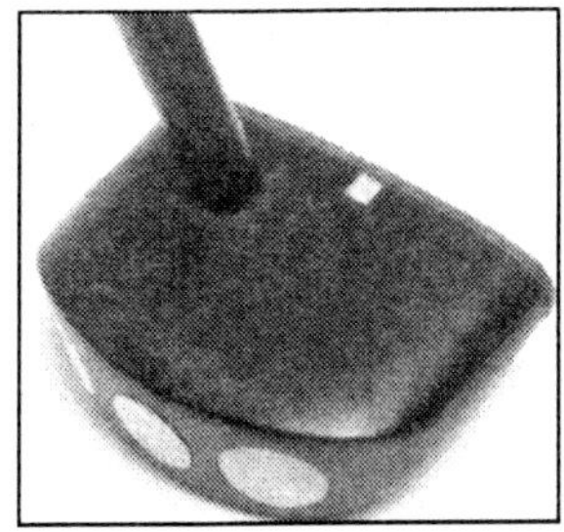

Willie Dunn designed this model putter which was made from the synthetic 'pyralin' by Kempshall Manufacturing Co. (also see the color plate page 2)

Willie Kidd, the Scotsman working in Minneapolis, sold this Stewart putter which collectors now call the "bassackward" model.

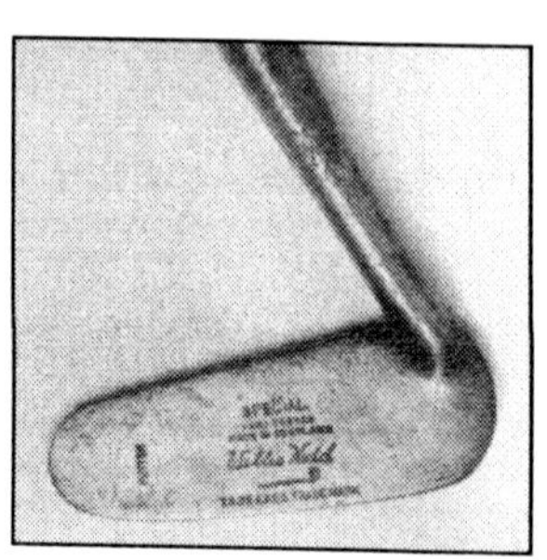

Driver—(U) Marked Rubber Core, pyralin face insert (Page B)... $400
Duplex Club--(U) Two face fairway club, ... $1,200
Putter--(U) Schenectady style head, black pyralin $500
Putter--(U) Dunn model, black pyralin
square head, center shaft, brass face $400
Putter--(U) As above but in white pyralin $600

Kenny, Daniel
Spoon--Socket head, fiber face insert $60

Kidd, Willie
[Minneapolis MN, et al]
Spade Mashie--Reg number, line face, WK in circle
on sweetspot $65
Mashie Niblick--Running stag CM, name in script $50
Named Irons-- Wm. Kidd model, Stewart pipe CM,
scored face .... $60 each
Putter--'Bassackward' model, hosel bent backward $3,500

Kilty Kersten Company+
[Milwaukee, WI]
Woods--Name in oval .... $40 each
Named Irons--Kilty Kersten series, K in triangle CM .... $25 each
Named/Numbered Irons--Lady Lucky Strike series,
K in triangle CM .... $25 each
Numbered Irons--Name in oval, K in triangle CM .... $25 each
Putter--Kilty Kersten series $35

King Hardware Company
[Atlanta, GA]
Iron clubs--King Bee model, bee CM, made by Burke .... $45 each

King-Horn
[William Gibson proprietary brand]
Iron clubs--Line face, star in circle CM .... $35 each

Kinnear, J.B.
Mashie--Deep face, line face, pipe CM $45

Kinnell, J. & D.
[Prestwick s]
Iron clubs--Prestwick brand, smooth face, two-sided K CM .... $85 each

Kinnell, David*
[Leven and Prestwick s]
Spoon--Splice head $200

Kinnell, James*
[Prestwick, s; Norwich and Purley e]
Brassie--Socket head, deep face $75
Putter--Own model, bar shaped blade, Stewart pipe CM $150

Kirk, R.*
[St. Andrews]
Putter--Fruitwood head, greenheart shaft $12,000

Kirk, R.W.
[Wallasey e]
Driver--Splice head, ash shaft $350
Driver--Splice head, short thick head $150
Iron--Smooth face, rose CM $100
Putting Cleek--(B) Steel blade with twisted neck, Anderson's reg. 277771, serial number at heel $200

Kirkaldy, Andrew*
[St. Andrews; clubs made by Martin & Kirkaldy]
Driver--Dreadnought model, large head, Kirkaldy autograph $175
Mashie--Autograph model, made by Wm. Gibson, line face $85
Putter--Splice wood head, fiber slip $250

Kirkwood, Joe

The Kismet putter achieved a certain amount of fame when Max Marston won the US Amateur Championship using one.

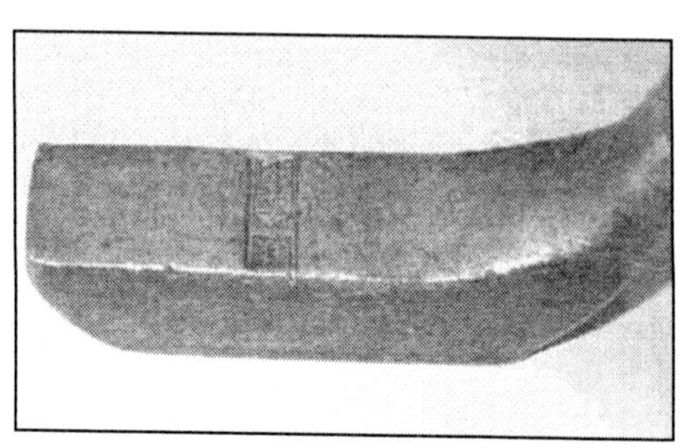

[San Francisco, CA]
Iron clubs--Line face, Gibson star CM $50

'Kismet'
[Made by Phosphor Bronze Smelting Co., Baltimore, MD]
Putter--Long rectangular metal head, shafted at heel $200

Klees, Charles J.+
[Chicago, IL]
Brassie--Socket head, name in script $40
Driving Iron--MacGregor Tomahawk series, dot face $60
Putting Cleek--Line face, Stewart pipe CM $65

Klein, Willie
Mashie Niblick--Zenith model 82, hand CM, dot face $60

Klin Brothers+
[Valparaiso, IN]
Driver--Stripe top socket head, bulger face $50
Driver--Socket head, name in script $50
Driver--Drive-Rite model, brass backweight, ivory insert $65
Brassie--Klin Club series, socket head $50
Jigger—Radio series, five petal flower CM, beveled edge $40
Mashie--Model K-32, dash face, flower CM, marked "Klin's" $45
Lofter--K-70 model, Klin Brothers flower CM $45
Numbered Irons--Spalding roses CM, stainless, dot face .... $40 each
Putter--Thick blade, offset head $50

Klin-McGill Golf Manufacturing Company+
[Valparaiso, IN]

The Klin Brothers made golf clubs in several locations south of Chicago and in Valparaiso, Indiana.

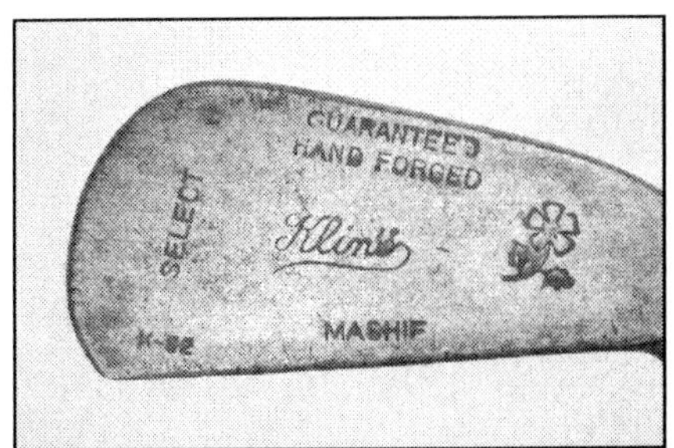

Driver--Socket head, Kiltie model $90
Iron Clubs—McGill metal, dash face, diamond-K CM .... $75 each
Iron Clubs—Eagle series, chromed , shamrock at sweetspot $30
Mashie--(D) McGill metal head, rustless bronze alloy, corrugated & brick pattern face $400
Mashie--Bakspin model K-5, stagdot face $65
Mashie Niblick--(D) Klin Klub series, deep slot face w/ comb grooves at sole, McGill metal $600
Mid Iron--(D) McGill metal head, corrugated face $200
Niblick--McGill metal head, line face, K in diamond CM $100
Putter--McGill metal blade $85

Klin, Eddie
[Chicago]
Mashie--Name in oval, dot face $30

Klin, Mike
[Chicago]
Putter--MacGregor R model, bamboo laminate shaft $125

Knight, A.H.
[Schenectady, NY; the inventor of the original Schenectady model aluminum putter. The first production models have a "Pat. Applied For" legend on the back side, later replaced with the patent date]
Putter--(A) Schenectady model, center shaft, diamond face, "Patent Applied For" on back $600

Knight, Ben
Mashie--(B) Vertically slotted face, open on bottom ('rake iron' type), Roger patent $6,000

Knox, A

Playclub--(S) Red-orange finish $1,500
Brassie--(S) C.1885, slightly hooked face $900
Spoon--(S) C.1890 ....$1,500

Knox, G.P.

Driver--Socket head, name in script $65

Knox, John

[Belfast i]

Driver--Socket head $95
Mashie--Line face, Gourlay moon-star CM $50
Putter--Forgan Scotia series blade $60

Kroydon Golf Company+

[Maplewood, NJ]

Woods--Ace model, batwing aluminum backweight ....$65 each
Driver--Stripe top, socket head $50
Driver--Super Kroydonite model, black finish $75
Brassie--Hy-Power model, socket head, 2 color face insert $60
Spoon--Model 6328, brass star in sole plate $60
Driving Iron--H 8, dot face $50
Mashie--N 7, dot face $45
Mashie--NO 7, ball face $75
Mashie--N 8, dot face $45
Mashie—40 degree, dot face $45
Mashie Iron--L 7, ball face $75
Mashie Iron--L 8, dot face $45
Mashie Niblick--P 7, tiny waffle pattern face $100
Mashie Niblick--PO 7, ball face pattern $75
Mashie Niblick--(D) Model U5, brick face $350
Mid Iron--J 7, ball face $75
Mid Iron--J 8, dot face $45
Mid Iron--J 9, diamond/dash face $50
Niblick--R 2, 50 degree, vertical lines on face $250
Niblick--R 7, ball face pattern $75
Niblick--R 8, dot face $50
Niblick--RO 9, diamond/dash face $50
Spade Mashie--P 7, ball face pattern $75

Most Kroydon carry the loft angle in degrees marked on the sole of the iron like this 40° mashie.

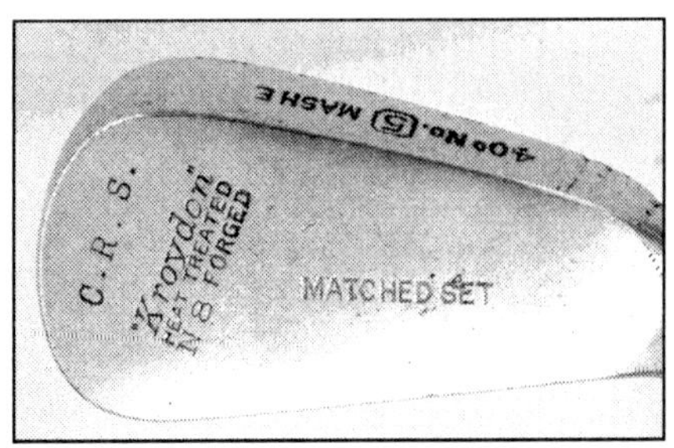

Spade Mashie--(D) U 5, Short Stop model, brick pattern face $350
Spade Mashie--U 6, tiny waffle pattern face $100
Jigger--M 7, ball face markings $100
4-Iron--MO 8, dot face $45
Putter--S 1, "7 degree" blade $80
Putter--S 7, ball face, blade $75
Putter--S 8, gun metal head, dash face $150
Putter--SO 8, shallow blade, round back, line face $50
Putter--S 10, ball face blade $100
Putter--(A) Model B, Ray-type head, dished chamber on top $100
Putter--(A) S 30A, mallet head $100
Putter--(A) S 30B, Ray-Mills style with recessed chamber on top ... $125
Putter--(A) S 31B, mallet head $75
Putter--(A) S 32, center shafted $150
Putter--(A) S 33A, center shafted $200
Putter--Panther model, iron blade, dash-diamond face $75
Putter—(U) Pendulum style, cross hatch face $600

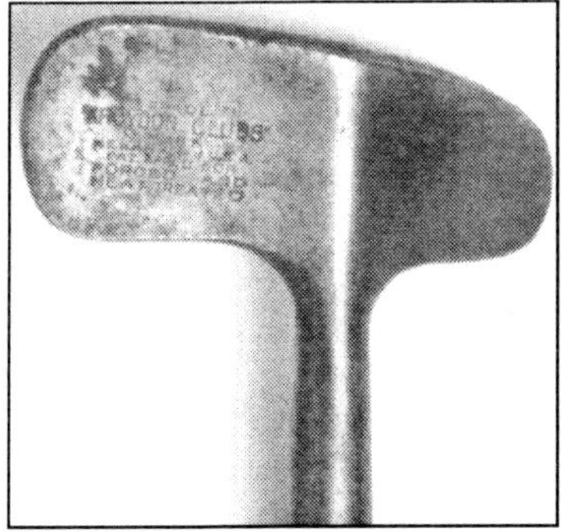

This Kroydon pendulum style putter never was well received by most golfers which makes it a desirable collectible today.

L

Laclede Brass Works+
[St. Louis, MO]
Putter--(U) Doerr Topem model, stainless, top flange $150
Putter--(U) Doerr Topem model, phosphor bronze, negative loft, bottom flange, deeply scored line face $300

'Lakewood'
Driver--Socket head $50

Lamino Golf Company
Driver--(U) Laminate construction head and shaft $750
Driver-Laminated shaft, black head, L in diamond CM $250
Putter--(U) Laminate construction, oversized mallet head and shaft (both laminated) $1,500

Lang, Bennett*
[Perth s]
Playclub--Beech head, light color finish $4,500

I'Anson, John
(listed in A section)

Large, William
Putter--Offset blade, stainless $40

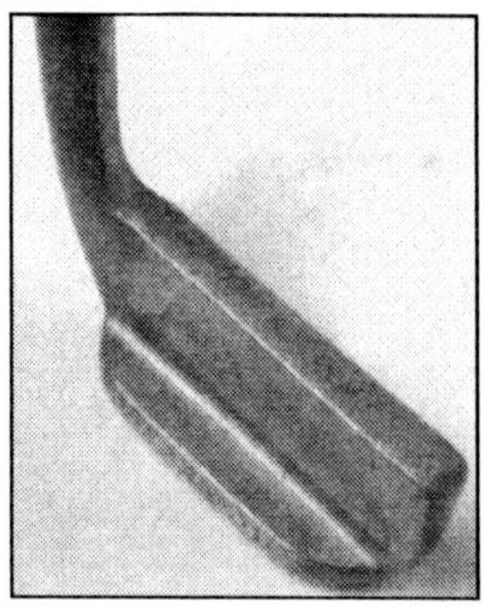

The Laclede Brass Works was one of those metal working companies that made golf clubs as a sideline, in this case, only topspin putters.

Page 35

Page 104

Bronze bent neck putter by Anderson (of Anstruther)

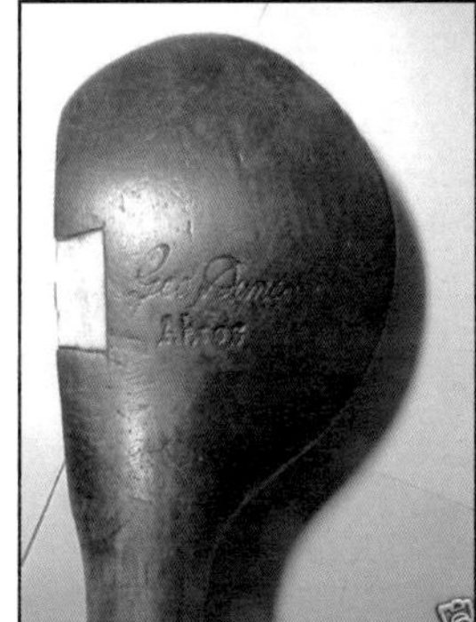

George Duncan "Akros" model driver with thick white ivorine face insert

Page 100

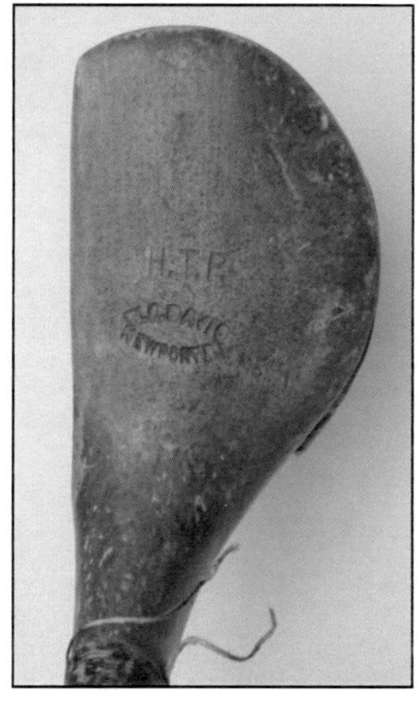

Willie Davis, Newport, Rhode Island splice head driver.

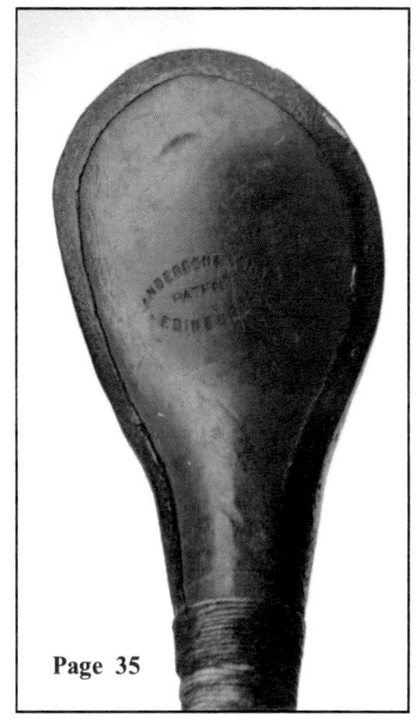

Page 35

R. Anderson, Edinburgh unusual patent driver with leather strip all around club head

Page 184

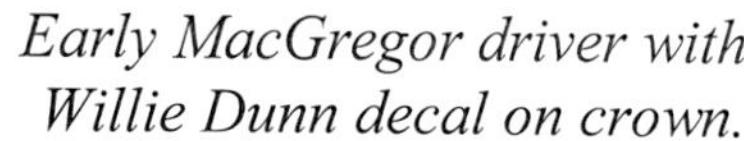

Early MacGregor driver with Willie Dunn decal on crown.

Kempshall rubber faced driver for use with the Kempshall rubber core ball.

Joe Lloyd juvenile driver.

Page 164

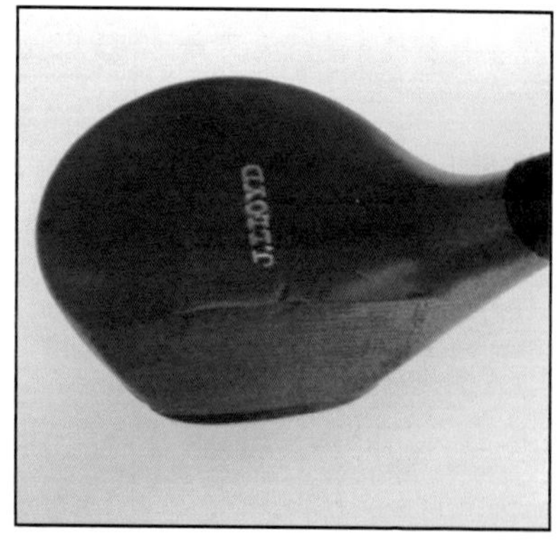

Page 174

Page 204

Tom Morris long nose grassed driver.

Page 309

Thomas Wilson Mac Smith model driver with fancy aluminum back weight and 5-spot face insert.

Alex Patrick well lofted short spoon.

Page 223

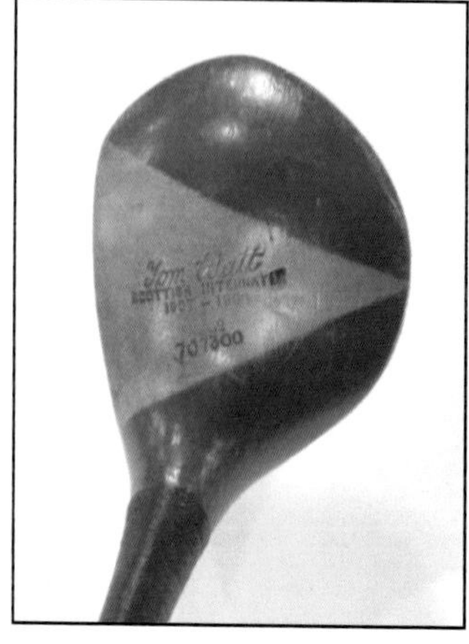

Tom Watt driver with an unusual stripe top stain design.

Page 301

John Reid, Atlantic City, New Jersey, bronze blade putter.

Page 234

Spalding George Duncan model driver.

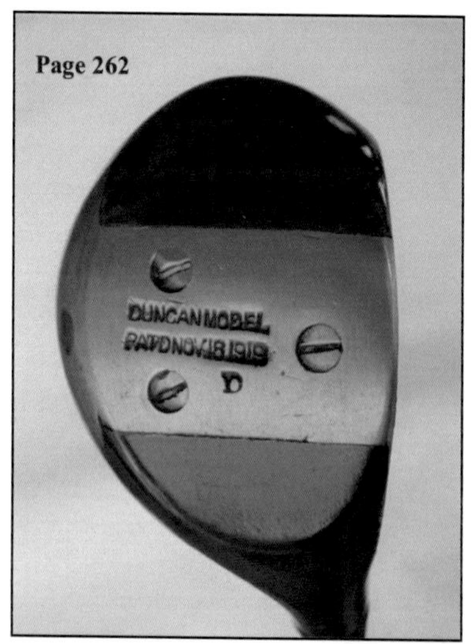

Page 262

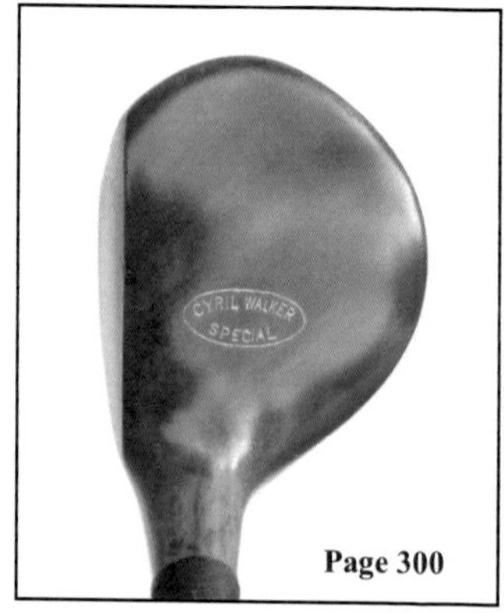

Page 300

Cyril Walker, 1924 US Open Champ, model driver.

Lee & Underhill+
[New York retail/catalog/import company]
Driver--(B) Split Socket model (fork splice head), leather insert $500
Brassie--George Sargent autograph, socket head $100
Driving Iron--Flower CM, dot face $35
Mashie--George Sargent autograph, dot face $75
Putter--Kilgour Match model $150
Putter--(A) Hammer head, Schenectady style $200

Lee Company, Harry C.+
[New York retail/catalog/import company; used an acorn CM on many of their imported clubs]
Driver--Dreadnought model, socket head, name in script $100
Baffy--(A U) Schenectady shaped head but with 17-degree lofted face........ $2,500
Iron clubs--Neptune model, stainless, dot face, 3 chain links CM .... $35 each
Iron clubs--Script "Lee" in circle CM. line face $35 each
Iron clubs-Script name, Lee+star CM .... $35 each
Iron clubs--Dexter series .... $30 each
Sammy Cleek--Smooth face $75
Putter--Iron blade, acorn CM $45
Putter--(A U) Schenectady model, band-crimped neck, marked 'sole licensee' $250
Putter--(A U) Schenectady model, September patent date stamped on back $125-300

◇◇Numbered irons (stainless, line face)
M-1--Mid iron $35
M-2--Mid iron, deep face $35
M-3--Mid iron, round sole $35
MA-1--Mashie, deep face $35
MA-2--Mashie, offset head $35
MM-1--Mid mashie $40
MN-1--Mashie niblick $35
N-1--Niblick, large head $45
P-2--Putter, regular blade $40
P-3--Putter, offset blade $40

Legh, Major Gilbert
[Kings Lynn e]
Driving Cleek—(B) Combination wood and steel head (like modern hybrid) $800
Irons—(B) The Leader, cavity back, hyphen face .... $150 each

Leith Golf Co.
Driver--Socket head $60

Leslie Co., R. & W.
Putting Cleek or Putter--Step down back $150

Leslie, Robert
[Glen View, IL]
Putter--Gun metal blade, Condie rose CM $100
Putter--Thick top of blade $350
Putter—Professional model, top weight but curved toward ends $150

Leslie, W.
Cleek--Smooth face, Condie rose CM $150

Letters, John*
[Glasgow]
Driver--Stripe top, socket head $80
Jigger--Newbridge series, shallow blade, dot face $75
Iron clubs--Stainless, line face, bridge CM .... $60 each

Lewis, A.J.
[Dudley e]
Putter—Bugle CM , shallow face $50

Major Gilbert Legh patented a number of clubs including this hollow back (or cavity back) iron, designed in 1912 and made by Robert Sellars.

The retail store Lillywhite's once they had their own club making department. This Whitehall series club was made for them by the Tom Morris shop.

Lewis, M.J.
[Sutton Coldfield e]
Putter--(B) The Perfect Putter, peacock CM, stainless $95

Leyland (Leyland & Birmingham Rubber Company)*
Woods--L L M B in triangle CM ....$60 each
Iron clubs--L L B M in triangle, dot face ....$35 each
Niblick--Jumbo model, extra large head, dot face bear CM $80
Niblick--Junior Giant model $100
Numbered Irons--Century series, bear CM, line face ....$35 each
Numbered Irons--Large 'spade' CM, line face ....$35 each
Putter--Century series, iron blade, bear CM $45
Putter--Truline series, musselback blade $45

Lillywhite's (J. Lillywhite, Frowd & Company)*+
[London]
Driver--Butchart model, V-groove splice head $500
Numbered irons--Whitehall series, mini-musselback, stainless, small triangle CM .... $40 each
Cleek—Aston series, weight & distance markings $50
Putter--(B) Blade with wood insert $900
Putter--(B) Winckworth-Scott model, autograph name stamp, square solid steel shaft $750

'Limber Shaft'
[see, Jimmy Thomson]

Lindgren Brothers+
Putter--Adjustable, center shaft, set screw in face $750

Litchfield Manufacturing Company+
[Connecticut]
Driving Mashie--Smooth face, deep face gun metal blade $300
Iron--Smooth face, gun metal blade, name in oval mark $200

Littledale, N.
[Houghton, MI]
Brassie--Pear shaped socket head $65

Lloyd, Joe
[1897 US Open Champion; served at clubs in England, France and US]
Driver--Socket head $140
Driver—Socket head juvenile (Page B)..$150
Lofter--Smooth face, marked "Pau" (France) $200
Putter--Name in straight line $150

'Lockenna'
Brassie--Socket head, red/black target face insert $100
Named/Numbered Irons--Chromed, line face $25

Lockhart, Gordon
[Gleneagles s]
Brassie--Stripe top socket head, eagle mark $100
Iron--(B)Smith model, dot face $150
Niblick--Line face, large Eagle CM $80

Lockwood & Brown*
[London]
Approaching iron--Jungle model, beveled sole, LB CM $100
Driving Iron--Maxwell pattern $50
Mashie Niblick--(B) Smith model (anti-shank), stainless,
Gibson star CM $150
Niblick--Giant head, dot face, "LB" on face $1,750
Iron clubs--LB in circle CM, stainless, dot face .... $45 each
Putter--Large wood head, Gassiat style $800

Lockwood, A.G.+
[Primarily worked French Lick, IN]
Driver--Socket head, insert $100
Driver--(A) Samson face insert, socket head, marked Boston $150

The Lovell Arms Company was typical of early sporting goods stores that once only handles hunting and fishing equipment before selling golf clubs.

Named Irons--Line face, pluto (devil) CM ....$55 each

Logan, Hugh*
[Wimbledon, St. Andrews, Glasgow, etc.; his most famous design, the Genii model iron, was manufactured by William Gibson]
Brassie--Splice head, small lettering $150
Named Irons--Connoisseur series, beveled sole, dot face $100
Putter--(A) Cherokee, mallet head, T aiming bar $400

London Golf Company*
[London]
Driver--Cuirass series, socket head, brass face plate $300
Driver--Cuirass series, juvenile size $350
Iron clubs--Name in small oval, dot face ....$60 each
Putter--Cuirass series, wood socket head, brass face
plate w/ 4 screws, dot face $250

Longsworth, I.R.+
[Somerset, KY]
Putter--(A) Adjustable, boat shaped head $1,500

Lovell Arms Company, John P.+
[Boston, MA]
Driver--Splice head $300
Brassie--Splice head $300
Iron--Name in block letters $150
Mashie--Lovell Diamond series, smooth face $150
Putter--Iron blade, gooseneck $150
Putter--Smooth face iron blade $100

Low & Hughes
[New York sporting goods house and importer]
Putter--Sure Shot model, Vaile style swan neck hosel $250

Low, George+
[predominantly Baltusrol, NJ, also NYC]
Driver--Small splice head, fiber insert $175
Driver--Socket head $100
Brassie--Socket head $100
Mashie--Marked for Dyker Meadow, smooth face $125
Mashie--Low & Hughes brand $75
Niblick—Marked for New York, smooth face $100
Putter--Gem model $100
Putter--(A) Mallet head, crossed clubs CM, lead face $300

Lowe & Campbell+
[Chicago, Kansas City]
Driver--Fairview series, socket head $40
Named/Numbered Irons--Ace brand, Wilson Range series .... $30 each
Named/Numbered Irons--Special, sterling forged .... $30 each
Numbered Irons--Dot face, stainless .... $30 each

Lowe, D.
Mashie--(B) Smith model (anti-shank), made by Gourlay $150

Lowe, George*
[St. Anne's-on-Sea e]
Spoon--(S) C.1895, well dished face, honey colored head $800
Cleek--(B) Styled after the Fairlie patent (anti-shank),
made from Hawkins Never Rust Steel $275
Cleek--(B) Styled after the Fairlie patent (anti-shank) $250

George Low was a popular and successful professional and club maker at Baltusrol GC and with a shop in New York City.

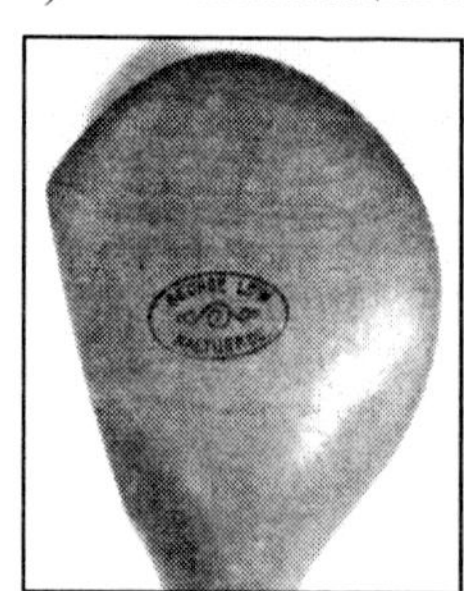

Iron--(B) Anti-shank type, by James Anderson, w/ serial number $200
Niblick--(B) Small head, as above, serial number $250
Putting Iron--(B) Steel blade with raised portion
along top edge $300

Set-(B) [cleek, mashie, lofter, niblick] smooth face
with matched serial numbers $1,000

Lumley's, Ltd.*
[Glasgow & Edinburgh]
Driver--Dreadnought Junior model, socket head $75
Iron clubs--Scottish Champion series, kilted soldier CM,
dot face ....$45 each
Mid Iron—Scottish Champion, shield CM $30
Iron clubs--Name in script, scored face ....$40 each
Iron clubs--Cochranes, knot CM, Lumley in script ....$50 each
Putter--Magic model,, beveled heel and toe, offset blade $75

Lunn & Company*
[London]
Driver--(S) C.1890, dark stain $800
Cleek--Balfour model, smooth face $150
Cleek--Smooth face, short hosel $150
Mashie--Smooth face, compact blade, heavy head $150

Lurcock, Murray
Putter--Socket head $125

Lurie, John
Mashie--Marked 'N Y Sport Klub', made by Burke $50

Lytton Company, The Henry
[Chicago]
Iron clubs--Made by MacGregor, rose CM, dot face ....$45 each
Putter--The Hub series, iron blade $40
Putting Cleek--Juvenile $50

M

M.L. Co.
[Urbana, OH]
Putter--Iron blade, primitive markings $25

M & S Company
[Batavia, NY]
Putter—Steel blade with unusual deep line score face pattern $75

The M & S Company made this putter with very unusual face markings.

Mac & Mac Company+
[Oak Park, IL]
Mashie--(D) Back Spin model, 19 holes drilled half way through face $450
Mashie Niblick--(D) Back Spin model, 22 holes drilled half way through face $450
Mashie Niblick--(D) Back Spin model, wide slots cut through face, German silver $2,000
Putter--Brass head, lead center exposed face and back, square hosel and grip $450

MacDonald, The
Putter--(A B) Long rectangular head, heel shafted, chamber with sliding lid housing removable weights $4,000

MacDonald, J.

[Musselburgh s]

Mashie Niblick--Line face $45

MacFarlane, Willie

[Tuckahoe, NY; US Open Champion 1925]

Driver--Socket head $75

Mashie--Name in oval, Spalding roses CM $50

Putter--Name in oval, MacGregor R model, top edge weight $75

MacGregor+

[Dayton, OH; officially called the Crawford, McGregor & Canby Co., they entered the business based on their woodworking abilities gained from 65 years in the wooden shoe-last business. Their primary CM was a rose, intended to imitate the mark of Robert Condie, the Scottish master cleek maker]

<><>Miscellaneous clubs

Driver--(B) Dunn one-piece, leather face insert $1,500-2,000

Driver--Lateral fork splice $1,250

Driver-Splice head, deep face $250

Driver--Model 2, dovetailed ivory face $175

Driver--Model 3, "six-spot" ivory face insert $80-125

Driver--Model 3 BB, red & white fiber face $75

Driver--Model 4, "fiber lock" insert with large white dot $100

Driver--Model 27, plain face $65-90

Driver--Model 27-F, fiber faced $125

Driver--Model 27-H, Samson face $275

Driver--Model 28, plain face $75

Driver--Model 30, plain face $75

Driver--Model 31, plain face $75

Driver--Model 125, short bulldog head, face insert $125

Driver--Model 203, plain face $75

Driver--Model 301, plain face $75

Driver--Model 302, plain face $75

Driver--Model 326, dreadnought, large head $125

Driver--Model 352, plain face $75

Driver--Model 478, steel face with 5 screws $80

Driver--Model 478 1/2, as above $80

Driver--MM model, plug fastened fiber face insert $60-100

Driver--WW model, plug fastened fiber face insert $60-100

Brassie--Short splice head, shamrock in circle CM $200
Brassie--Short splice head, deep face $200
Brassie--BAP model, fiber insert $65
Brassie--BAP Bulger model 17 .... $65
Brassie--Model 2, ivory face, 2 fiber pins $175
Brassie--Model 4, "fiber lock" insert with large white dot $100
Brassie--Model 4 BB, red & white fiber face $65
Brassie--(A) Model 17, "white dot" dot face insert $200
Brassie--Model 27, plain face $60-100
Brassie--Model 27-F, fiber face $125
Brassie--Model 27-H, Samson face $275
Brassie--Model 28, plain face $75
Brassie--Model 30, plain face $75
Brassie--Model 31, plain face $75
Brassie--Model 203, plain face $75
Brassie--Model 225, short bulldog head, face insert $125
Brassie--Model 301, plain face $75
Brassie--Model 302, plain face $75
Brassie--Model 326, dreadnought, large head $100
Brassie--Model 352, plain face $75
Brassie--Model 479, steel face insert $80
Brassie--Model 479 1/2, as above $80
Brassie--Model MA1, 5-dot Yardsmore face inlay, socket head $80
Brassie Cleek--Model 344, plain face $75
Brassie Cleek--Model 355, plain face, wide head $75
Brassie Cleek--Model 421. plain face $100
Brassie Spoon--Model WW, face insert, brass backweight $100
Spoon--Model 32, Plain face $80
Spoon--Model 312, plain face $80
Spoon--Model 325, bulldog style short socket head,
pegged face insert $125
Spoon--Model 373, plain face $80

MacGregor "white dot" model driver with white fiber face insert.

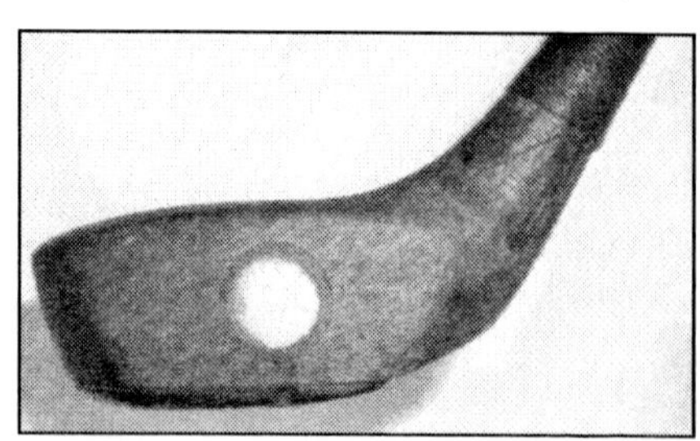

The MacGregor (left hand) concentric lofter was thickest at the center of the sole, smooth faced and had only this second generation shamrock mark.

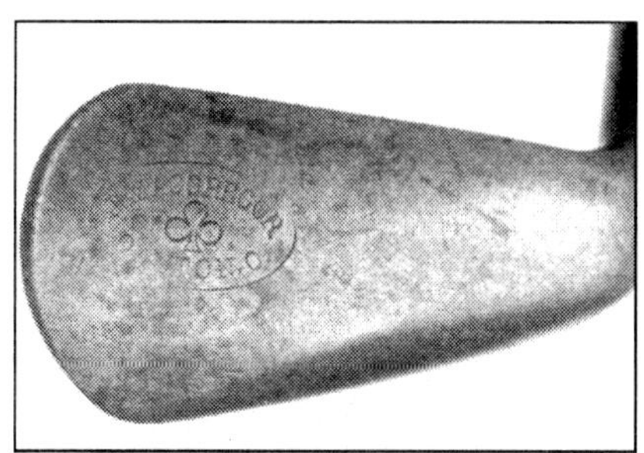

Wooden Cleek-(U) Wedge shaped brass backweight $175
Approach Iron--Model 31 1/2, Em-An-Em metal, dot face $150
Driving Niblick--Gun metal head, name in oval, smooth face $750
Iron--Model B, smooth face, shamrock CM $75
Lofter—Concentric back, shamrock CM, number 205 on hosel $85
Mashie--Model 29, thick toe, Em-An-Em metal $150
Mashie--Deep face, smooth face, shamrock in circle CM $125
Mashie--Model OA, flange sole, stagdot face $60
Mashie--Model SC1, slotted hosel, dot face $125
Mashie—Model B, rose CM, smooth face $75
Mid Iron--Model OA, flange sole, stagdot face $60
Mid Iron--Model 25, Em-An-Em metal $125
Mashie Niblick--Foulis-type, through bore hosel,
Em-An-Em Metal $250
Mashie Niblick—Foulis-type, shamrock in oval CM $85
Niblick--Model OA, flange sole, stagdot face $60
Niblick--Smooth face, very thick head & hosel,
shamrock in circle $300
Niblick--(B) Smooth face, Fairlie style,
shamrock in circle CM $300
Niblick--Smooth face, medium head, shamrock in circle CM $150

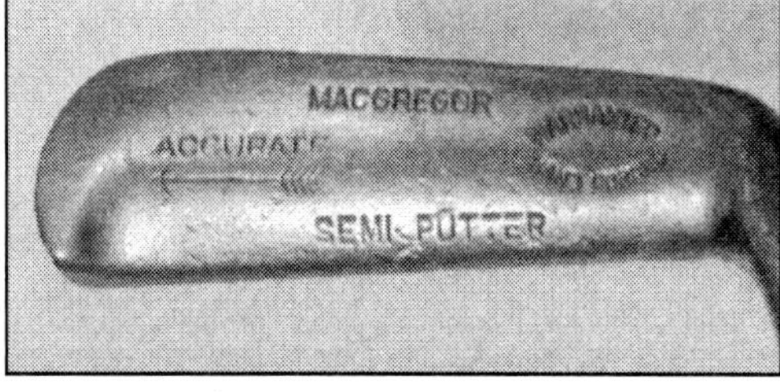

The Semi-Putter was a heel and toe weighted, lofted chipping club used around the greens.

After the Willie Dunn 'Bowtie' mark, the next oldest series has the small shamrock mark in the double circle, like this smooth face niblick.

Semi-Putter--Shallow face, bent neck, thick toe $175
Semi-putter--Duralite metal, line/dot face $150
Putter--(A) Mallet head, lead face insert $350
Putter--(A) Lead face insert, square hosel, flat side shaft $400
Putter--(A) Model RA, mallet head, vulcanite T line $250
Putter--(A) Model 1, short mallet head, dot face $75
Putter--(A) Model 2, mallet head, dot face $100
Putter--(A) Model 3, Ray-Mills style, dot face $75
Putter--(A) Model 3 1/2, small Ray-Mills style $100
Putter--(A) Model 4, Schenectady style $150
Putter--(A) Model 11, mallet head $100
Putter--(A) Model 12, Ray-type head $100
Putter--(A) Schenectady-type, 4-leaf clover CM $150
Putter--Model 20, gun metal blade $75
Putter--Model 20-J, swan neck, gun metal blade $250
Putter--Model 20-W, extra wide gun metal blade $150
Putter--Model 20 ½, gun metal blade with raised weight ridge across center of back $300
Putter--Model 30, gun metal gooseneck $150
Putter--Model 52, gun metal, gooseneck blade $125
Putter--Model 60, gun metal, flange sole with top edge weight $100
Putter--Model 70, gun metal dominie style, round back $225
Putter--Model 90 gun metal, flange sole $100
Putter--Model B5 Ivora, gunmetal blade with round ivorine insert, 'sunset' face markings $150-300
Putter—Gun metal copy of Chicopee with hollow back $250
Putter--Model 331 Cimetric, Schenectady style wood head $250
Putter--Model 331 1/2 Cimetric, wide head $250
Putter--Model 486 Down-It, wood mallet head, brass face $250
Putter--Right Angle model, wood mallet head, black fiber insert $200

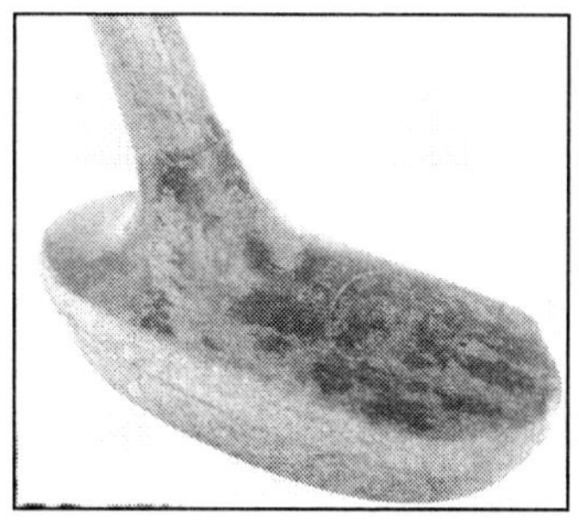

The MacGregor Cimetric model 331 putter was a wood copy of the Schenectady. This example has lost about half its original finish. It is the same model club pictured on the book cover.

Putter--Model 486 1/2 Sink-It, 1/2 wood mallet head, aluminum face $200
Putter--Model 490 Sink-Em, wood mallet head, aluminum face, brass backweight $250
Putter--WW model, wood Schenectady style, brass face $200
Putter--Yardsmore Inlay model, wood mallet head, green fiber face $250
Putter--Model OA, flange sole, stagdot face $65
Putting Cleek--Model 33, rustless Em-An-Em metal, line face $125

◇◇Willie Dunn marked clubs
Driver--Splice head, Willie Dunn 'bowtie' CM $350
Cleek--Smooth face, short blade, Dunn 'bowtie' CM $175
Iron--Smooth face, Dunn 'bowtie' CM $150
Lofter--Smooth face, Dunn 'bowtie' CM $175
Mashie--Smooth face, Dunn 'bowtie' CM $150
Niblick--Smooth face, small head, Dunn 'bowtie' CM $450
Putter--Iron blade, Dunn 'bowtie' mark $175

◇◇Early clubs (post-Willie Dunn)

MacGregor made this gun metal putter very similar in shape to the Spalding Chicopee. This example is stamped for Lance Servos, an early Canadian/American pro.

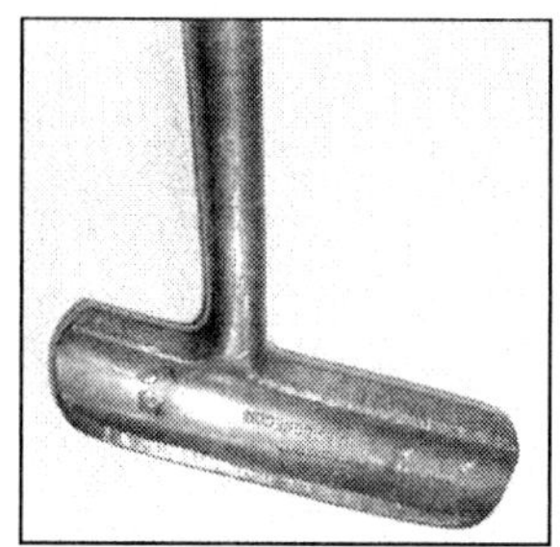

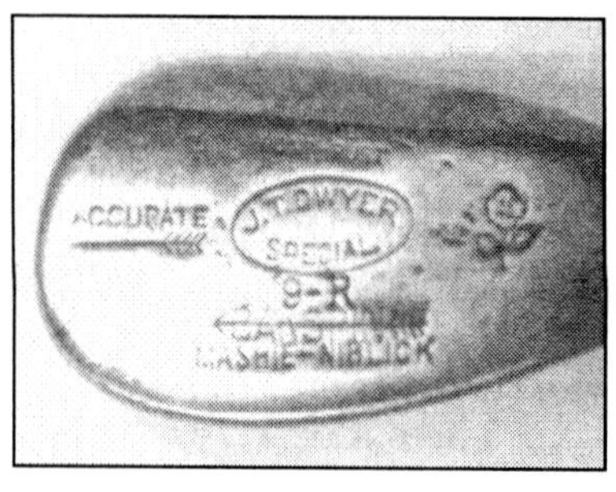

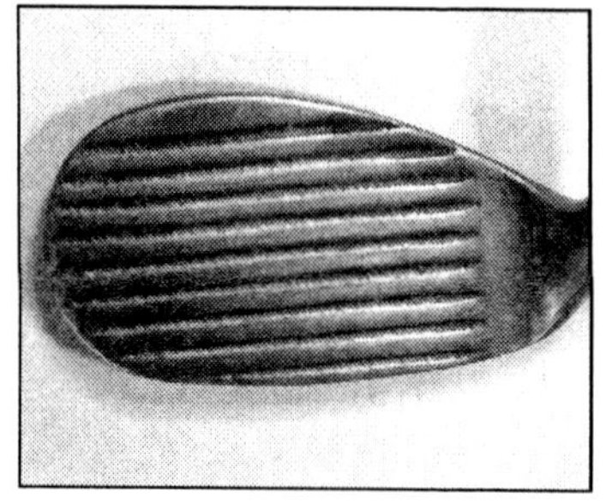

Driver--Splice head, MacGregor 'bowtie' mark $350
Driver—Willie Dunn decal on crown (Page B)... ....$400
Cleek--Smooth face, short blade, MacGregor 'bowtie' CM $175
Iron--Smooth face, MacGregor 'bowtie' CM $150
Lofter--Smooth face, MacGregor 'bowtie' CM $175
Mashie--Smooth face, MacGregor 'bowtie' CM $150
Niblick--Smooth face, small head, MacGregor 'bowtie' CM $450
Putter--Iron blade, MacGregor 'bowtie' mark $175

◇◇"Bakspin" clubs
Jigger--(D) Model RB, ribbed face $200
Mashie--(D) Model 10R, Radite ribbed face $100
Mashie--Model B4, stagdot face $45
Mashie--(D) Model G1, grooved face $125
Mashie--(D) Model G2, grooved face $125
Mashie--(D) Model M1, grooved face $125
Mashie--(D) Model R2, ribbed face $110
Mashie--(D) Model XC, ribbed face $150
Mashie Niblick--(D) Model 9-R, Radite ribbed face $100
Mashie Niblick--Model B, stagdot face $45
Mashie Niblick--Model B4, stagdot face $45
Mashie Niblick--(D) Model C2, grooved face $100
Mashie Niblick--Model F, stagdot face $45
Mashie Niblick--(D) Model R1, ribbed face $100
Mashie Niblick--(D) Model R4, ribbed face $100
Mashie Niblick--(D) Model R5, ribangled face.................................. $150
Mashie Niblick--(D) Model R6, ribbed face $100
Mashie Niblick--(D) Model R7, ribangled face $150
Mashie Niblick—(D) Model 9-R, corrugated face $100
Mashie Niblick--(D) Model RC2, ribbed face $125

Opposite page:
MacGregor R-9 Bakspin Mashie Niblick

Deep groove, 'backspin' irons were enormously popular in the years 1915-1921. MacGregor sold several different types and styles.

The R-9 Mashie Niblick, was made in both steel and Radite, a brand of stainless steel. The Radite club is stamped ***"Won't Rust."***

The MacGregor model numbers began with an 'R' for "ribbed" and a 'G' for "grooved," the wider, deeper grooves.

Mashie Niblick--(D) Model RZ, ribangled face $150
Mashie Niblick--(D) Model G4, grooved face $125
Mashie Niblick--(D) Model XA Bakspin, corrugated face $150
Niblick--(D) Corrugated face $125
Niblick--Model B4, stagdot face $45
Pitcher--(D) Model G3, grooved face $125
Spade Mashie--Model 11-R, Holdem series, Radite, baby waffle face $250
Putter--(D) Model 20, gun metal blade, ribbed face $250

◇◇Edgemont series (introduced 1909)
Driver--Socket head, plain face $45
Brassie--Socket head, plain face $45
Approach Mashie--Dot face, shallow face $30
Driving Cleek--Dot Face (diamond shaped pattern) $25
Driving Iron--Dot face $25
Lofter--Dot face $30
Mashie--Dot face, centraject back $30
Mashie--Dot face, thick sole, deep face $25
Mid Iron--Dot face $25
Mid-Iron--Juvenile $35
Niblick--Round, medium head $30
Putter--Gooseneck blade $40
Putting Cleek--Iron blade, dot face $25

◇◇Em-An-Em metal irons
Approach Iron--Model 31 1/2, Em-An-Em metal, dot face $150
Mashie--Model 29, thick toe, Em-An-Em metal $125
Mashie Niblick--Foulis-type, through bore hosel, Em-An-Em Metal $250
Mid Iron--Model 25, Em-An-Em metal $125
Putting Cleek--Model 33, rustless Em-An-Em metal, line face $125

◇◇Juvenile clubs
Driver--Model 323, socket head $45
Brassie--Model 324, socket head $45
Driving Cleek--Model 304 .... $35
Driving Mashie--Model 312 .... $35
Lofter--Model 306 .... $35

Lofting Mashie--Model 305 .... $35
Mashie--Two shamrocks CM, marked "Juvenile" $25
Mid Iron--Model 309 .... $35
Mid Iron--Marked "MacGregor Junior" $30
Mid-Iron--Edgemont $35
Putting Cleek--Model 310 .... $45

<><>Par series
Driving Cleek--Model XB, short blade, dot face $75
Driving Cleek--Model XK, long blade, dot face $75
Driving Iron--Model XA, beveled heel, dot face $75
Driving Mashie--Model XC, medium blade, dot face $75
Lofter--Model XC, centraject back $75
Mashie--Model XA 1/2, dot face $75
Mashie--Model XB, dot face, deep face $75
Mashie Jigger--Model XD, concave face $100
Mid Iron--Model XB, heavy blade, dot face $75
Mid Iron--Model XM, dot face $75
Niblick--Model XA, large head $90
Niblick--Model XW, large head $90
Putter--Model XB, narrow blade, flange sole, dash face $90
Putting Cleek--Model XA, dot face $80
Named/Numbered Irons(1-9, Putter 10)--Stainless,
"Balanced" with stars at heel .... $35 each

<><>Peerless series
Approach Iron--Model A-1, dash face $45
Driving Cleek--Model A-1, dash face $40
Driving Iron--Model A-1, dash face $40
Jigger--Model A-1, dash face $45
Mashie--Model A-1, dash face $35
Mashie Iron--Model A-1, dash face $40
Mid Iron--Model A-1, dash face $35
Niblick--Model A-1, dash face $40
Putter--Model A-1, gooseneck blade, dash face $45

<><>Perfection series
Driver--B4 model, plain face $60-80
Driver--Model B6, plain face $60-80
Driver--Model B8, plain face $60-80

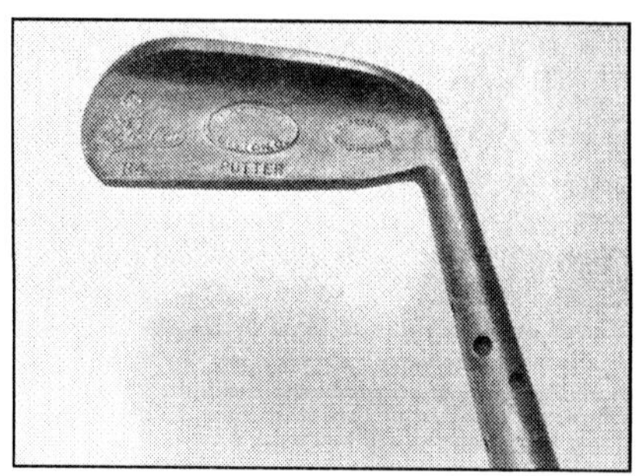

This putter from the MacGregor Perfection series had a drilled hosel and flange sole, copying the Maxwell Pattern. It also has stagdot facing.

Brassie--Model B4 .... $60-80
Brassie--Model B6 .... $60-80
Brassie--Model B8 .... $60-80
Brassie Spoon--Model B10, plain face $75-90
Spoon--Model B4 .... $60-80
Approach Iron--Model B4, Maxwell style, full stagdot face, centraject back $75
Approach Jigger--Model B4, as above $85
Approach Mashie--Model B4, as above with straight back $75
Bobby Iron--Model B4 as above with round back $125
Driving Cleek--Model B4, as above with centraject back $75
Driving Iron--Model B4, as above $75
Mashie Iron--Model B4, as above with centraject back $85
Mashie Niblick--Model B4, Maxwell style Bakspin, half stagdot concave face $75
Mid Iron--Model B4, as above $75
Niblick--Model B4, as above with round sole $85
Pitcher--Model B4, as above $100
Sammy Iron--Model B4, as above with round back $100
Putter--Model B4, Maxwell style, full stagdot face, flange sole $100
Putting Cleek--Model B4, as above with regular sole $100

<><>Pilot series
Driver--Model 1, plain face $50-75
Driver--Model 2, plain face $50-75
Driver--Model L4, lady's, plain face $50-75
Brassie--Model 1, plain face $50-75
Brassie--Model 2, plain face $50-75
Brassie--Model L4, lady's, plain face $50-75
Brassie Spoon--Model 3, plain face $65-80

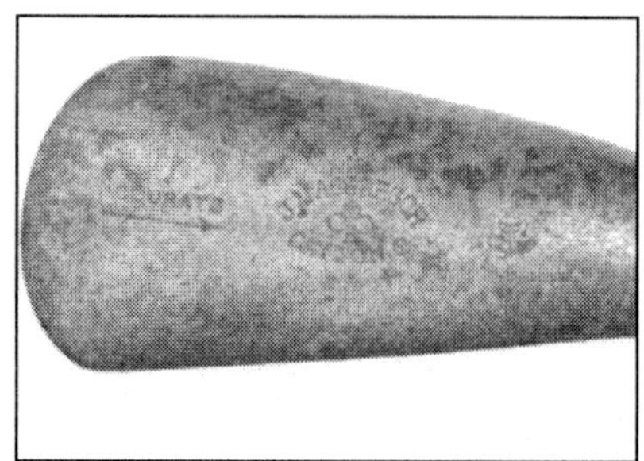

This MacGregor model B mashie dates from 1905-1910 and is one of the earliest clubs to show the rose cleek mark.

Driving Cleek--Model 4, line face $35
Driving Cleek--Model 104, lady's, line face $35
Driving Iron--Model 1, line face $35
Mashie--Model 8, line face $35
Mashie--Model 105, lady's, line face $40
Mashie Niblick--Model 15, Foulis style, concave face $85
Mid Iron--Model 9, line face $35
Mid Iron--Model 109, lady's, line face $35
Niblick--Model 11, line face $35
Niblick--Model 111, lady's, line face $35
Putter--Model 10S, line face $40
Putter--Model 110, lady's line face $40

◇◇Popular series
Driver--Model 27, plain face $50-75
Driver--Model 27J, plain face $50-75
Driver--Model 31, plain face $50-75
Driver--Model 203, plain face $50-75
Driver--Model 492, plain face $50-75
Brassie--Model 27 .... $50-75
Brassie--Model 27J $50-75
Brassie--Model 31 .... $50-75
Brassie--Model 203 .... $50-75
Brassie--Model 492 .... $50-75
Brassie Cleek--Model 344, plain face $75-90
Brassie Cleek--Model 355, plain face $75-90
Brassie Spoon--Model 312, plain face $75-90
Approach Cleek--Model G, musselback, dot face $60
Approach Iron--Model A 1/2, straight back, dot face $50
Approach Iron--Model B, round back, dot face $50

Approach Mashie--Model AA, Carruthers hosel $75
Approach Mashie--Model E, centraject back $50
Approach Mashie--Model G, thick toe $75
Approach Mashie--Model J, diamond back $60
Approach Mashie--Model S, slightly round back $50
Driving Cleek--Model A, straight back, short blade, dot face $35
Driving Cleek--Model B, round back, dot face $40
Driving Cleek--Model C, diamond back, dot face $45
Driving Cleek--Model D centraject back, short socket, dot face $45
Driving Iron--Model A, straight back, dot face $40
Driving Iron--Model A 1/2, centraject back, dot face $40
Driving Iron--Model B, round back, dot face $35
Driving Iron--Model C, diamond back, dot face $45
Driving Mashie--Model A, straight back, dot face $40
Driving Mashie--Model B, weighted on top edge, dot face $50
Driving Mashie--Model C 1/2, diamond back, dot face $50
Jigger--Model A, straight back $50
Jigger--Model A 1/2, concave face $100
Jigger--Model B, centraject back $50
Jigger--Model 8-B, notch hosel $75
Lofter--Model A, straight back $50
Lofter--Model B, round back $50
Lofter--Model C, centraject back $50
Lofting Mashie--Model F, extra wide blade $60
Mashie Iron--Model A, straight back, dot face $50
Mashie Niblick--Model A, straight back, wide toe $45
Mashie Niblick--Model B, round back, concave face $100
Mashie Niblick--Model C, Foulis style, dot face $75
Mashie Niblick--Model E, Foulis style, concave face $150
Mid Iron--Model A, straight back, dot face $35
Mid Iron--Model A 1/2, diamond back, dot face $50
Mid Iron--Model AA, Carruthers hosel $75
Mid Iron--Model C, centraject back, dot face $45
Mid Iron--Model E, straight back $40
Mid Iron--Model F, heavy blade $45
Mid Mashie--Model C, "Bull Dog", dot face $75
Niblick--Model A, dot face, straight back $45
Niblick--Model B, small head, smooth concave face $300
Niblick--Popular series, Model B, medium size head,
concave face $150

Niblick--Model C, large head, dot face $50
Niblick--Model G, large heavy blade $50
Sammy Jigger--Model C 1/2, beveled heel and toe $75
Putter--Model A 1/2, wide back, beveled edge $45
Putter--Model H, slight gooseneck, dot face $50
Putter--Model HH, gooseneck $75
Putter--Model K, gooseneck, narrow blade $60
Putter--Model M, shallow face $50
Putter--Model R, top edge weight $60
Putter--Model OA, flange sole $60
Putting Cleek--Model H 1/2, long blade, dot face $50
Putting Cleek--Model A, straight back, dot face $50
Putting Cleek--Model B, diamond back, dot face $60
Putting Cleek--Model BB, musselback $50
Putting Iron--Model A 1/2, deep face, beveled top edge $60
Putting Iron--Model C, back and face have same loft $50

Named/Numbered Irons (1-9, putter 10)--Line face,
small club pip CM $35

◇◇Superior series
Driver--Model 7, plain face, brass backweight $75-90
Brassie--Model 7, plain face, brass backweight $75-90
Approach Iron--Model S-C-1, stagdot face, slotted hosel $100
Bobbie Iron--Model S-D-1, round sole, stagdot face,
slotted hosel $150
Cleek--(U) Model S-D-1, stagdot face, slotted hosel $100
Driving Iron--(U) Model S-C-1, diamond back, slotted hosel,
stagdot face $125
Jigger--Model S-B, stagdot face, slotted hosel $125
Jigger--Model S-C-2, stagdot face, slotted hosel $125

MacGregor's Chieftain woods were their super-premium model with ivory backweights and crown inlays.

Mashie--Model S-C-1, stagdot face, slotted hosel $100
Mashie--Model S-C-2, stagdot face, slotted hosel $100
Mid Iron--Model S-C-1, stagdot face, slotted hosel $100
Mid Iron--Model S-C-2, stagdot face, slotted hosel $100
Mid Mashie--Model S-C, stagdot face, slotted hosel $100
Mashie Niblick--Model S-C-1, stagdot face, slotted hosel $100
Niblick--Model S-C-2, stagdot face, slotted hosel $100
Putter--Model S-C-2, blade, stagdot face, slotted hosel $125
Putter--Model S-X-B, Orion style, broad sole, stagdot face, slotted hosel $150
Putter--Model S-B-V, Brown-Vardon style, rounded back, stagdot face, slotted hosel $150

◇◇Airway series irons
Named irons--Dot face, slightly concave .... $65 each

◇◇Chieftain model
Woods (driver, brassie, spoon)--Ivory backweight, ivory inlay on top of head .... $750-1,200 each
Set of 3 matched woods.. $3,000-4,000

[Chieftain woods with ***steel or coated steel*** *shafts .... $200-400 each]*

◇◇Duralite series irons
Named Irons--Stainless .... $35 each
Numbered Irons--Stainless .... $30 each
Semi Putter--Duralite metal, line/dot face $150
Set of six or more consecutively numbered clubs .... $40 each

◇◇Go-Sum series irons
Numbered Irons--Stainless .... $30 each

◇◇Lady Mac series irons
Numbered or named irons--Stainless .... $25 each

◇◇Nokorode series irons
Numbered or named irons--Stainless .... $30 each

◇◇Premier series irons
Named irons--Line face .... $35 each

Mashie--(D) Corrugated face $125

<><>Radite series irons
Numbered or named irons--Stainless .... $30 each
Set of six or more consecutively numbered clubs .... $45 each

<><>Tomahawk series irons
Named Irons--Soft steel, shield design in dots on face, tomahawk and star CMs .... $65 each

<><>Yardsmore series
Woods--Black & white ivorine face insert .... $85 each
Numbered Irons--Stainless .... $30 each
Set of six or more consecutively numbered clubs .... $45 each
Putter--Yardsmore Inlay model, center shaft wood mallet head, green fiber face $250
(The Yardsmore putter was produced in a limited edition replica by MacGregor in the late 1990s)

MacKay, D.
[North Berwick s]
Driver--Socket head $75
Brassie--Stripe top, socket head $75

Mackie, Isaac
[Staten Island, NY]
Brassie--Socket head, name in oval $100

Mackie, J.
Mid Iron--Stewart pipe CM, line face $50

Mackrell & Simpson
Mashie--Line face, Stewart pipe CM $50

Mackrell, James+
[Aiken, SC]
Brassie--(U) Very l large head, signature name stamp $100
Mashie--Model 20, flange sole, line face, Winton diamond CM $65
Niblick--Medium head, smooth face $150

MacNamara, Dan
[Boston, MA, et al]
Driver--Socket head $75

Macnamara, W.
[Lahinch i]
Driver--Longish socket head $100

MacPherson, A.F.
Niblick--Dot face $40

MacPherson, Duncan*
[Manchester e]
Spoon--Bulldog style short socket head, fiber face insert $90
Mashie—Terrier brand, dot face $50
Approaching Putter--Terrier Brand, model 17 blade $75
Putter--Terrier Brand, model 7, dog CM, line face $60
Putter--Terrier Brand, musselback blade $60

MacPherson, J.
Niblick--Arrow & Heart CM, line face $60

Macy Company, R.H.
[New York City department store]
Woods--all models .... $50 each
Riverside brand irons, stainless, dot face $35
SupreMacy brand irons, stainless, line face $35

Maiden, Jimmy+
[Nassau, NY; Atlanta, GA]

Duncan MacPherson made and sold Terrier brand clubs from his Manchester shop.

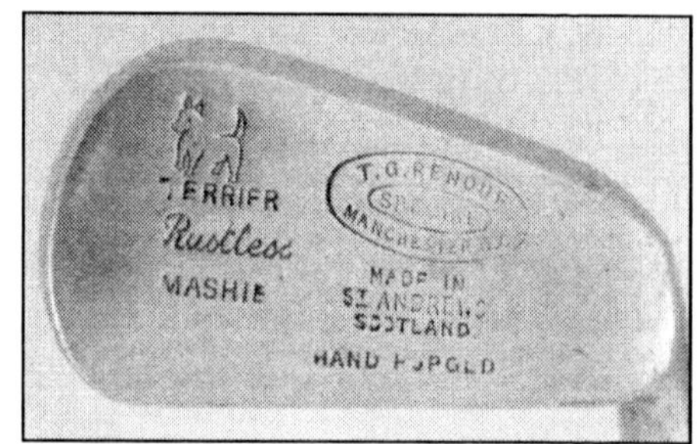

Putter--Stewart pipe CM, bent neck $80

Maiden, Stewart+
[Nassau, NY; Atlanta, GA]
Brassie--Dalglish pattern, rounded sole, face insert $300
Mashie--Diamond back, line face, Pipe CM $65

◇◇Stewart Maiden series by Hillerich & Bradsby
Numbered Irons--Stainless $40
Putter--# 10, stainless blade $75
Numbered Irons--Stainless with B-Bow shaft $60
Putter--# 10, stainless blade with B-Bow shaft $90

'Majestic'
[see Burr-Key]

Malpass, Harry
[Detroit, MI, et al]
Driver--Ivorine face with five black pegs, socket head $90
Mashie--Dot face, 3 bar CM $35

'Malvern, The'
Putter--(A B) Braid-type head $80

'Marathon'
[Chicago; brand name from the Montgomery Ward Company department store]
Numbered Irons--Stainless, line face ....$25 each

Marling, Alex
[Aberdeen s]
Putter--Magic model, bent neck blade, broad sole $75

Marling & Smith*
[Aberdeen s]
Driver--Splice head $150
Mashie Niblick--Dot face, Cochrane knight CM $50

Marriott & Ransome
Putter--(B) Triangular gun metal head, three hitting faces $2,500

Marsh & Co., Jordan
[Boston, MA]
Putter-Model 18, Avona brand $60

Marshall, William
[Onwentsia, Chicago]
Lofter--Smooth face, long blade $125

Martin & Kirkaldy*
[Edinburgh]
Driver--Andrew Kirkaldy autograph model, dreadnought socket head $175
Brassie--Pug model, short socket head with thick toe $125
Brassie--Sovereign model, socket head $75
Spoon--Superb series, ivorine insert, socket head $125
Spoon--Splice head, name in script $175
Baffy--Splice head, full sole plate $225
Mashie--Elite model, dot face $60
Mid Iron--Kirkaldy autograph model, dot face $75
Niblick--Elite series, large head, line face $75
Pitcher-Elite series, Kirkaldy autograph $75
Putter--Elite series, Andrew Kirkaldy Excelsior, triangular backweight, line face $100

Martin & Patrick*
[Edinburgh]
Driver--Sovereign model, socket head $75

Martin, R.B.
[Edinburgh and Kirkaldy, Fife s]
Mashie--The Golf Depot, dot face $75
Niblick--Smooth face, small head $150

Martin's Velometer Golf Clubs
[Herne Bay e]
Driver--(B) Velometer model, socket head $450
Brassie--(B) as above $450

Martin, W.

Irons--(U) Step back design , matched set....................................$60 each

Massy, Arnaud
[Open Champion 1907; worked several locations in France]
Named Irons--Autograph model, Gibson star CM ....$75 each
Putter—Autograph model, Gibson star CM, bent neck $85

May & Malone
Iron clubs--Bogey model, M+M in shield CM ....$45 each
Putter--Bogey model, dash face blade $50
Putter--80P, Eagle series, flange sole, eagle head CM $50

May, Dick
[Newcastle e; later U.S.]
Putter--(B) Bulge face blade, line face $175

Mayo, Charles*
[Southampton, Long Island]
Driver--Socket head $50
Putting Cleek--Premier model, hosel notch $80

McAndrew, J.
[Aberdeen s]
Brassie--Splice head, narrow head $175

McAndrew, Robert
[St. Andrews s & New York]
Cleek—SF, long blade, St. Andrews $250
Mashie--Smooth face, name stamp in italics $125

McDaid, Martin*
[Edinburgh]

Robert McAndrew worked in Scotland for many years before coming to American in the late 1890s.

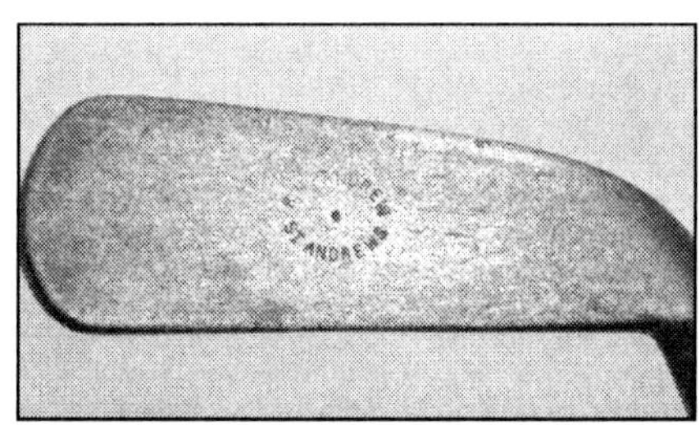

Driver--Small splice head, horn slip $200
Driver--(A) Mills style compact head $250

McDermott, John J.
[Atlantic City, NJ, et al; US Open Champion]
Brassie--Jumper model, socket head, fiber face insert $150
Brassie—Little Johnny model, ivorine insert $200
Mid Iron--Diamond back, arrow CM dot face $80
Iron--Little Johnny model, 6-pointed star CM $100
Jigger--Little Johnnie model, notched hosel, narrow blade, dash face $100
Putter--Little Johnny model, mallet head $125

McDonald, C.
[Glengarry s]
Putter-Glengarry bonnet (cap) CM $50

McDonald, William
Driver--Short splice head $150

McDonald, W.*
Driving Putter--(L) Slender thorn wood head $6,000

McDowall, J.
Mashie--Spalding anvil CM $40

McEwan & Sayner
Brassie--Short socket head $75
Niblick--Smith model anti-shank, stainless, Ayres CM $200

McEwan & Son*
[Bruntsfield (Edinburgh) & Musselburgh s; this firm founded in 1770 worked continuously until 1895. Six generations of McEwans made golf

Johnnie McDermott was the first native born American to win the US Open.

clubs up to WWII]

◇◇Feather ball period clubs

Playclub--(L) C.1780, large thistle stamp $25,000-50,000

Playclub--(L) C.1840, dark finish $10,000-20,000

Long Spoon--(L) C.1850, dark finish $7,500-10,000

Putter--(L) C.1840, slightly hooked face $10,000-20,000

◇◇Guttie ball period clubs

Playclub-(L) C.1860, leather face insert $3,000-6,000

Playclub--(L) C.1880, leather face insert $2,500-4,500

Playclub--(L) C.1890, slightly shorter head $1,000-2,500

Driver--(S) C.1895, short head, leather face insert $750-1,000

Long Spoon--(L) C.1880, dark finish $2,500-4,000

Short Spoon--(L) C.1880, broad, dark colored head $2,500-4,000

Baffing Spoon--(L) C.1880, well lofted face $3,500-5,500

Brassie--(S) C.1895, shorter head $750-1,000

Cleek--C.1895 smooth face, oval stamp, Stewart serpent CM $125

Cleek--Smooth face, Condie fern CM $150

Iron--C.1890, smooth face, straight line name stamp $200

Lofter--C.1895, smooth face, oval stamp, Condie rose CM $150

Lofting Iron--Smooth face, Condie fern CM $225

Mashie--C.1890, smooth face, straight line name stamp $150

Niblick--C.1890, small head, oval name stamp $400

Niblick--C.1895, medium size head, Stewart pipe CM $200

Niblick--C.1895, very small head, Stewart serpent CM $600

Niblick--Medium head, smooth face, Stewart serpent CM $200

Putter--(L) C.1880, long slender head $1,500-3,000

Putter--(L) C.1890, shorter, broader head $1,000-2,000

Putter--(S) C1895, short head $750-1,000

Putter--C. 1895, gun metal blade, straight name stamp $150

Putter--C.1895, bent blade style, oval name stamp $150

Putter--C.1900, regular iron blade, oval name stamp $125

McEwan, David*

[Birkdale]

Driver--Birkdale model, small socket head, name in oval $100

McEwan, Peter*

[Nairn s]

Iron clubs--Line face, name in script $50

Fred McLeod waon the US open Champion ship in 1908 at Myopia Hunt.

McEwan, Stewart
[Harrisburg, PA]
Driver--Socket head, steel face insert with screws $100
Mashie--Smooth face $75
Mashie--Dot face, 3 bar CM $35
Mashie--Dot face, centraject back, 3 bar CM $40

McEwan, William*
[Formby e]
Driver--(B) Dunn patent $1,500-2,000
Driver--Socket head $125

McGregor
[see MacGregor]

McGill Golf Co.
[Valparaiso, IN]
Mashie Niblick--(D) Klin Klub, deep hyphens only on middle 1/3 of face $200

McIntosh, David
Driving Iron--Smooth face, Stewart pipe CM $75
Pitcher--Smooth face, Celtic oval head $150
Putter--Gun metal blade $80

McKenna, J.
Brassie--Splice head $100

McLeod, Fred

[Chicago, IL, et al; US Open Champion]
Brassie--Very short splice head $250
Mashie Niblick--Autograph model $80
Putter—Steel blade $60

'Meadowlark'
[MacGregor store brand]
Iron clubs--Dot face, 2 club pips CM .... $25 each

Meaker, R.H.
Driver--Splice head $100

Melville, Jack
Driver--Stripe top, socket head $45

Metal & Alloy Specialty Co.
[Buffalo, NY]
Niblick--RadiName model, circular dot face pattern $65

'Metropolitan'
Putter--Blade, made by JH Williams, W in diamond on hosel $175

Mieville-Lancier
[England]
Numbered Irons—Flanged sole, bamboo shaft, house CM.... $100 each

Miles, A.
Brassie--Handkraft brand, socket head $50

Millar, Charles L.*
[Glasgow; also proprietor of the Glasgow Golf Company and the Thistle

Mieville Lancier clubs were fitted with laminated bamboo shafts.

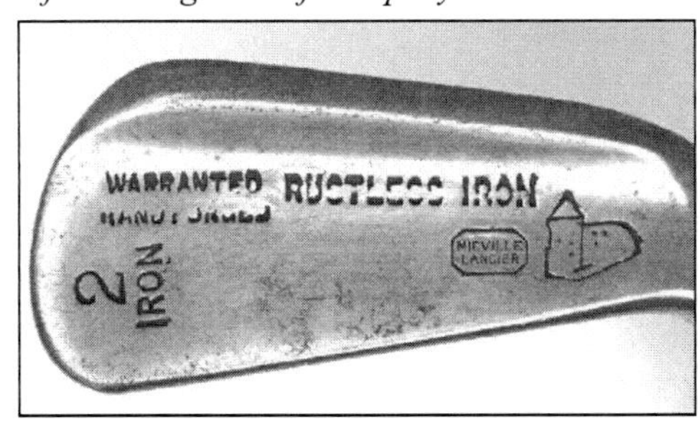

Golf Company]
Driver--Socket head, thistle CM, patent training rubber grip $300
Iron--Smooth face, small thistle (Reg'd.), smooth face $90
Lofter--Smooth face, round back, marked 'C L Millar' $100
Mashie--Smooth face, short blade, small thistle CM $150
Mashie--Thistle Brand, thistle in circle CM $50
Putter--Gun metal blade, thistle CM $100

Miller & Taylor*
[Glasgow]
Mashie--(B) D & T Spinner Mashie, concave face, half dots $250
Mashie Niblick--(B) Concave face, half dot face, curling stone CM $250

Milne, John*
[Neasden, London]
Driver--Socket head $80

Minton
[Barbourville, KY]
Putter-Steel blade, thumb-groove handle (like Huntly) $150

Mitchell & Ness+
[Philadelphia, PA]
Driver--Socket head, stripe top $60
Mashie Niblick--Stewart pipe CM, line face $50
Mid Iron-Flange sole, Monel $65

Mitchell & Weidenkopf+
[Cleveland, OH]
Brassie--Socket head, circular ivorine insert $125

Mitchell, Joe+
[Cleveland & Jacksonville, FL; also see P.G. Manufacturing Co.]
Driver--Socket head, palm tree CM $65
Mid Iron--Smooth face, anvil CM, made for P.G. Mfg. Co. $65

Mitchell's
[Milwaukee, WI]
Iron clubs-Name in oval, boxing gloves CM .... $45 each

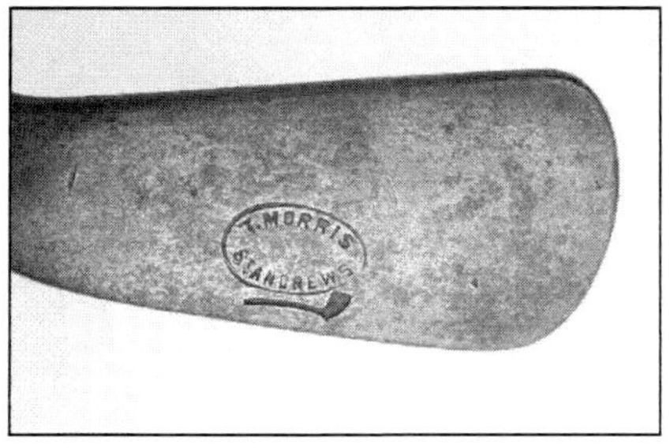

Early Tom Morris clubs made by Tom Stewart were very simply marked, like this mashie circa 1900.

'Monarch'
[Great Lakes Golf Company brand]
Iron clubs--Dash face, crown CM .... $25 each
Putter--Iron blade, crown CM $30

Monk, Arthur
Mashie--Stainless, dot face $30

Morehead Golf Company+
[Milwaukee, WI]
Driver--Socket head, crescent shaped vulcanite face insert $250
Jigger--Model S, dash face, swastika CM $45
Mashie--Ship's wheel CM, stainless, dot face $40
Mid Iron--Swastika CM, line face $80
Putter--Glen Eagle series, flange sole, eagle head CM $50

Morgan, E.
Mashie Niblick--Dot face, oval head $50

Morris & Youds*
[Hoylake e]
Mashie--(B) Smith model (anti-shank), Spence &
Gourlay club pip CM $250
Mashie-Pipe brand, name in double outline oval, line face $85

Morris, John (Jack)
[Hoylake e; nephew of Old Tom, he was professional and club maker to the Royal Liverpool G.C. for over 60 years]
Driver--Splice head $200
Driver--Socket head $90

Cleek--Smooth face, Stewart pipe CM $90
Niblick--Medium size head, smooth face $150
Named Irons--John Morris model, Stewart pipe CM, scored face$75 each
Named Irons--Name in oval, no other marks .... $65 each
Putter--Wood transitional splice head $850
Putter--Iron blade, mark in oval $80
Putter--Wood mallet head, stork CM $300

Morris, Tom*

[St. Andrews; he was four times Open Champion in the 1860s and his moniker became The Grand Old Man of Golf. Originally trained as a ball maker, he opened his club making business in 1867 though his popular Autograph series was not introduced until several years after his death]

◇◇Long nose (guttie ball) period clubs
Playclub--(L) C. 1870, thin narrow head, light color $10,000-15,000
Playclub—Grassed driver, c.1870 (Page C).................................. $2,500
Playclub--(L) C.1875, narrow head $2,500-5,000
Playclub--(L) C.1885, wider head than above $1,500-3,500
Driver--(L) C.1895, leather face insert $1,000-2,000
Driver--(S) C.1900, as above $600-1,000
Spoon--(L) C.1875, narrow head $3,500-6,000
Spoon--(L) C.1885, wider head than above $1,500-3,500
Brassie--(L) C.1895, leather face insert $1,500-3,000
Brassie--(S) C.1900, shorter head, thicker neck $500-1,000
Baffy--(L) C.1890, well spooned face, stamped shaft $1,500-2,500
Putter--(L) C.1880, wide shallow head, ... $1,500-3,000
Putter--(L) C.1895, more compact head, deeper face $1,000-2,000
Putter--(S) C.1900, transitional shaped head $400-800
Cleek--Smooth face, Stewart pipe CM, oval stamp $300
Cleek--(B) Smooth face, round sole, pat. # 5039 .... $400

Tom Morris's "round sole cleek" was patented in 1892 and carries its patent number 5039.

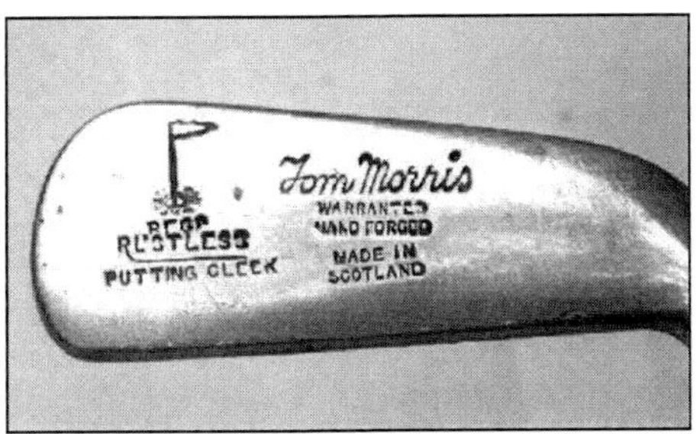

Irons made for the Morris Shop's Autograph series came from a variety of makers like this Putting Cleek from Forgan.

Iron—Pre Stewart era, name in oval, large letter I for iron $600
Mashie--Smooth face, Stewart pipe CM, oval stamp $250
Niblick--(B) Concave face $500
Niblick--Smooth face, medium size head $300
Niblick--Smooth face, small head $500
Putter--Gun metal blade, Stewart serpent CM $200
Putter--Cylindrical iron head, 'drainpipe' model $3,500

◇◇20th century clubs
Driver--Short splice head, long scare $300
Driver--C.1910, short splice head $250
Driver--Elongated splice head, Autograph series, fibre insert $200
Driver--Socket head, stripe top, Autograph series $150
Brassie--Socket head, Autograph series $125
Cleek-Monarch series, beveled toe $100
Driving Iron--Autograph series, dot face, pipe CM $75
Iron--Autograph series, dot face $60
Iron--Autograph series, juvenile $100
Iron--Monarch series, Brodie CMs $125
Jigger--Autograph series, Stewart pipe CM, dot face $75
Mashie--Autograph series, line face, Condie rose CM $75
Mashie—(B) Smith patent, stainless, Brodie BSA triangle CM $300
Mashie--St. Andrean series, musselback, Old Tom CM, stainless $75
Mashie--(D) Dedum model, Brodie triangle CM $175
Mashie Niblick--Autograph series, line face, Condie rose CM $75
Mashie Niblick--'Morris Model', Stewart pipe CM, dot face............. $150
Mashie Niblick--Autograph series, stainless, triangle/BS&A & Tom Morris CMs, line face $75
Niblick--Autograph series, Old Tom CM $75
Niblick--Autograph series, Stewart pipe CM $75
Spade Mashie--Autograph series, Old Tom CM,

line face, stainless $75
Spade Niblick--Autograph series, head of Old Tom &
Brodie CMs, dreadnought size head $150
Putter--(B) Straight Line model, Old Tom and Brodie CMs $150
Putter--Autograph series, Stewart pipe and arrow CMs $75
Putter--Autograph series, Wellington model, Old Tom CM $125
Putter--Socket wood head, Autograph series $250
Putter--Autograph series, Stewart large Old Tom CM $150
Putter--The Davie model $125
Putter-(B) Broadclair model, round back blade, grooved sole $250
Putting Cleek—Autugraph series, Forgan flagstick CM $125
Numbered Irons-Elect series, line face, Brodie CMs .... $60 each
Numbered Irons—Whitehall series, made for Lillywhite .... $40 each

Motion, J.G.
[Minneapolis, MN]
Driver--Splice head $250

Mules, W.*
[Penarth w]
Driver--(B) Leather cushion behind metal face plate $800
Iron--(B) Leather cushion behind metal face plate $1,200

Munro, Alexander*
[Aberdeen s]
Playclub--(L) Thornwood, light finish $4,000-5,000

Munro, Robert*
[Wimbledon, Chislehurst e]
Driver--Bulger splice head, leather face insert $150
Driver--Large socket head $100
Putter--(S) C.1895, large splice head $600

Murray, Albert
[Montreal, QUE]
Iron clubs--Diamond back, Moosehead CM .... $75 each

Murray, Charles+
[Montreal, QUE]
Driver--Socket head $75

Mashie Niblick--Spalding Gold Medal, right angle face lines $75
Mid Iron--Blade with maple leaf CM $75
Putter--Iron blade, offset head, name in oval $60

Murray, D.
Brassie--Splice head $100

Murray, J.
[Pitlochry s]
Brassie--Socket head $75
Putting Iron--Iron blade, line face $45

Murrie & Sons*
[Methven s]
Mid Iron--Smooth face, Joe Anderson OK CM $75
Putter--Concentric back, dash face $60

Murton, J.
[Newcastle e]
Niblick--Smooth face, heavy medium size head $100

'Mutt'
Niblick--X-23, smooth face, dog head mark $45

Myles, David*
[Dundee s]
Driving Iron--(B) Nipper model, circle on face $400
Driving Iron--(B) Placer model, circle on face $500
Driving Iron--(B) Paxie model, circle on face $400
Driving Iron--(B) Rexor model, circle on face $500

David Myles produced four short blade driving irons designed to be used from the tee by people having difficulty driving with

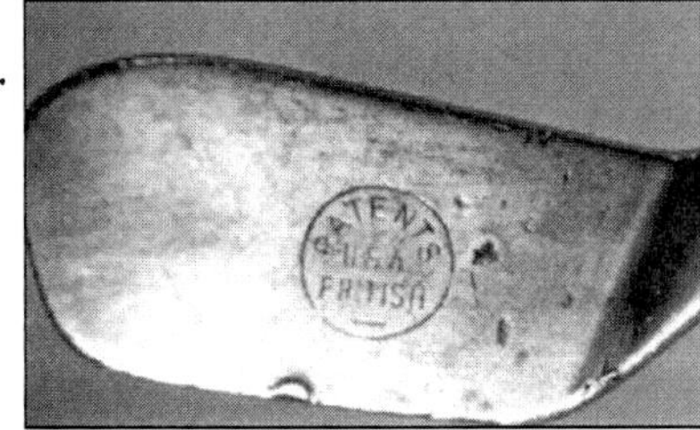

N

'Nassau'
[Brand name from New York Sporting Goods]
Putter--Gun metal blade....$150

National Golf Company+
[Chattanooga, TN]
Named Irons--Moccasin series, line face ....$30 each
Named Irons—Shot Maker series, line face, chromed ....$25 each
Putter--Homer model, blade $35

Neaves, Charles*
[Leven & Lossiemouth s]
Driver--Splice transitional head $200
Driver--Socket head, fiber insert $80
Driver--Long Tom model, large socket head $85
Spoon--Splice head, full sole plate $225
Cleek--Smooth face, marked for Leven $80
Mashie Niblick--(B) Genii model, smooth face $75
Mid Iron--Smooth face, name in oval $50
Putter--Large socket wood head $200

Neilson, Robert*
[Musselburgh s]
Driver--Splice head $150
Driver--Socket head $80
Cleek--Line face $60
Iron--Condie rose CM, dot face $60
Niblick--Smooth face, Condie rose CM $80

'Nesco'
Putter--Brass head with aiming fin, aluminum insert $1,800

New York Sporting Goods Company+
[New York]
Driver--Splice head, stag over shield CM $275

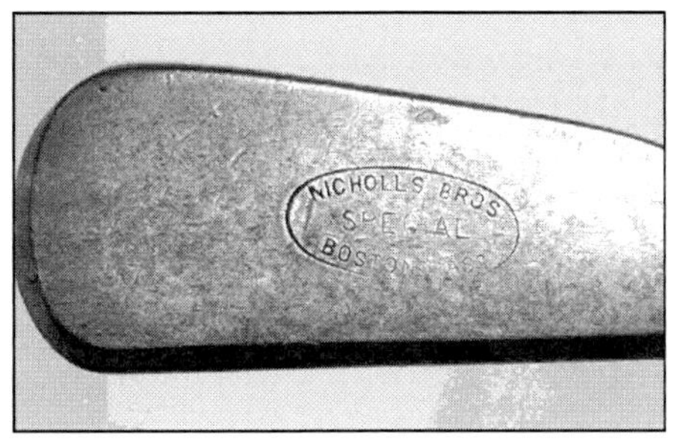

Ben and Gill Nicholls sold clubs, like this cleek, as Nicholls Brothers and as individual club makers.

Cleek--Running stag CM, dot face $125
Lofter--Smooth face, oval mark $125
Mashie--Running stag CM, dot face $125
Niblick--Small head, concave, name inside Maltese cross, smooth face $500
Putter--Gun metal blade, "N.Y.S.G." $150
Putter--Hillside model, name in decorated oval $125

Ness, O.M.
Putter--MacGregor R model, top weight $150

Newbery, Ernest*
[Strawberry Hill e and Italy]
Sammy--Stewart pipe CM, line face $75
Putter—(B) Half moon series $350
Named Irons--(B) Half-moon model, crescent-shaped weighted portion on back .... $300 each

Niblett-Flanders
Iron clubs--Life Saver model, stainless, dot face .... $50-60 each

Nicholls Brothers+
[The firm of F. Bernard (Ben) Nicholls and Gilbert Nicholls, English professionals working around Boston, MA C.1900. Clubs were marked Nicholls Brothers or Nicholls Special]
Driver--Splice head $200
Driver--Special bead splice head $350
Driver--Socket head, steel face insert $150
Driver--Socket head $95
Cleek--Smooth face, Boston address $75

This Nicholson Brothers' club came from Brodie forge. Others were made by George Nicoll.

Cleek--Yellow rustless metal, smooth face $100
Lofter--Short round back blade, smooth face $70
Mashie--Concentric back, smooth face, name in oval $75
Mashie Niblick—18, script name, Brodie triangle CM $50
Niblick--Name in oval, smooth face, Hunt Co. shaft stamp $500
Putter--Gun metal blade $85
Putter--Iron blade, marked "Nicholls Special" $60

Nicholls, F. Bernard "Ben"+
Iron clubs--Smooth face, name in block letters .... $75 each
Cleek—Name in block letters, short hosel, bore through $100

Nicholls, Gilbert "Gil"+
Mashie--Name in oval, Spalding Gold Medal $45

Nichols, W.
Putter--Gun metal, Burke model G4, flower & bee CMs $125

Nicholson Brothers
[Anstruther s]
Iron clubs--Nicoll hand CM, stainless .... $60 each
Iron Clubs—BSA triangle CM, stainless $65

'Nicola'
Putter--(A B) Two faced hammer head with
semi-circular cut-out for bridging ball $1,200
Putter--(B) Two faced hammer head in gun metal with
semi-circular cut-out for bridging ball $1,500

Nicoll, George*

[Leven s; founded in 1881, this firm was one of the premier cleek making companies, making only metal headed clubs. Their CM was a hand, which came in several versions over the years]

◇◇Clubs made prior to use of hand CM (1898)
Cleek--Smooth face, small circular name stamp $175
Cleek--(B) Leather face insert $2,000
Cleek--(B) Gutta percha face insert $2,250
Iron--Smooth face, name in arc $200
Lofter--Smooth face, long blade $300
Mashie--Smooth face, round back $200
Niblick--Small head, name in arc $350
Putter--(B) Nicoll patent model $250
Putter--Swan neck model $350
Putter—Gun metal blade $200

◇◇Irons with Hand CM
Cleek--F.G. Tait model, dot face $125
Driving Iron--Nap model, line face $50
Driving Iron--Precision series, flange sole, stainless $30
Iron--Smooth face, name in arc, small hand CM $100
Iron--Clinker series, oval head $60
Iron--Nap model, concave face $75
Iron--San Souci series $50
Jigger--Musselback, hand CM, dot face $75
Mashie--Smooth deep face, name in arc, small hand CM $100
Mashie--Braid model, musselback, dot face, hand CM $80
Mashie--Recorder series, dot face $40
Mashie--Fairlie's patent, small hand CM $175
Iron--Nicoll autograph, made for Donald Ross $150
Mashie Niblick--Marked Playklub, small diamond &

The oldest irons made by George Nicoll were marked with his name and Leven for 17 years before he utilised the 'Hand' cleek mark.

The Indicator series of clubs was one of the first modern matched sets. It was also one of the first for Nicoll to offer woods.

hand CMs, chromed $40
Mashie Niblick--(D) Name in script, corrugated face $75
Mashie Niblick--Zenith series, dot face, oval head $60
Mashie Niblick--Big Ball series, stainless, deep face $35
Mashie Niblick--Big Shooter series, stainless, line face $35
Mashie Pitcher--Zenith series, line face $80
Mid Iron--Sure series, dot face $40
Niblick--Able series, line face $40
Niblick--Indicator series, dot face $50
Push iron—Recorder series $75
Pitcher--(D) Corrugated face $125
Pitcher--(D) Zenith series, corrugated face $125
Putter--Trusty model, musselback blade $75
Putter--Gem style head $75
Putter--Whippet model, long hosel $60
Putter--Gray series, line face $50
Putter--Nap model, beveled heel and toe $75
Putter--The Gray, model name in script, long blade $100
Putter--Zenith series, long blade $75
Putter--F.G. Tait model $100-150
Putter--Park model, bent neck $150
Putter--Recorder series, long blade, dot face $50
Putter--Philp model, beveled heel and toe $95
Putter--Indicator series steel mallet head $275

Named Irons--George Nicoll in script .... $45 each
Numbered Irons--George Nicoll name in script,
stainless, line face .... $35 each
Named Irons--Big Ball series .... $35 each
Named Irons--Big Shooter series .... $35 each

The Nicoll F.G. Tait putter was a tribute to the late Freddie Tait, the Amateur Champion.

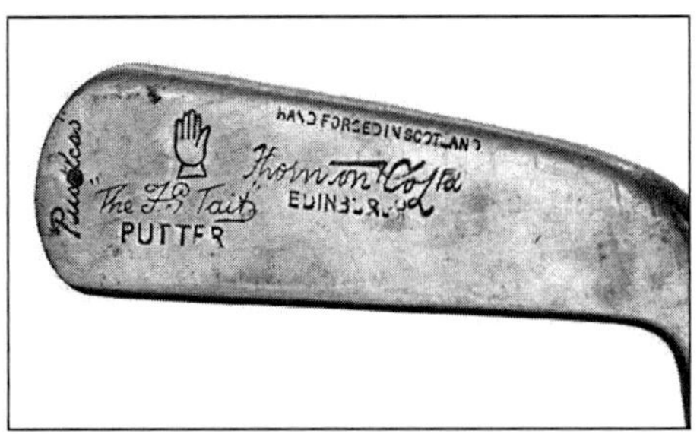

Numbered Irons--Cracker Jack series, Carruthers hosel, dot face .... $40 each
Numbered Irons--Compaction Blade, dot face .... $35 each
Numbered Irons--Akurasy series, musselback, line face .... $40 each
Named/Numbered Irons--Indicator series, dial CM .... $45 each
Set (1-9, Putter)--Indicator series $600-700
Woods—Individual Indicator series woods .... $125 each
Set—Indicator woods, driver, brassie, spoon $450
Named/Numbered Irons--Mac Smith Duplicate Set, stainless .... $50 each
Named or Numbered Irons--Precision series, stainless, flange sole .... $35 each
Named/Numbered Irons--Recorder series, name in script, hand CM .... $45 each
Numbered irons--Viking series, Viking ship CM .... $35 each

Nicolson, T.*
[Pittenweem s]
Iron--Line face $75
Mashie--Smooth face, Edinburgh Gold Medal stamp $125
Putter--Bent neck, Edinburgh Gold Medal CM $150
Putter--Juvenile, marked B, Gold Medal CM $100

Noirit, E & A
[Walsall e]
Putter--(A) Model 123, round back with lead face insert $175
Putter--(A) BMR model, lead face insert $250
Putter--(A) TTS model, Ray-type with three plateaus and spider web face $250

Norrie, R.*
[Johnstone s]
Putter--(B) Cochrane Castle model, overspin-type, gooseneck hosel $125

Northwestern Golf Co.
[Chicago, IL]
Iron clubs--Ace series, winged propellor CM, line face .... $35 each

Norton, Tom
[Llandrindod w]
Lofter--Ariel series, smooth face $60

Norton, William
[New Jersey]
Driver—Transitional shape splice head $200
Driver--Short splice head $150
Mashie--Dot face, two pine cones CM $75
Mashie--Dot face $40
Mashie--(U) 2 star CMs, Spalding Lard 'whistler' shaft $4,000
Niblick--Small round head, smooth concave face $350

Novak, Joe
[San Francisco]
Adjustable Iron--(U) Novakclub, line face $1,000
[Similar Novakclub with steel shaft .... $100-150]

Noyes Brothers
[Boston, MA retail store]
Driver--Transitional splice head $250

Willie Norton worked at several American clubs over his 30 year professional career. This driver dates from 1905-1910

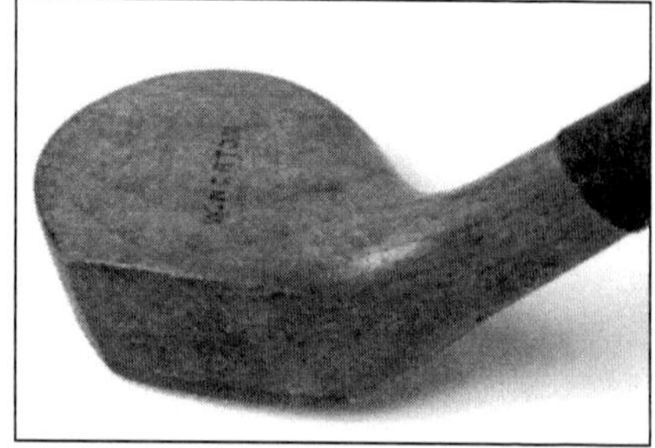

O

'O-V-B'+
[Sears Roebuck, Chicago, IL]
Driver--Model 571, socket head $75
Brassie--Model 531, socket head $75
Cleek--Model 731, Carruthers hosel $100
Mid Iron--Model 831, line face $50
Mashie--Model 781, 1/2 dot concave face $85
Mashie--Model 841, line face $50
Mashie Niblick--Model 852 .... $50
Niblick--Model 711, line/dot face $60
Putter—801, steel blade $50
Putter--931, gun metal blade $75
Putter--Model 931, initials in shield, flange sole $60
Putter--Model 932, iron blade $60

O.W.C.+
[see Overman Wheel]

Ockenden, James
[Raynes Park, London, et al]
Driver--Socket head $50

Ogg, Willie
[Worcester, MA, et.al.]
Spoon--Socket head, bull dog-type, fiber insert $100

The Sears Roebuck company had a store brand they named O-V-B for "Our Very Best."

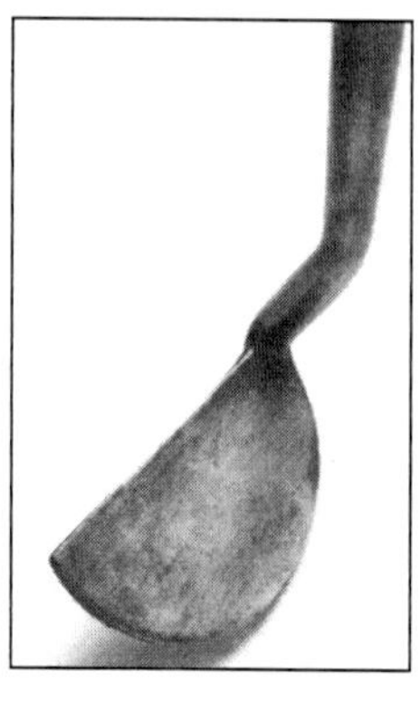

Dave Ogilvy sold this unique anti-shank style lofting or bunker iron. The semi-circular shaped blade was intended to slide under the ball very quickly. Markings on the club head indicate it was made by Spalding.

Mashie--Spalding Dedstop 6, waffle face $300
Irons—Spalding Kro-Flite PGA model, Willie Ogg autograph . $40 each
Irons—Wilson Ogg-mented, thick toe weight, chrome .... $35 each

Ogilvie, Dave
[Morris County, NJ and Augusta, GA, et.al.]
Brassie--Pick-up model, sole protrudes from face $300
Spoon--Pick-up model $400
Irons--Stewart pipe models, line face .... $60 each
Niblick--Extreme gooseneck anti-shank type hosel, round sole $450

Oke, J.H.*
[Sutton Coldfield e, et al]
Mashie--Smooth face $75
Putter--Offset blade $45
Irons—Stewart made with pipe CM, line face .... $75 each

Oke, W.G.*
[Honor Oak, London, et al]
Mashie--Oak Brand, oak tree CM, dot face $50
Putter--Staynorus stainless head, long thin hosel $100
Putter--Oak Brand, oak tree CM $80
Putter-Oak Brand, oak tree CM, extra long hosel $175

Ollarton, R.
Brassie--Small splice head $100

'Olympia'

[MacGregor store brand]
Putter--Line face, 2 club pips CM $25

O'Neill, G.A.
[Auburn Park, IL]
Cleek—Round sole MacGregor model, smooth face $400

O'Neill and Naylor
[Chicago, IL]
Cleek—MacGregor rose CM, thick toe $150

Ornum Putter Company
[St. Andrews]
Putter--(B) Round wood mallet socket head, brass face plate $250

Osborn
Mid Iron--"Osborn's Rustless", tiny hand & heart CM $60

Ouimet & Sullivan
[Boston]
Driver--Socket head $250
Jigger-Stewart pipe brand, line face $150
Niblick-Stewart pipe brand, line face $150
Putter—Round back, low profile, line face $175

Outing Goods Manufacturing Company+
[Brookfield, CT]
Driver--(S U) Brooklawn Special model, splice head, markings in red paint, fiber face $1,250
Brassie—(S U) Brooklawn Special $1,100

George O'Neill sold this round soled cleek (or driving niblick) which was probably made by MacGregor.

Overman Wheel Company+
[Springfield, MA; also see Victor-O.W.C.]
Cleek--Smooth face $250
Niblick--Smooth face, small gun metal head $2,000

This MacGregor cleek sold through O'Neill & Naylor shows early use of the rose cleek mark.

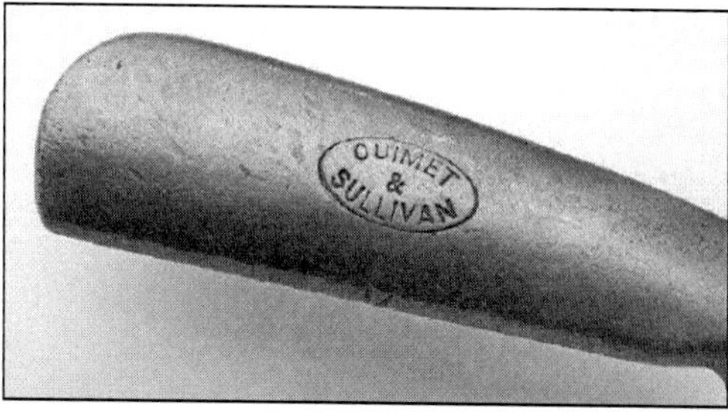

Francis Ouimet was involved for a short time with a club company before quitting to preserve his amateur status.

One of the earliest American club manufacturers, Outing Goods Mfg. Co. painted its name on the crown of its woods instead of stamping.

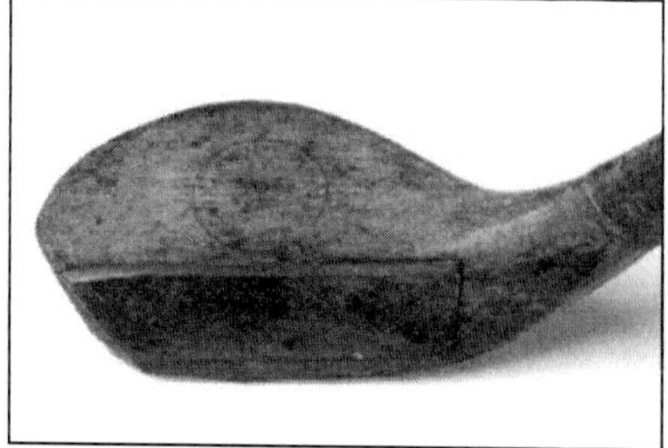

This mashie was made for the PGA of America, by Spalding, to sell to its member professionals.

This mid iron was made by MacGregor for the P.G.A. professionals co-op. (This Tom Morris was an Illinois pro)

P

P.G.A. or 'Professional Golfers Association'+

[Clubs made by Spalding and MacGregor marked "P.G.A." were sold by member professionals of the P.G.A. of America. The P.G.A. acted as a co-op and obtained volume discounts, passing the savings on to pros with smaller shops]

Driving Iron--P 10, line face $40
Jigger--P 81, crossed clubs CM, line face $40
Mashie--Kro-Flite CM, dot face $30
Mashie Iron--P 41, dot face $35
Mashie Iron--P 40, line face $35
Mashie--P 50, line face $40
Mashie--Acorn & hammer CMs $45
Mashie Niblick--P 60, line face $40
Mashie Niblick--P 61, Dedstop ribbed face $100

Mid Iron--P 22, deep cut line face, crossed clubs CM $35
Niblick--P 91, line face $40
Numbered Irons--Spalding roses,
arrow and long golf club CMs .... $30 each
Numbered Irons--Kro-Forged model, crow CM .... $30 each
Numbered Irons—PGA Standard with acorn
and hammer CMs .... $35 each
Putter--Kro-Flite series, long golf club CM $40
Putter--P-1, crossed clubs CM $40
Putter--P-3, blade, crossed clubs & shamrock CMs $40

P.G. Manufacturing Company+
[Homewood, IL; marketing co-operative for several Midwestern club makers of Scottish descent]
Mashie--Made for Joe Mitchell, anvil CM $65
Mashie Niblick--Marked "Genuine Foulis Mashie Niblick",
smooth concave face, anvil CM $200
Mid Iron--Dot face, anvil CM, Homewood, IL $60
Mashie—Marked for Robert White, Homewood $75
Mashie—Marked for A.J. Christie, Rochester $60
Mashie—Marked for E. Way, Cleveland $80
Niblick--Homewood model, smooth face, anvil CM $60
Putter--Birdie series, iron blade, anvil and trophy CMs $60

Park, John "Jack"+
[Essex County, NJ; young Willie Park's younger brother]
Driver--Socket head $125

Park, Mungo*
[Alnmouth e; Open Champion 1874, younger brother of Auld Willie Park]

The PG Manufacturing Co. was the first co-op of golf club makers in the United States. Occasionally a maker's name also is stamped on the club.

Playclub--(L) Dark head $3,500-5,000
Putter--(L) C.1880, beech head $3,000-4,000

Park & Son, William*

[Musselburgh s; founded by Open Champion Old Willie, the firm had very small output until Young Willie assumed leadership in 1885. Then the firm became one of the largest in Scotland]

◇◇Early clubs made by Willie, Sr.
Playclub--(L) Long head $5,000-15,000
Spoon--(L) Long head $6,000-15,000
Putter--(L) Long head $5,000-15,000

◇◇Clubs made during the time of Willie, Jr.
Playclub--(L) Late long nose, stamped "D" for driver $1,250
Driver-(S) Transitional splice head $1,000
Driver--(S) Bulger head, bowed face, shaft stamp $1,500-2,500
Driver--Splice head, straight face $250-350
Driver--Short socket head, shaft stamp $150-200
Brassie--(S) Bulger head, bowed face, shaft stamp $1,500-2,500
Brassie--(B) Compressed patent splice head $300-500
Brassie--(B) Pik-up model, grooved sole $450-600
Baffy--Transitional splice head $700
Putter--(S) Transitional head, shaft stamp $1,000-2,500
Putter--(S) Wood head, modern manufacture C. 1970 .... $75
Cleek--Smooth face, oval stamp $200
Driving Cleek--(B) Smooth face, round back $200-300
Driving Mashie--Extra deep face, small oval stamp $750
Iron--Smooth face, oval stamp $125
Iron--Line face, line stamp $75
Lofter--(B) Smooth concave face $300-600
Lofter--Smooth face, oval stamp $150-200
Lofter--Smooth face, straight name stamp $200
Mashie--Smooth face, oval stamp $100
Mashie--Smooth face, name in oval with outline $125
Mashie--Stock exchange model, thick heavy blade, smooth face $175
Mashie—Smooth face, marked Deep Face $150
Mashie Niblick--(B) 'Step Face', made by Spalding $3,500
Niblick--Small head, smooth face, straight name stamp $400-500

The normal Park oval cleek mark is simple yet elegant and easily recognizable. It is the most often used of his several marks.

Niblick--Medium head, smooth face, oval stamp $250-350
Niblick--Large diamond back head $150
Putter--(B) Bent neck, "patent" marking, shaft stamp $150-300
Putter--Marked "Original Bent Neck Putter" $85
Putter--Iron blade, oval stamp $100
Putter--Gun metal blade, oval stamp $150

Park & Son
[Mungo and Son; Gullane s]
Putter--(A) Mallet head $150

Parker, William
[Carnoustie s]
Mid Iron--Royal Crown model, crown CM, dot face $60
Mashie--Defiance Brand, lion CM, Maxwell pattern $65
Putter--Blade, eye CM $75

'Parlor Putter'
[See Wellington-Stone Company]

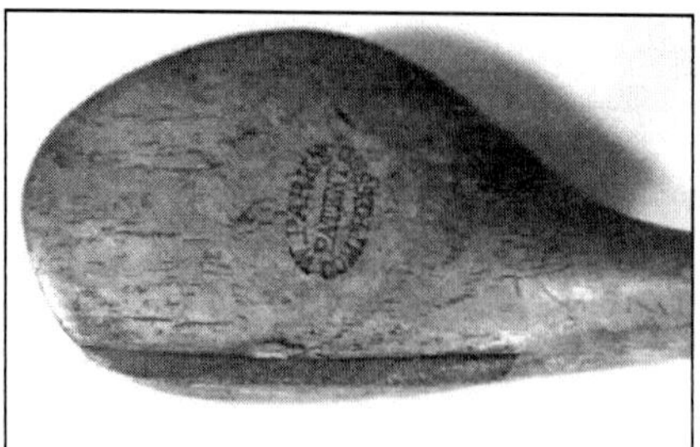

The Park Compressed Patent driver has its neck steamed and bent to make it stronger.

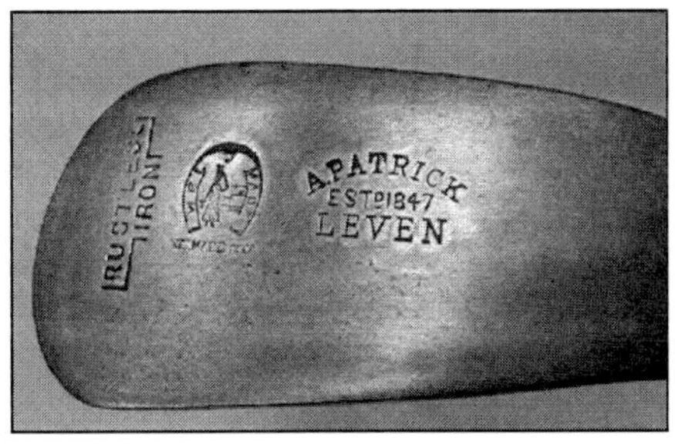

This Alex Patrick mashie carries the 'Wel-Made' cleek mark, which was registered in 1911.

Parr, Jack
Spoon--Socket head, fiber insert $85
Mashie--Dot face $35

Parr, Tom*
[Heswall e]
Driver--Superb model, socket head, face insert $65
Putter--Centre-Balance model, gun metal blade $80

Parr, S.
Mashie--Stainless, line face $30

Partridge Company, Horace
[Boston, MA]
Brassie--Socket head $60
Mashie--Diamond back, line face $40
Mashie Niblick--Foulis-type, monogram CM, concave smooth face ..$85

Patrick & Son, A.*
[Leven s; this firm was actually founded by Patrick's father, John in 1847. It continued in business until the 1930s]
<><>19th century clubs
Playclub--(L) Dark head, shallow face $2,500-4,500
Driver--(S) Bulger head $1,250-2,000
Driver--Splice head, leather face insert $300-400
Short Spoon—C.1870, dark satin (Page C) $2,000
Brassie--(S) Transitional head $1,000-1,800
Spoon--(L) C.1880, dark head $2,500-4,000
Putter--(L) Beech head $2,000-3,000
Putter--(S) Semi-long nose splice head $1,250-1,750

Patrick Bros. was a New York City golf house run by the Patrick family of Leven, Scotland. This mashie is juvenile size

Putter--Gun metal blade, thick hosel $150

<><>20th century clubs
Driver--Short splice head $200-300
Driver--D.J.S. model, socket head $80
Driver--The Robbie model, socket head, aluminum face insert $150
Brassie--Short splice head $200-300
Brassie--(B) Perfector model, triangle face insert $250
Brassie--Popular model, socket head, fiber insert $50
Brassie--Acme model, fiber face insert with 5 pegs $100
Spoon--Apex model, bulldog style short head, 6 peg fiber face insert $125
Spoon--"Est'd 1847" markings, socket head $85
Approach Mashie--Own Model, Welmade horseshoe CM $45
Driving Iron--Half musselback, spur CM, line face $100
Driving Iron--Tivoli series, thick toe, spur CM $125
Iron--Juvenile with gun metal head, spur CM $75
Mashie--Diamond back, spur CM, line face $75
Mashie—Line face, Wel-made CM $60
Mashie--The Bass Rock model, dot face $60
Mashie Niblick--Nicoll hand CM $50
Niblick--Popular series, "P" CM, "Est'd 1847" markings $80
Numbered Irons--Blade marked "Est. 1847" .... $50 each
Numbered Irons--Own Model, Wel-made horseshoe CM, line face .... $35 each
Putter--Gun metal mallet head, steel face insert $300
Putter--The Robbie model, wood socket head, steel face plate $300
Putter--Wel-made series, stainless dot face blade,

horseshoe mark $60
Putter--Wel-made series, stainless dot face blade,
gooseneck hosel $75

Patrick Brothers
Iron--Smooth face, name in oval $75
Mashie—Juvenile smooth face, name in arc $75

Patrick, Alex
[New York]
Driver--(S) Bulger shaped head, leather face insert $350

Patrick, D.M.
[Leven s]
Driver--Socket head $100
Brassie--Splice head $300
Putter--(B) Foster's model, wood socket head $650
Putter--Iron blade $80

Patrick, David
[Leven s]
Jigger--Pefector series...$75

Patrick, John
[Leven s; brother of Alex Patrick, Sr.]
Spoon--(L) Beech head $2,500-5,000

Patrick, John
[Tuxedo, NY]
Iron--Smooth face, pipe CM $90

Peter Paxton worked at Tooting Bec from 1898 to 1900, making age of this cleek fairly accurate.

Niblick--Large head, circular deep grooves on face $600
Putter--Deep face blade, gun metal $150

Paxton, James*
[Romford e, et al; nephew of Peter Paxton]
Brassie--Socket head, Paxtonite insert $150

Paxton, Peter*
[Raised in Musselburgh, Paxton was a fine golfer who preferred business to competitive golf. His firm was located in several English towns and his clubs were highly sought]
Playclub--(L) C.1885, long head $1,500-3,500
Driver--(S) Transitional head $900-1,500
Driver--Ealing model, socket head $150
Brassie--(S) Bulger head, crown CM $1,000-1,500
Brassie--(S) Bulger head $600-1,200
Brassie--(S) Transitional head $750-1,500
Short Spoon--(S) Medium short head,
well lofted face $1,000-1,500
Putter--(S) Short transitional head $750-1,000
Cleek--Smooth face, Eastbourne address,
made by W. Wilson $400
Cleek—Smooth face, Tooting Bec address $150
Iron--Smooth face, Tooting address $300
Lofter--Smooth face, Eastbourne address,
made by W. Wilson $4000
Mashie--Smooth face, short heavy blade,
made by J. Anderson $300
Mashie Iron--Smooth face, oval name stamp $200
Putter--Long iron blade $275
Putter--Gun metal blade $150

Peacock, J.M.
Putter--Gun metal blade $75

'Peacock'
Mashie--Line face, large bird CM $25

Pearson, J.S.
[Southall, London]

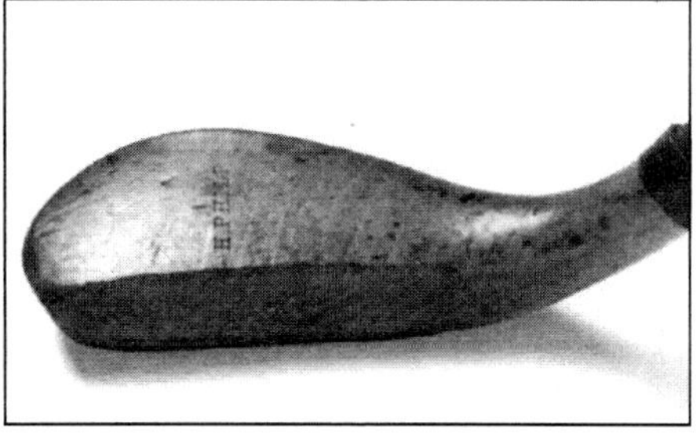

Hugh Philp was the club makers' club maker. Today, his clubs are the most prized of the 19th century woods.

Mashie Niblick--Slots cut through face $2,200

Pederson+
[New York]
Mashie Niblick--(U) Convex face, line face $250
Niblick--(U) Convex face, line face $300
Putter--(A) Own Model, 2 dials on top of head $250

Peeples, Thomas
[Pittenweem s]
Cleek--Name in circle, smooth face, Masonic compass CM $250
Mashie--Name in circle, smooth face $200

'Pegasus'
[see Seales Allen]

Penick, Harvey
[Austin, TX]
Semi-Putter--MacGregor rose CM, Penick name in script $200

Philp, Hugh
[St. Andrews; possibly the most famous club maker of all time. His clubs were prized as collectibles by the end of the 19th century. The wide price range reflects demand for clubs in varying states of condition. Clubs in fine or excellent condition are rare and extremely valuable]
Playclub--Long head, straight face $5,000-25,000
Putter--Long head, slight hook face $5,000-25,000

Phosphor Bronze Smelting Company+
[Baltimore, MD]

Putter--(A) Kismet model, rectangular head,
shafted at heel $150-250

'Piccadilly'
[W.T. Grant Company (New York) brand name]
Iron clubs--Chrome head, line face .... $25 each
Putter--Model P-2, twin diamond mark $30

Playgolf, Inc.+
[Cleveland, OH]
Iron clubs--Chrome head, "P G" on face .... $25 each

'Playwell'
Iron clubs--Chrome head, line face .... $25 each

Pope, W.R.
[Chorlton-cum-Hardy, Manchester e]
Putter--Short headed blade $125
Putter--(A B) Center shafted, square head $300

Potts, W.H.
[Briarcliff, NY]
Mashie--Line face, small Spalding thistle CM $40
Putter--Gun metal mallet head, cork face insert,
made by Spalding $1,250

Premier Golf Company, Ltd.*
[Battersea, London]
Driving Iron--Dot face, 3 crowns CM $75

Premier Golf Club Company*
[Glasgow]
Cleek--Rustless, dot face $50
Putter--The Premier model, name in script,
bar shaped blade, oval hosel $100

'Prestwick'
[There were several users of this name, most notably Burke and J. & D. Kinnell]

'Pro-Made'
[B.C. Leather & Findings Co., Vancouver]
Driver--Socket head, stripe top $75

'Pro-Made'
[Leather Parts & Golf Manufacturing Co., Detroit, MI]
Iron clubs-Peacock mark, line face ....$25 each

Pryde, R.D.
[Hartford, CT]
Driver--Bull Dog model, bulldog head CM, socket head $50
Brassie--(U) Socket head, one piece aluminum sole plate & head weight $300
Iron--Dash face, Nicoll hand CM $40
Brassie--Dash face, bulldog head CM $50

Pulford, George
[Hoylake e]
Brassie--Splice bulger head $200

Purkess, J.
Niblick--Excelsior model, eye CM, line face $60

RD Pryde patented a set of wooden clubs with uniquely shaped aluminum back weight.

R

R.G.C. Co.+
[see Rustless Golf Club Company]

Ramsbottom, Robert*
[Manchester e]
Driver--(A B) Wood face dovetailed into head, horn slip $900
Iron--(B)Smooth face, claw hosel $800
Lofter--Smooth face, slightly concave $300
Mashie—Smooth face, Ayres Maltese cross CM $125

Randall, John*
[Sundridge Park, London]
Driver--Short splice head $100
Driver--(B) Grand Slam model, socket head, grass fiber insert $125
Driver—(B) The Jehu, triangular face insert, round sole $100
Iron clubs--Stewart pipe CM, dot face .... $45 each
Putter--(A B) Long mallet head, lead filled plug holes $250
Putter--(A) Flallie model, mallet head $100

Randall, Robert*
[Herne Bay, Kent e]
Driver--(B) Velometer model, large socket head $350
Driving Iron—Diamond shaped CM with lion, Stadium GC anchor CM $60
Mashie Niblick--Asp model, line face $60

Robert Ramsbottom ran the Golf Depot of Manchester around the turn of the century.

Horace Rawlins occupies a special place in American golf history since he won the first USGA Open Championship in 1895.

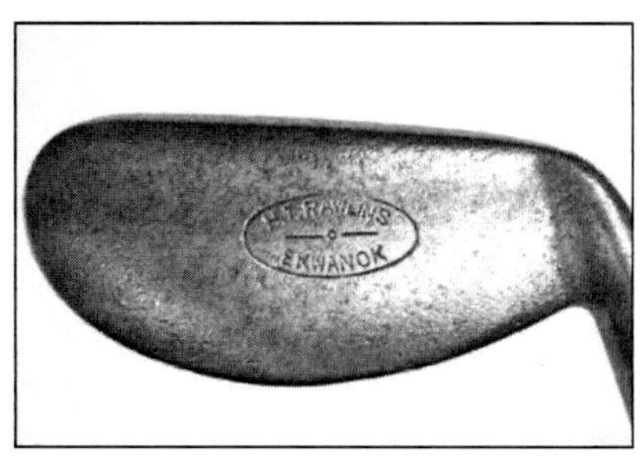

Pitcher--Line face, hatchet CM $75
Putter--(B) True Sight model, iron blade, oval hosel $150
Putter-(B) True Sight model, square grip with thumb depressions, broad sole, name in script $100

Rawlings Sporting Goods+
[St. Louis]
Brassie--Small socket head $100
Putting Cleek--Dot face blade $60
Putter—Target model, bronze, Chicopee-style head $80
Numbered Irons--Siege Gun series, line face, cannon CM ....$50 each

Rawlins, Horace+
[U.S. Open Champion 1895, worked at various east coast clubs]
Driver--Horace Rawlins stamp, deep face splice head,
Spalding Special shaft $350
Driver--Socket head $250
Brassie--Splice head $250
Iron--Smooth face, hand struck name stamp $300
Iron—Smooth face, oval stamp $175
Mashie Niblick—Fairlie anti-shank style, smooth face $250
Lofter—Short blade, smooth face $200
Putter—Park style bent neck $150

Ray, Edward (Ted)*
[Open Champion 1912, US Open Champion 1920; professional at several important English clubs]
Driver--Socket head $100
Driver--(B) Steel face insert, socket head $300
Driving Iron--Autograph model, marked for Oxhey GC $60

This extra-deep face, bent neck putter was made for Ted Ray by Tom Stewart around 1904.

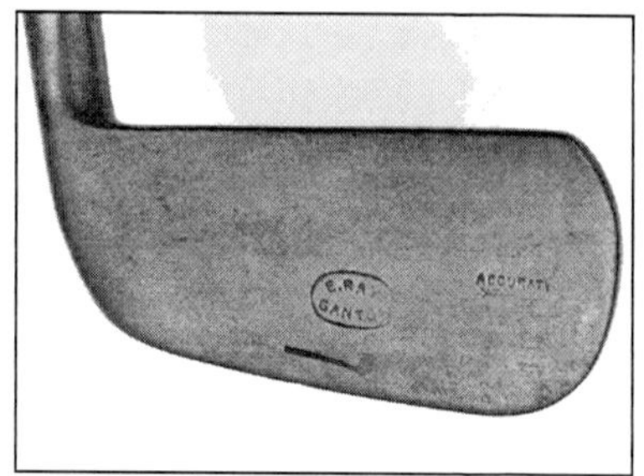

Mashie Niblick--Everbrite brand, stainless $75
Named Irons--E. Ray model, Stewart pipe CM, scored face .... $65 each
Named Irons--Autograph series, made by Wilson Co. .... $60 each
Putter--(A) Schenectady style, marked for Ganton $250
Putter—Extra deep face, Stewart pipe CM $150

'Rayl, The'
Irons or putter--Heather model, offset blade $50

Reach Company, A.J.+
[Philadelphia sporting goods company owned by the Spalding Company]
Driver--Model 56R, splice head, keystone CM $125
Driver--Socket head, double stripe top $50
Driver--Model X95, long socket head $85
Driver--Fairway series, socket head, keystone CM $50
Driver—Name in script $60
Woods--Model 598, black/white diamond pattern fancy face, bamboo shaft .... $100 each
Wood Set--Model 598 .... $350
Woods (dr, br, sp)--Warwick series, socket head, keystone CM .... $75 each
Wood Set--Warwick series $275
Mashie--Red Brand, stainless, line face $35
Mashie--Superior Grade series, dot face $35
Mashie Niblick--(D) Chek-Rite model C92R, corrugated face $100
Mashie Niblick--(D) Dedstop model C51R, corrugated face $100
Mid Iron--Model 1R, large keystone CM $40
Mid Iron--Line face, hammer & anvil CM $35
Mid Iron--Reach series, keystone CM $35

Niblick--(D)Check-Rite model C98R, corrugated face $100
Niblick--(D) Hammer brand, corrugated face $100
Named Irons--Warwick series, keystone CM $30
Putter--Hammer & anvil CM $40
Putter--Willie Mack model, iron blade, line face $50
Putter--(A) Model R4. keystone CM $90
Putter--Model 8P, Super Grade series, flange sole $60
Putter--Warwick series, blade, keystone CM $35
Putter--Eagle Grade series, line/dot face $50
Numbered Irons--Eagle Grade, Expert Model,
eagle CM ....$40 each

Read Golf Company
[Boston, MA]
Spoon--(U) Barnes-Read model, brass face insert $150
Spoon--(U) Read Balanced model, bulldog socket head $150
Irons--Name in diamond, scored face ....$40 each

Read, William
Driver--Splice head, diamond monogram CM $150
Brassie--Read model, socket head, diamond CM $60
Putter--Bent neck blade, broad sole $65

Redpath & Co.
[Glasgow]
Mashie--Dot face $35

Reekie, Tom
[Elie s]
Driver--Socket head, plain face $60
Iron--Brodie triangle/BS&A CM $50
Mashie--Line face, Stewart pipe CM $40

Reflex Manufacturing Company
[Cincinnati, OH]
Driver--(U) Socket head, special rotating grip $400

Reid, John
[Atlantic City, NJ]

Brassie--(U) Compressed, bulger splice head $400
Mashie--Smooth face, short head, name in arc $150
Niblick--Atlantic City model, medium face $300
Putter--Gun metal blade (Page D) $100

Reid, Wilfred
[Banstead, London, later Detroit, MI]
Driver—Splice head, early 20th century $150
Driver--Pear shape socket head $80

Reith, W.R.
[Eltham e]
Brassie--(S) Splice bulger head $300

Remson Company+
[Erie, PA]
Putter--Gun metal head, hump in center of blade,
plastic face inlay at sweet spot $400

Renouf, T.G.*
[Manchester e]
Driver--Stripe top, socket head, ivorine face insert $75
Cleek--Diamond face $65

'Rev-O-Noc'
[Conover (spelled backward) Hardware Co., St. Louis, MO]
Driving Iron--Smooth face, Carruthers hosel $85
Mashie--Model 36, line/dot face $55

Rhino Cupples Company
[St. Louis, MO]
Iron clubs--Scored face, rhinoceros CM $40
Putter--Blade, rhinoceros CM $45

Rhodes, F.
Baffy--(B) Shoebury patent, cup face $400

Rigden, F.E.
[Garden City, NY]
Driver--Short splice head $150

Mid Iron--Smooth face $80
Niblick--Perfect model, smooth face, two stars CM $100
Putter--Bent neck blade $125

Righter, Walter "Turk"
Putter--(A U) Center shaft pendulum style, special finger bar in grip $800

Ritchie, W.L.*
[Addington, London]
Driver--Socket head, signature stamp $85
Mashie--(D) Stopded model, flower CM, concave face, dot punched $125
Mashie Niblick--Own Model, WLR Brand, flower CM $60
Putter--The Uncanny model, round topped blade, notched at hosel $75
Putter--The "Uncanny," prism shaped blade sloped back $175
Putter--Gem model, flower CM $75

'Rob Roy'
[MacGregor economy series]
Mashie--Dot face, name in arc $25
Mid Iron--Line face, name in arc $25

Robertson, Andy
[Burr-Key series]
Iron clubs--Autograph series, Burr Key Bilt, line face .... $30 each

Robertson, Fred
[Cooden Beach e]
Driver--Socket head $60

Originally from Scotland, Peter Robertson patented several original designs like this notched hosel iron.

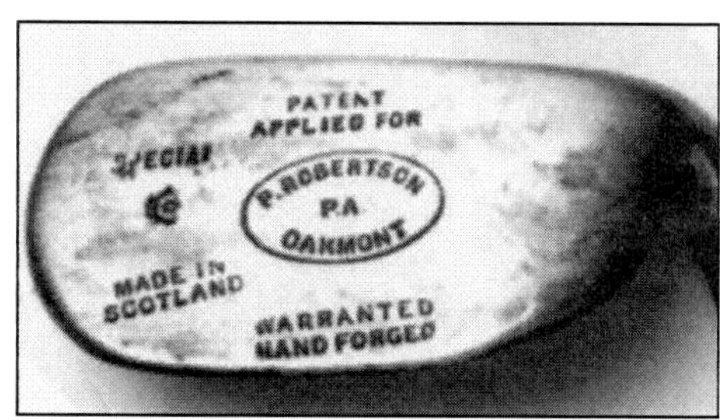

Mashie--Stainless, line face, "PROJ" CM $50

Robertson, Peter
[Oakmont, PA, et. al.]
Brassie, Spoon--Socket head, one piece sole plate+ backweight $225
Cleek--(U) Notched at hosel, Nicoll hand CM $250
Mashie--(U) Notched hosel joint, dot face, Gourlay CM $250
Niblick--Large head, line face, Nicoll hand CM $80
Niblick-Line face, hand and spade CMs $100
Putter--Wood Schenectady-type $200

Robertson, William
[Oakmont, PA]
Brassie--(U) The Leader model, socket head, one piece sole plate-backweight $225

'Robo'
Putter--(A) Mallet head with notch cut out of toe $300

Robson, Fred
[Cooden Beach e, and other locations]
Brassie--Splice bulger head $200
Mashie--Proj model, stainless head, dot face, sold by Harrods $50

Rodwell & Company, Charles*
[London]
Mashie--Flange sole, offset blade $50
Niblick--(B) Fairlie model (anti-shank), diamond/dot face $200
Putter--(A) Rodwell model, mallet head with aiming dial on top $175

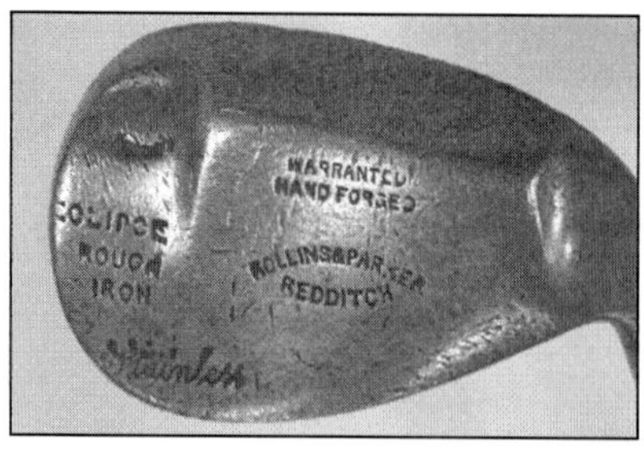

Rollins and Parker produced this "Rough Iron" which was a low loft, deep faced trouble club.

Rogers Peet Company
[New York City]
Iron clubs--Scored face, RPCo monogram CM .... $40 each
Putter--Offset blade $25

Rollins & Parker*
[Redditch e]
Mashie--Maxwell pattern, line face $75
Mashie--(B) Smith model (anti-shank), line face $200
Mashie Niblick--Excelsior series, eye CM, round back $60
Niblick--Excelsior series, round back, eye CM $80
Rough iron—Musselback, dot face $125
Putting Cleek--Dash face blade, eye CM $75

Rolls, A.E.
Mashie--Dot face $40

Ross, A.M.*
Putter--(B) Negative loft, thickened sole $250

Ross, Alex (or Alec)
[U.S. Open Champion 1907; Donald's younger brother]
Driver--Socket head, marked Pinehurst $100
Mashie--Spalding hammer CM, name in oval $50
Iron clubs--Burke fleur-de-lis CM, dot face $50

Ross, Donald
[Oakley (Boston), MA & Pinehurst, NC]
Driver--Socket head, name in script $200
Brassie--Socket head,

Alex Ross was 1907 US Open Champion, 10 years before this Burke Golfrite mashie niblic was sold.

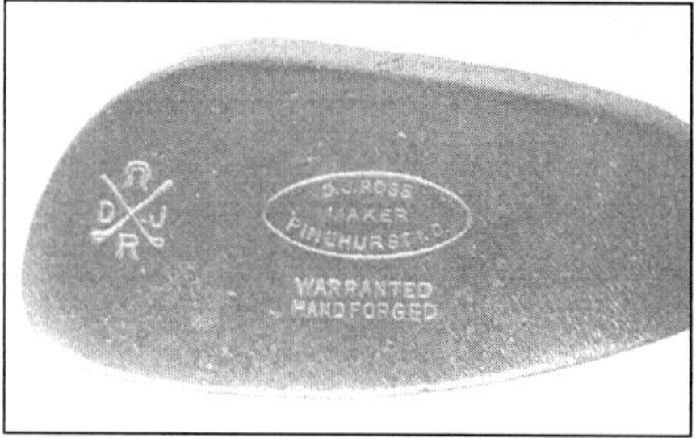

Donald Ross is best known for his course architecture but as a pro in Pinehurst he sold many clubs bearing his name

crossed clubs CM $150
Spoon--Small splice head $500
Spoon--splice head, stripe top, name in script,
Spalding Reach patent model date marking $200
Cleek--Smooth face, Dornoch stamp $300
Iron--George Nicoll, lie face, Ross name in script $100
Mashie--Smooth face, name in arc $100
Mashie--Name in oval, Stewart pipe CM, dot face $85
Mashie--Straight line name stamp, dot face $100
Mashie--(D) Bakspin model (MacGregor), slotted face $150
Mashie--Smooth face, MacGregor rose CM $100
Mashie Niblick--Smooth face, name in arc $125
Mashie Niblick--Kro Flite model, Ross name in script $100
Mid Iron--Line face, crossed clubs CM $125
Mid Iron--Line face, Burke scales CM $90
Niblick--Small head, smooth face $500
Niblick--Medium head, smooth face name in arc $150
Pitcher—DJR cross clubs CM, line face $150
Chipper--Pinehurst model run-up iron, line face
(like semi-putter) $250
Putter--Iron blade, name in oval $125
Putter--Spalding Monel blade $150
Putter--Wood Schenectady-type, brass face $300
Putter—Aluminum Schenectady $225

Ross, John
[various locations including St. Andrews]
Driver--Splice head, face insert $150
Iron--The Creek model, shorebird CM $60

Rothschild Company
[Chicago retail store]
Irons—Made by MacGregor, small shamrock CM .... $40 each

Rowe, Jack*
[Ashdown Forest e]
Driver--Small splice head $200
Driver--Splice head, extra long fishing rod shaft $300
Mashie--Pipe brand, dot face $60
Mashie Niblick-Aero model, bi-plane CM, rustless $65
Putter--Wood socket head $200

'Royal'
Mashie--Line face, chrome head $25
Iron clubs--Chrome, shield CM .... $25 each

'Ruso'
Driver--Socket head, rooster CM $45
Iron clubs--Line face, rooster CM $40

Rustless Golf Club Company+
[Chicago]
Mashie--Thick toe, sun CM $90
Mashie Iron--Smooth face, face CM $75
Mashie Niblick--Rustless, marked "Genuine Foulis",
concave smooth face, sun CM $200

The Rustless Golf Club Co. produced some of the first stainless steel clubs in the US.

S

S.B.F.
[Stix, Baer & Fuller, St. Louis, MO department store]
Brassie--Socket head, S.B.F. in shield CM $75
Mashie--Smooth face, company crest mark $65
Putter--Gun metal, company crest CM $95

S.D. & G.+
[Schoeverling, Dailey & Gales, Boston, MA retail store]
Driver--(B) Compressed model, made by R. Simpson $350
Brassie--Splice head $150
Brassie--Socket head, flag stick CM $80
Cleek--Smooth face, marked "Best Quality" $80
Iron--Name in box, smooth face $75
Mashie--Smooth face, "Best Quality" $75
Mashie--Model 1, Ringer series, flag CM $35
Pitcher--S D & G trademark, dot face $50
Pitcher--Rounded sole, line face $60
Iron clubs--Ringer series, flag in hole CM, dot face .... $35 each

S.G.C.M. Co.
(see Scottish Golf Club Mfg. Co.)

S-V-B +
[Scruggs, Vandervoort & Barney, St. Louis, MO hardware and sporting goods retail store]
Iron Clubs--Scored face, made by Spalding .... $45 each

The New York and Boston sporting goods house of Schoeverling, Dailey & Gales produced their own brand of clubs in the late 19th century.

Putter--Gun metal, MacGregor model 60, flange sole $100

St. Andrew Golf Company*
[Glasgow, later Dunfermline s]
Driver--Synchrometric series, socket head $60
Driver--Name in variable height letters $60
Driver--HBC model, stripe top, ivory face and backweight $200
Driver--Bobby model, juvenile socket head $40
Driver--Kiddy model, juvenile socket head $40
Brassie--Scottie, juvenile socket head $40
Brassie--Super Stag series, stripe top $65
Brassie--Socket head, patented Grypta grip $350
Cleek--Super Stag series, stainless, line face $35
Driving Iron--Smooth face, stag head CM $60
Iron--Stag head CM, smooth face $60
Mashie--Scottie brand, stainless, line face $35
Mashie--Standard series, line face $40
Mashie Niblick--Challenge series, Maxwell pattern,
stainless, sun CM $40
Mashie Niblick--(D) Straight name stamp,
leaping stag CM, corrugated face $100
Mashie Niblick—(D) Dedum model, corrugated face $150
Mid Iron--Stag head CM, dot face $50
Mid Iron--St. Andrew in variable height letters, line face $40
Niblick--Model 32, Maxwell pattern, leaping stag CM $50
Niblick--Thick sole, medium head, leaping stag CM $40
Niblick--(B) Fairlie model (anti-shank), line face $150
Niblick—Gourlay moon-star CM $75
Spade Mashie--Suxes series, stainless $40
2-Iron--Choix series, stainless, line face $30
Putter--Dick May model, convex face $150

The stag head is the earliest of the St. Andrew Golf Company's many marks.

Putter--Bobby model, juvenile gun metal blade $40
Putter--(A) XXX model, black sight line $75
Putter--Jupiter model, heavy iron blade $50
Putter--Standard series, bent neck, line face $50
Putter--Hawkins Never Rust steel, flange back,
running stag CM $60
Putter--Gun metal mallet head, steel face insert $250
Putter—(A) St. A model, blade style $85
Putter—Long shallow blade with round back $150

'St. Andrews Special'
[MacGregor store brand]
Jigger--Convex back, crown CM, name in arc $40
Putter--Iron blade, crown CM, name in arc $40

'St. Regis'
Irons--Chrome head, shield CM $25

Sales, Ernest
[Sunningdale e]
Irons—(B) Stoneded model, weighted sole ....$30 each
Irons—Thin sole and thick top edge, wedge shaped ....$200 each
Putter--(S) Wood socket head $125

Sandison, Ludovic*
[Aberdeen s]
Playclub—1880s vintage $2,000
Putter--(L) Thorn head $5,000

'Sandy Mac'
Putter--Lion CM, made by Burke $40

Saunders, Fred*
[Birmingham and Highgate, London]
Driver--Red fiber face insert, socket head $60
Mashie--Diamond back, dot face $40
Putter--(A) Straightline model, large back lobe $800
Putter--Long iron blade $50
Putter—(A) Northwood model, mallet head $100

Saville Company, Ltd., J.J.*
[Sheffield e]
Iron Clubs--Saville model, stainless, dot face $50

Sayers, Bernard (Ben)*
[North Berwick s; Sayers was a fixture in N. Berwick for over 50 years. His son Ben, Jr. ran the firm after Ben Senior's retirement]
Driver--(S) C.1885, light colored head $500
Driver--Splice transitional head $200
Driver--Autograph model, socket head $75
Driver--Socket head $75
Driver--Dreadnought model, large socket head $150
Brassie--(B) Domex model, rounded sole, stripe top $150
Brassie--Socket head, stripe top $75
Spoon--Small socket head, wooden cleek $150
Baffy--(B) Masta model, splice head with protruding sole front edge $500
Spoon--(B) Gruvsol model with grooved sole plate, socket head $150
Spoon--(B) Socket head, stripe top, marked for the N-B Exhibition $200
Wooden Cleek--Autograph model, socket head $125
Wooden Cleek--(B) Gruvsol model, socket head, grooved sole plate $175
Benny--Stewart pipe CM, dot face, Stewart pipe CM $75-110
Benny--Spalding Anvil CM $65-100
Cleek--Redan model, Maxwell hosel $100
Iron--Tweenie model, round sole, Stewart pipe CM $100
Lofter--Special Benny, Stewart pipe CM $75-100
Lofter--Smooth face $85
Mashie--(D) Stop um model, corrugated face, H & B

Ben Sayers made clubs in North Berwick for 35 years before passing the business to his son Ben, Jr.

mitre CM $200
Mashie--Maxwell pattern, holes in hosel $60
Mashie Iron--Dunedin series, dot face $70
Mashie Niblick--(D) Stop um model, corrugated face $200
Mid Iron--Redan model, Maxwell pattern $75
Niblick—Redan Maxwell model $80
Niblick--Large stainless head, line face $50
Niblick--Digger model, thick top edge, thin bottom $150
Young Benny--Smaller Benny iron, line face, Stewart pipe CM $85-125
Named Irons--Ben Sayers model, Stewart pipe CM, scored face $70
Named Irons--Waverley series, flange sole, line face, robin CM .... $60 each
Numbered Irons--Autograph series, stainless .... $50 each
Numbered Irons--Craig series, robin CM, pointed toe, line face .... $50 each
Numbered Irons--Crest series, stainless, line face .... $35 each
Numbered Irons--Domesole series, stainless .... $40 each
Numbered Irons--Regent series, stainless .... $35 each
Numbered Irons--Target series, bull's eye on sweet spot .... $40 each
Numbered Irons--Waverley series, stainless .... $35 each
Putter--(L) Late period, long head $450
Putter--(S) Splice head, brass sole $300
Putter--Wood mallet head $300
Putter--(B) Benny model, grooved sole, stainless $100-175
Putter--(A B) Benny model, mallet head $150
Putter--Wood socket head, fiber sole slip $80
Putter--Straight gun metal blade, name in block letters $150
Putter--Gun metal blade $125
Putter--(B) Gassiatt-style wood putter $450
Putter--Gun metal mallet head, steel face insert $250
Putter--Gun metal blade, name in block letters $75

Sayers, Ben Jr.
[Cuckfiend, Royal Wimbledon, e; son of Ben Sayers, left Wimbledon in 1911 to join his fathers firm]
Driver--Dreadnought, socket head $125

Sayers, George

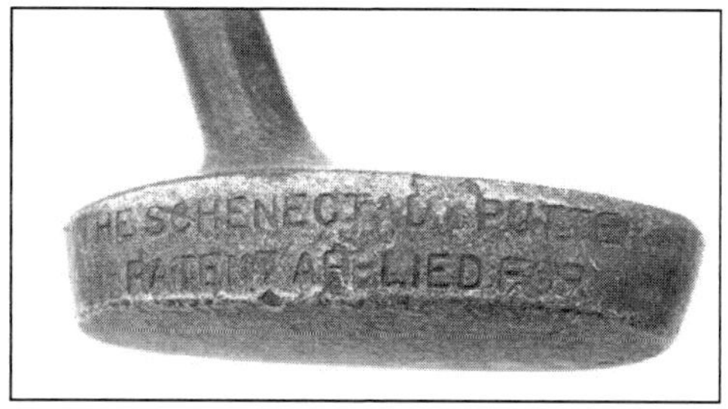

The original model of the Schenectady putter has "Patent Applied For" markings on the back.

[Merion, Philadelphia, PA; old Ben Sayers' son]
Brassie--Stripe top $125
Benny--Stewart pipe CM, dot face $75-110
Mashie--(D) Stop um model, corrugated face,
H & B mitre CM $200
Niblick--Dot face, Stewart pipe CM $50
Putter--Blade, 2 Spalding rose CMs $50

Saynor, Cedric
[Duffield e]
Putter--(A B) Raised face and rounded back toe and heel,
back shaped like Mickey Mouse ears $1,000

Schenectady Putter Company
[Schenectady, NY]
Putter-(A U) Center shaft, patent legend on back $200
Putter—(A U) "Patent Applied For" on back $500

Schmelzer's
[Kansas City hardware company]
Iron--M-12, Pilot Series, diamond back, dash face $35
Mashie--Dot face $30
Mashie--Anderson arrow CM, dash face $45
Putter--P-1, Pilot series, Burke model 69 .... $75

Schoverling, Daly & Gales+
[see S.D. & G.]

Schwarz, F.A.O.
[New York toy store]

A.H. Scott's model DSO putter was a take off on the Mills aluminum long nose clubs.

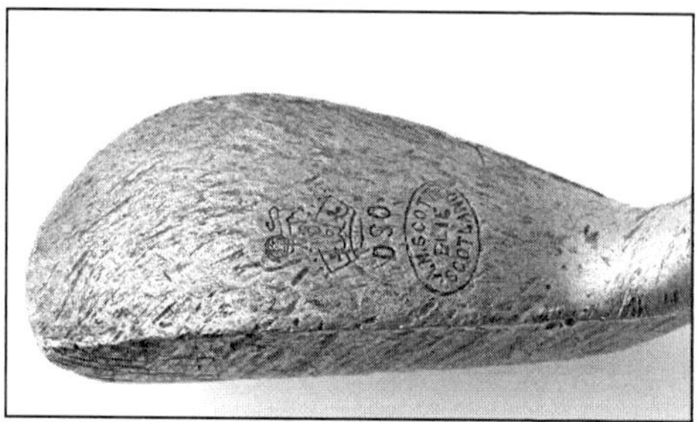

Driver-Clan series, bell CM, juvenile size socket head $60
Mid Iron--Clan series, bell CM, juvenile size $45
Mashie-Clan series, bell CM, junior size $40
Lofter--Clan series, bell CM, juvenile $55
Putter--Clan series, bell CM, juvenile $75

Scott, A.H.*
[Elie s; Scott was appointed club maker to the Prince of Wales in 1901 and obtained a royal warrant just as Robert Forgan had for an earlier prince]
Driver--(B) Fork splice head $300-500
Driver--Socket head, lion over crown CM $80
Driver—Scoto model, lion crown CM, socket head $95
Brassie--(B) Fork splice head $300-500
Cleek--Signature, plume of feathers CM, smooth face $150
Iron--Monarch model, ridge on back $85
Mashie--The Midget model, short blade $150
Lofter--Line face, lion over crown and Brodie triangle CMs $75
Spade Mashie--Line face, lion over crown CM $50
Stymie Mashie--Lion CM, concave face $125
Putter--(A) Monarch model, mallet head $100
Putter--(B) Straight-Line model, blade with top edge weight $150
Putter--(B) The Leslie model, two level back $75
Putter-(B) Broadclair model, round back,
groove sole, lion/crown CM $250
Putter--Stymie model, concave face $150
Putter--Park model, lion and (Hewitt's) heart CMs $100
Putter—(B) Monoplane model, broad sole, biplane CM $200
Putter—(A) DSO model, lion crown CM, semi-long nose style $100

Scottish Golf Club Manufacturing Company, Ltd.*
[Edinburgh]
Driver--Splice head, face insert $250-400
Driver--(S) Transitional splice head, fishing rod style grip $750
Driver--Socket head $150
Cleek--Smooth face $150
Iron--Round back, thick hosel $200
Lofter--Smooth face, long blade $200
Mashie--Smooth face, monogram w/ arrowheads CM $125
Putter--(S) Wood splice head $400
Putter--Iron blade $200
Putter--Gun metal blade $250

Scottish India Rubber Company
Iron—Name in double arc, smooth face $100

'Scotty'
Driver--Name in diamond, socket head $30

Seager, Jack
Putter—Own model, weight bar along sole, circle CM, offset head ...$75

Seales Allen
Mashie--Pegasus model, winged horse CM, diamond back, line face ..$30

Sellars, Robert J.
[London]
Niblick—(B) The Leader model, Legh patent, hollowed back $175
Iron clubs--Horseshoe shaped CM, dot face ....$100 each
Iron clubs—(B) Legh patent, hollow back .... $150 each
Putter--Gun metal blade, horseshoe CM $125

Sellars, W.
Putter--Wood mallet head, aluminum face insert $175

Shaler Company+
[Waupun, WI]
Woods--Marked with fancy Shaler S $40
Named Irons--Overbrook series, chromed ....$25 each
Named Irons--Tailor Made series, line face ....$30 each

Numbered Irons--Tailor Made series, line face, S in circle CM .... $30 each

Sheffield Steel Products, Ltd.
[Sheffield e]
Iron clubs--Name in large oval, club weight stamped on head .... $50 each

Shelly, W.H.
[Anstruther s]
Brassie--Socket head $60

Shepherd, Alex*
[Inverness s]
Iron clubs--Line face, hand holding shepherd's crook CM .... $75 each

Sherlock, Ray & Turner*
[Abingdon e]
Brassie--(B) Metal face, SRT in circle CM $300
Mid Iron--Stainless, line face SRT in circle CM $60

Sherlock, H.G.
[Worlington & Newmarket e]
Brassie--Socket head, triangular insert $75

Sherlock, James*
[Oxford, Stoke Poges & Hunstanton e]
Driver—Socket head, aluminum sole plate, Oxford CM $100
Driver—Long thin splice, marked for Stoke Poges $150
Brassie--Socket head $60
Spoon--Small splice head $300
Iron--Montmorencie model, Gibson star CM $75
Mashie--Smooth face, Stewart pipe CM $75
Semi-Putter--Shallow face chipper, Oxford CM $125
Putter--Small bar shaped head, Oxford CM $125

Sherratt, B.
[Saddleworth e]
Iron clubs--Riding saddle cleek mark .... $50 each

Clubs made by John Shippen are extremely rare. He was the first native born American to play in the US Open and the first African American golf professional.

Sherwood, W.C.
[Memphis, Toledo]
Niblick—S-10, made by Burke, ...$80
Putter—Gun metal, made by MacGregor, roes CM $75

Shippen, John
[Aronomink et. al.]
Driver—Splice head, reddish finish $1,200
Putter—Iron blade, offset head $800
Putter—(A) Schenectady type $1,500

Silverite Company
Iron clubs--High nickel stainless, arm CM $40

'Silver Ace'
[Robert E. McClure patent]
Putter-(A) Round center shaft head with front blade $400

Simmons Hardware Company

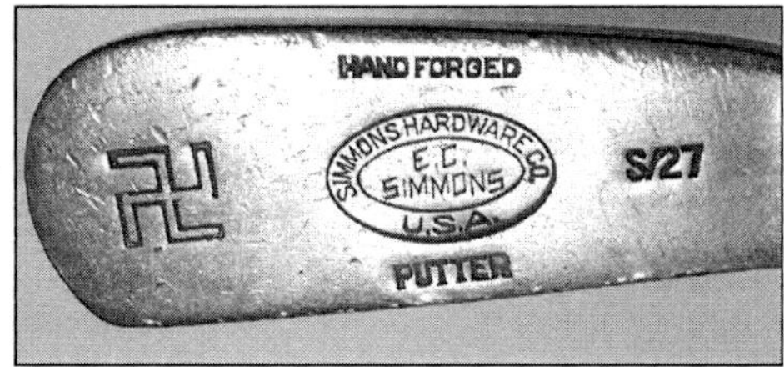

The Simmons Hardware Company bought many of their clubs from the Great Lakes Golf Co., who used the mark that later became known as the "Swastika."

Brassie--Socket head, oval name stamp $35
Approach Iron--Model S/18, swastika CM $75
Mashie--(D) Model S/33, corrugated face $75
Mid Iron--Line face $30
Putter—S27, blade style, swastika CM $60

'Simplex'
[Clubs with this name were produced by Francis Brewster, Robert Simpson and others; see Brewster, Simpson]

Simpson, Alex*
[Maidenhead e]
Putter--(B)Maidenhead model, iron blade, square hosel $250

Simpson, Archie*+
[Aberdeen s; various locations in U.S.]
Driver--Small splice head, ash shaft $300
Brassie--Socket head, marked for Aberdeen $100
Niblick--Small head, smooth face $350
Putter--Offset blade $75

Simpson, G.O.
Mashie--(D) 'Stop em' model (Spalding), corrugated face $100

Simpson, J. & A.*
[Edinburgh]
Cleek--Full musselback, Carruthers hosel, mitre CM $125
Iron--Name inside oval, smooth face $65
Putter--Maxwell pattern, star/moon CM, line face $50

Before the sand wedge players had many choices for sand play, like this bunker mashie

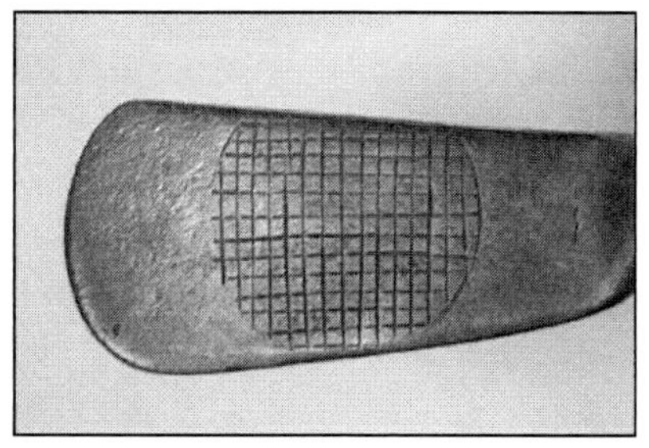

Robert Simpson patented the ball face iron in 1903. It was available in a cleek and iron, as well as this

Simpson, Robert*

[Carnoustie s]

Playclub--(L) C.1885, medium length head $1,500-2,000
Long Spoon--(L) Lancewood shaft $1,500-2,000
Driver--Short splice head, face insert $200
Driver--(S) Bulger splice head, ash shaft $900
Driver--Socket head, straight name stamp $100
Driver--(B) Marked 'Compressed' $400
Driver--H H model, socket head, face insert $125
Driver--Perfect Balance model, brass backweight,
socket head $100
Driver--Paragon model, socket head $75
Driver—HH model, black insert-diamond shape $100
Driver--Ivorex model, socket head, ivorine face insert $100
Driver--Matchless series, socket head $75
Driver--Malinka model, socket head $75
Driver--(B) Celluloid splice head $2,500
Driver—Long thin splice, made for Elvery $175
Brassie--(S) Bulger splice head $750
Brassie--(S) Transitional splice head $600
Brassie--(B) Laminated splice head $750
Brassie--Ivorex model, ivorine face insert $100
Brassie--Medalist model, socket head, aluminum face insert $100
Brassie--(B) Reliance model, socket head $100
Spoon--Simplex model, socket head, brass backweight $65
Bunker Mashie—Line face, anchor CM $100
Driving Iron--Line face, anchor CM $60
Driving Mashie-Line face, anchor CM $75
Iron--(B) Perfect Balance model, large bulge on back
of sweet spot $450
Lofter--(B) Ballingall's model, smooth face, flange sole $300

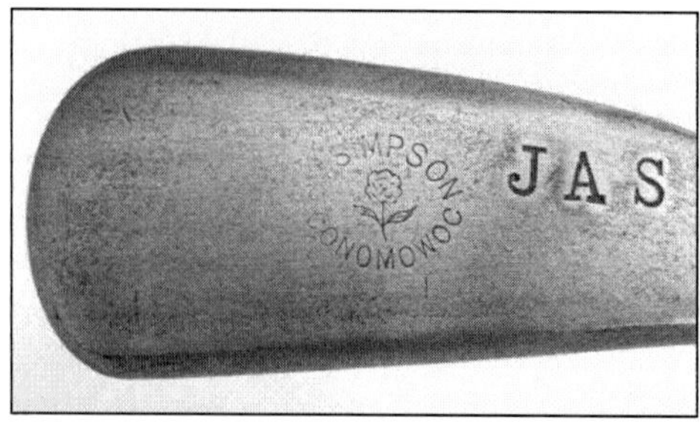

Robert "Bob" Simpson was western Open Champion but started his career at Oconomowoc, Wisconsin.

Mashie--(B) Ball face model, oversized round sweet spot on face $1,250
Mashie--Concentrated model, V-shape thickened back $150
Mashie--(B) Malinka series, faceted back $80
Niblick--(B) Malinka series, faceted back $100
Niblick—(B) Reliance model, heavy head $85
Putter--(S) C.1890, transitional head $800
Putter--(S) C.1900, fiber sole slip $350
Putter--(S) Wood socket head $300
Putter--(B S) Premier model, hollow steel head $450
Putter--Gem model, vertical line face $80
Putter--Teacher model, offset head, hump on top $150
Putter--(B) Perfect Balance model, large bulge in center of back, S in circle CM $500
Putting Cleek--Iron blade, S in circle CM $65
Putter--Low profile blade, pointed nose $125
Putter--Teacher model, offset gem-type $100

Simpson, Robert S. "Bob"
[Oconomowoc, Memphis, Milwaukee, Kenosha, San Diego, et.al.]
Cleek—Short hosel, marked for Oconomowoc $125

This Slazenger extra-deep face mashie came from Tom Stewart circa 1905.

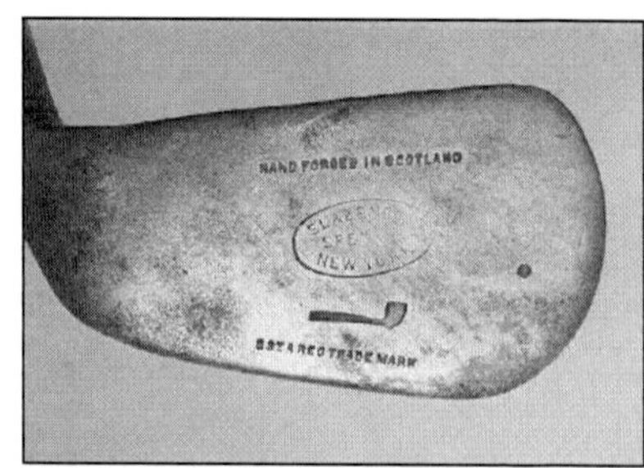

Slazenger flange sole putter from the new York store, circa 1915.

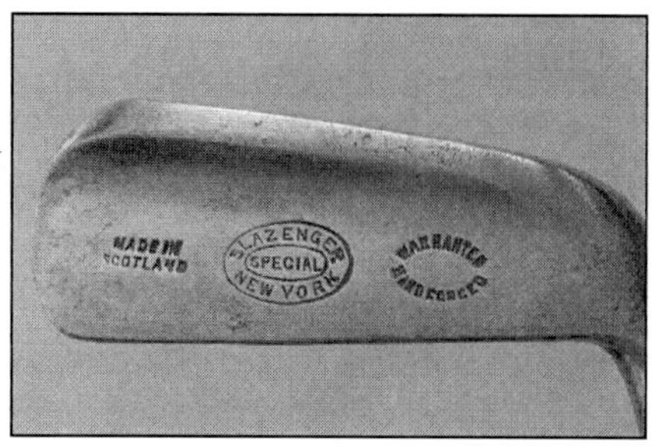

Iron--Smooth face, Gibson star CM, marked for St. Louis $60
Mashie--Marked "Champion", name in double oval, dot face $100

Simpson, Tom
[Southport e]
Mid Iron--Stainless, VK CM, dot face $40

Slater, F.
Mashie Niblick--Propellor Brand, propeller CM, line face $45

Slazenger & Sons*+
[London and New York]
Driver--(B) Demon model, patent face insert $950
Driver--(B) One piece, leather face insert $1,500-2,000
Driver--(B) Screw socket head (#682960) $200
Driver--(B) Screw socket head in large dreadnought size $300
Driver--Splice head $175
Driver--Socket head, pear shape, New York address $125
Driver—(A) Pipe stem neck, socket head $400
Brassie--(S) Elongated socket head $100
Brassie--Vardon model, small splice head $300
Cleek--Smooth face, 6 point star CM $125
Cleek--The Ball Model, thick toe, smooth face,
large circular CM $250
Iron--Centraject series, thick blade $150
Iron--Smooth face, name in oval, rose CM, Condie
name in oval $100
Irons—Nicoll Zenith stamped for Slazenger ....$50 each
Iron--Line face, Craigie rifle CM $80
Mashie--Boodie series, smooth face $125

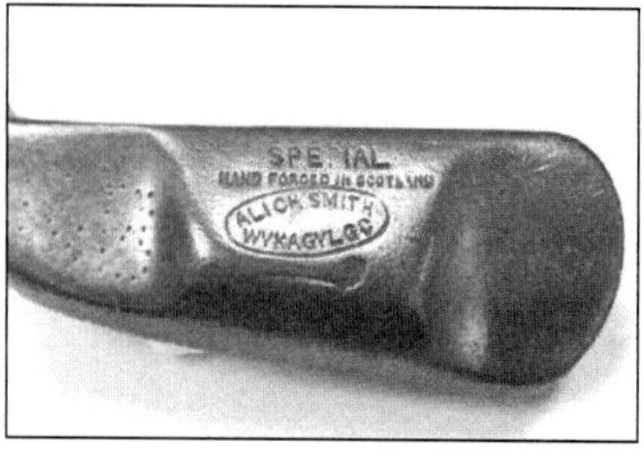

This approaching cleek has an extra-heavy musselback. Most of the time Alex Smith used the 'x' in his spelling. The use of Alick here is unusual.

Mashie--Smooth face, St. Andrews series, name in arc $150
Mashie—Flange sole, made in Scotland $75
Mashie—Extra deep face, Stewart pipe CM $150
Mashie Niblick--dot face, Gourlay moon/star CM $60
Niblick--Tiny concave head, centraject back,
6 point star CM $600
Niblick--Small head, smooth face, Stewart serpent CM $300
Niblick--Concave face, thick sole, stainless,
6 point star CM $200
Putter--Iron blade, Stewart pipe CM $60
Putter--Iron blade, Condie rose CM, NY address $75
Putter--Oak Brand (W.G. Oke), extra long hosel $175
Putter-Gem style, Nicoll hand CM, dash face $75
Putter--Gun metal blade, marked "Slazenger & Sons" $175
Putter--Centraject series, gun metal blade $175
Putter--(A U) Triangular head with center shaft $550
Putter--(A) Mallet head, cross hatched face $100
Putter--Wood socket head, swan neck bent hosel,
marked Slazenger on toe $600
Putter—Center Balance model, head marked "gun metal" $150
Putter—Flange sole, name in double circle $60
Putting Cleek—Gibson star CM, NY address $80

Smalldon, W.G.
Niblick--Tru-Flite model, stainless, line face, swallow CM $35

Smart, J.
[Chicago]
Putter--Smooth face iron blade, Stewart pipe CM $50

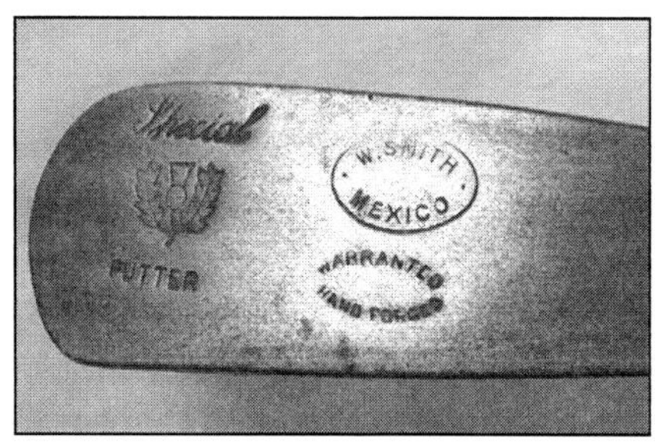

Willie Smith was the first of the Carnoustie Smith brothers to come to America. He was US Open Champ in 1899, later moving to Mexico.

Smethwick Golf Company*
[Smethwick Birmingham e]
Cleek--X 33, smooth face, shield CM $75
Mid Iron--Valor series, line face, bench wheel CM $75

Smith, Alex+
[Nassau, later Wykagyl, NY; US Open Champion]
Driver--Socket head, Nassau mark $100
Approaching Cleek—Heavy musselback, pipe CM, name spelled 'Alick' $150
Jigger--Smooth face, name in circle $60
Mashie--(D) Baxpin, made by Wilson $150
Mashie—Stewart pipe CM, diamond back $100
Putter—Stewart pipe CM, blade style $100
Named Irons--Alex Smith irons, name in oval, scored face ....$50 each

Smith, C. Ralph
[W. Middlesex e; later U.S.]
Mashie--Pipe brand, line face $45
Lofter--Center shafted anti-shank style, smooth face $750
Putter-(A,B) Medalist model, tapered back, square grip $125
Putter—(B) Truesite model, aiming fin on top, bullseye face $400

Smith, E.
[Halifax e]
Mashie--(B) Smith model (anti-shank), name in small oval, smooth face $150

Smith, G.F.
[Amateur golfer and patentee of the goose neck anti-shank iron]

Alex Smith, Fred Herd and William Yeoman worked together for a year in 1899. They had all come to Chicago from St. Andrews.

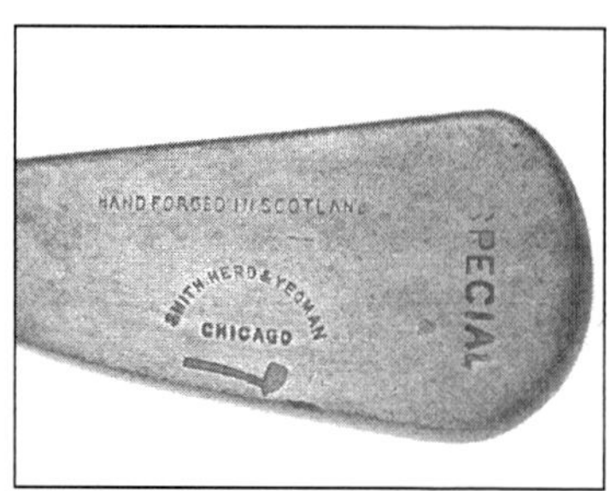

Mashie--(B) G.F. Smith model (anti-shank), hollow back, line face, made by D. Anderson $200

Smith & Sons, J. C.*
[Monifieth s]
Named Irons--Line face, Stewart pipe CM $45

Smith, Willie+
[Chicago, Mexico, et. al.; US Open Champion]
Putter--Marked 'W. Smith, Mexico', Millar thistle brand CM $150

Smith, W.B.
Sammy--Approach Eagle model, dot face $60
Putter--Long blade and hosel, pointed toe, shallow face $150

Smith, W.P.*
[London]
Putter--(A) Maxmo model, mallet head $125

Smith, Herd & Yeoman
[Chicago]
Iron Clubs—Stewart pipe model, name in arc, smooth face $150

Somerville, Andrew
[Dunbar s]
Driver--(S) Transitional splice head $500
Cleek--Smooth face $200

'Southern Cross'
[Australian made]

Mid Iron--Stainless, dot face, constellation CM $75

Sooutar, Davie
Numbered Irons—Approved by PGA of Australia ....$40 each

Spalding & Brothers Company, A.G.*+
[Chicopee, MA, London e and Dysart s; Spalding quickly became the leading supplier of golf equipment in the US due to their established sports marketing network. They entered the British market about 1900. Spalding produced a seemingly infinite number of combinations of markings and club types not all of which can be itemized here]

<><>Spalding (block letters) series
Driver-(S) Bulger type splice head $400
Cleek--Smooth face $150
Iron--Smooth face $125
Mashie--Smooth face long blade $150
Niblic--Small head, smooth face $850
Putting Cleek--Iron blade $200

<><>'The Spalding' series
Driver--Splice head $150-300
Brassie--Splice head $150-300
Cleek--Smooth face, Carruthers hosel $150
Cleek--(U) Cran model, wood face $600-900
Cleek--Diamond back, gun metal, smooth face $125
Driving Mashie--Smooth face $100
Driving Niblic--The Spalding series, large oval head,
smooth face $2,750
Iron--Convex back, smooth face $125
Lofting Mashie--(U) Center shafted, round head $3,250

The Spalding Vardon series was heavily marketed along with Vardon's tour of America (1899 -1900) which Spalding sponsored.

Mashie--Short heavy blade, smooth face $100
Niblic--Smooth concave face, medium size round head $500
Niblic--Large head, smooth face $150
Putter--Extra deep face, gun metal blade $250
Putter--Gun metal diamond-back blade $175
Putting Cleek--Gooseneck iron blade $175

<><>'Spalding Special' series
[Name can appear in block letters or more infrequently in a more stylized font, almost script]
Driver--Splice head, name in script $300
Driver--Horace Rawlins stamp, deep face splice head,
Spalding Special shaft $350
Cleek--Name in block letters $125
Driving Iron--Name in script $250
Iron--Name in arc, smooth face $250
Mashie--Name in block letters $250
Lofter--Name in block letters $275
Putter--Name in script, gun metal blade $225
Putter--Name in small block letters gun metal blade $200

<><>Vardon series
Driver--Small splice head $250-400
Brassie--Short splice head $250
Cleek--Name in small oval, diamond (X) face scoring $125
Driving Mashie--Smooth face $125
Jigger--Smooth face $100
Lofting Mashie--Smooth face $125
Mashie Iron--Smooth face, short blade $125
Mashie--Line face $75
Mid Iron--Line face, shaft stamped with Vardon autograph $150
Mid Iron--Smooth face $125
Mid Iron--Line face $75
***Niblic--Small heavy head, smooth face $5*00**
Putter--Iron blade $150
Putting Cleek--Offset iron blade $100

<><>Other Early Club model lines
<>Clan series
Driver--Splice head $450

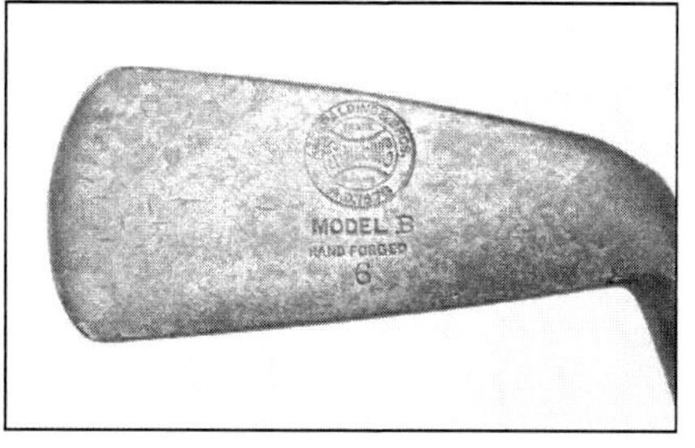

Made right after the turn of the century this model B iron with the double line 'baseball' mark also had a through-bore hosel.

Driver--Socket head $200
Cleek--Juvenile model, smooth face, stamped shaft $250
Lofter--Smooth face, stamped shaft $300
Mashie--Smooth face, name in block letters $300
Niblick--Smooth face, medium size head $500
Putter--Iron blade $400

<>'Spalding' in a horseshoe shaped mark
Brassie Niblick--Splice head, horseshoe CM $1,250
Spoon--"A.G. Spalding & Bros." in horseshoe $750
Iron--Smooth face, "Syracuse" in arc shaped CM $125
Iron--Spalding name in horseshoe $250

<>S.M.Co. series
Driver--Splice head $400
Brassie--Splice head $400
Cleek--Smooth face, short hosel $300
Iron--Smooth face, long hosel $300
Mashie--Smooth face $250
Niblic--Smooth concave face $650
Putter--Iron blade $300

<>Single outline 'baseball' mark
Cleek--Smooth face, shaft stamp $200
Mashie--Smooth face, shaft stamp $250
Lofter--Smooth face, knurled hosel $300
Putter--Gun metal blade $250

<>Doubleline 'baseball' mark
Driver--Model F, socket head $90

Also from the turn of the century, this Spalding Crescent series round sole cleek is a scarce club.

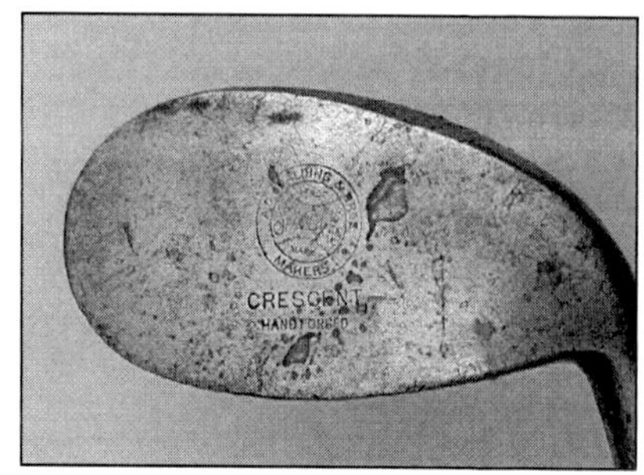

Cleek--(U) Cran model, wood face $600-900
Cleek--Flat diamond back shape, 'baseball' CM,
smooth face $150
Iron—Model B Long blade, through bore, smooth face $125
Iron--(U) Spring face $750-1,000
Jigger--Model A 17 .... $65
Lofter--Model B 3, deep smooth face, short blade $100
Mashie Niblic--Model N4, Monel $55
Mid Iron--Model V, heavy line face $50
Putter--Model D, bent neck $60
Putter--(L) Long slender splice head $1,650

<><>Crescent series
Brassie--Socket head, 'ball' CM $80
Cleek--Flat diamond back shape, 'baseball' CM, smooth face $150
Cleek—Round sole model... $250
Lofter--Baseball CM, smooth face $80
Mid Iron--Smooth face $45
Putter--Deep face, gun metal blade, 'baseball' CM $250
Putter--H model, small steel head, similar to BV model $175

<><>Morristown series
Driver--Bulger spliced head $275
Driver--Morristown series, splice head $175
Brassie--Small splice head $175
Cleek--Morristown series, 'ball' mark, smooth face $60
Driving Mashie--Morristown series, smooth face, shaft stamp $100
Niblic--Morristown series, round head, smooth concave face,
shaft stamp $500
Putter--Morristown series, gun metal blade $95

The Gold Medal series was introduced in 1905 as a result of the Gold Medal the company's display of sports equipment won at the 1904 World's Fair in St. Louis.

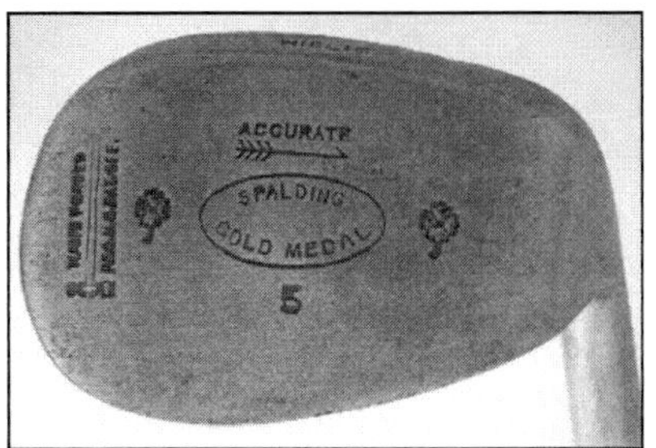

<><>Gold Medal series
Driver--Model C, shaft stamp $60
Driver--(U) Model J, compressed socket head $400
Driver--(U) Model J, socket head, 3 wood plugs in face $275
Driver--(U) Model JR, Rigden backweight,
3 circular Jacobus wood face blocks $300
Driver--(U) Model R, brass backweight $125
Driver--(U) Model RN, brass backweight $125
Driver--Model 7, real ivory insert, 2 screws $400
Driver--Model 18, splice head, oval stamp $150
Driver--Steel face insert, 4 screws $150
Cleek--Carruthers hosel, centraject back $100
Driving Iron--Model B93, flange sole, dash face $200
Iron--(U) Seely model, with reinforcing ridge $650-850
Iron--(U) Seely model, without reinforcing ridge $750-900
Iron--RS model, rounded sole $125
Mashie--(U) Model DF, angled two surface face $600
Mashie--(D) Model 1 Dedstop, corrugated face, 2 roses CM $100
Mashie--Right angled face lines (90 degree) $65
Mashie--Hammer CM near toe $50
Mashie Niblic--(U) Park's 3-step face $3,250
Mashie Niblic--Model 3, Foulis model with patent date $250
Mashie Niblic--Model series, Foulis style concave face $125
Mid-iron--(U) Leitch patent with raised ridge on center of back,
dash face........ .... $150
Mid Iron--(U) Fitted with Lard perforated metal shaft $2,000-4,000
Mid Iron--Model F, hammer CM, smooth face $60
Mid Iron--Model 2, dot face, hammer & roses CMs $45
Niblick--Model D, smooth face $75
Niblick—Model 5, large head, line face $80

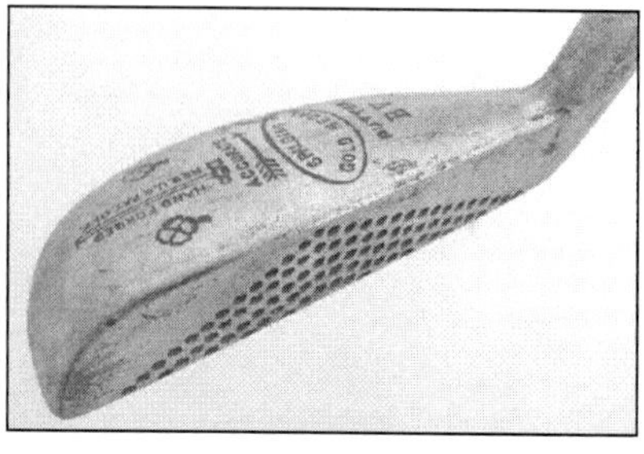

The Brown-Vardon putter was popular enough that almost every major maker offered its own model.

Putter--(U) Model C, brass mallet head, cork face insert $1,250
Putter--Model BV, Brown-Vardon style, oval hosel, rounded top to back, dot face $250
Putter--Model G, gun metal blade, oval stamp $75
Putter--Model H, rounded back $150
Putter--Model LW, broad sole, 2 roses CM $150
Putter--Model 2, 2 roses and hammer CMs $45
Putter--Model 6, 2 roses and hammer CMs $45
Putter--Model 9, gun metal, flange sole, oval stamp $65
Putting Cleek--Model C, straight stamp, hammer CM $65

◇◇Miscellaneous clubs
Driver--Socket head, leather insert slotted into head $500
Driver--(U) Travis patent, "P", "S" or "R" stamped on sole $175
Driver--(U) Duncan model, one piece sole plate & backweight, socket head (Page D)... $85
Driver--S925W model, socket head $65
Driver--Autograph, Maltese cross insert, stripe top $65
Driver--Spalding Autograph, stripe top $50
Driver--Model F, small socket head $50
Driver--Fire Brand, arm holding torch CM $150
Brassie--Socket head, Cyril Walker autograph $100
Brassie--Model C, socket head, straight line stamp $50
Brassie--(U) Model EM three piece splice $200-400
Brassie--(U) Duncan model, one piece sole plate backweight $125
Brassie--(U) Skooter model, brass sole edge plate $275
Brassie--(U) Barrel sole, Dalgleish pattern, fiber face insert $300
Brassie--(U) Model R925, Autograph, Rigden brass backweight $75
Brassie--Autograph marked head, raised ring shaft (looks like pseudo bamboo) $1,500

Spoon--(U) Model EMS, three piece splice $425
Spoon--Model 16, socket head $55
Driving Mashie--Deep face, two roses & hammer CMs, dot face $200
Iron--Indian head CM $80
Mashie--Model 3, bronze head, 2 roses & hammer CMs, circle dot face $300
Mashie--Model M3, Monel, winged ball CM $60
Mashie Niblic--Model C 4, smooth concave face, boat shaped head $250
Mashie Niblic--Model G-3, Monel, round sole, super gooseneck hosel $400
Mashie Niblic--Name in block letters, Foulis style in bronze $350
Mid Iron--Model Irons series, Autograph, hammer CM, dot face $40
Niblic--Fire Brand 9-H, hand holding torch CM, line face $50
Niblic--Heather series, line face, 2 roses CM $40
Niblic—Cyril Walker autograph, dot face $150
Sky Iron--Model M-8, two roses & hammer CMs, wide line face $75
Putter--Model 1-H, Fire Brand, hand holding torch CM $75

<><>Aluminum clubs
Driver--(A S) Model D $250
Driver--(A U) Vehslage patent, marked "The Spalding", wood face $2,500
Brassie--(A S) 1U model, fairway club $300
Brassie--(A) 3 U model, fairway club $300
Brassie--(A S) B model, fairway club $250
Cleek--(A S) C model, fairway club $250
Cleek--(A) CC model, ... $750-1,000
Cleek--(A) Gold Medal series, spring face $750-1,000
Driving Iron--(A S) Model 2, fairway club $250
Lofter--(A S) L model, fairway club $250
Mashie--(A S) M model, fairway club $200
Mid Iron--(A) Fairway club $175
Putter--(A U) American Putter model, Schenectady style, Dysart anvil CM $250
Putter--(A) CK model, offset mallet head, 'ball' mark $250
Putter--(A) Model 4, 2 roses CM, mallet head $125

Putter--(A) Gold Medal 5 model, mallet head, lead face insert $300

Putter--(A) HH model, Schenectady style head $150

Putter--(A) RM model, Ray-Mills style head $100

Putter-(A) Fownes-type, long mallet with heel $400

◇◇Deep Groove irons

Mashie Iron--(D) Forged Model, ribbed face $100

Mashie--(D) Gold Medal 1 Dedstop, ribbed face, 2 roses CM $100

Mashie--(D) Gold Medal M 1 Dedstop, ribbed face $100

Mashie--(D) Stop'Em model, ribbed face $125

Mashie--(D) Dedstop model C91, ribbed face $100

Mashie Niblick--(D) Jock Hutchison, Pittsburgh in double oval ... $150

Mashie Niblic--(D) Stop'Em model, ribbed face $125

Mashie Niblic--(D) Dedstop 1, waffle face $300

Mashie Niblic--(D) Dedstop 6, waffle face $300

Mashie Niblic--(D) Medal C51, Dedstop, corrugated face $100

Mashie Niblic--(D) Dedstop model C54, ribbed face $100

Mashie Niblic--(D) Dedstop model C67, ribbed face $100

Mashie Niblic--(D) Dedstop model C69, ribbed face $100

Mashie Niblic--(D) Dedstop model C92, ribbed face $100

Mashie Niblic--(D) F 6, double waterfall face, crow CM $3,000-4,000

Mashie Niblic--(D) F 6, waterfall face, crow CM $250-400

Mashie Niblic--(D) F 6, corrugated face, crow CM $150

Mid Iron--(D) Forged Model, ribbed face $100

Niblic--(D) Medal C98, Dedstop, corrugated face, 2 thistles CM . $100

Niblic--(D) Stop'Em model, ribbed face $175

Pitcher--Model M 7, ribbed face $125

Pitcher--(D) Dedstop Kro-Flite, ribbed face $100

Pitcher--(D) F 7, waterfall face, crow CM $250-400

Pitcher--(D) F 7, corrugated face, crow CM $150

Pitcher--(D) F 17, waterfall face, crow CM $250-500

Sky Iron--(D) Dedstop Kro-Flite, ribbed face $150

◇◇Putters not belonging to other model series

Putter--A.G. Spalding 10, Schenectady style, wood head, brass face plate $200-350

Putter--(A) Model 4, 2 roses CM, mallet head $125

Putter--(A) Gold Medal 5 model, mallet head, lead face insert $300

Putter--Model C5, small Monel mallet head with

Spalding Kro-Flite Series "Waterfall" Face Irons

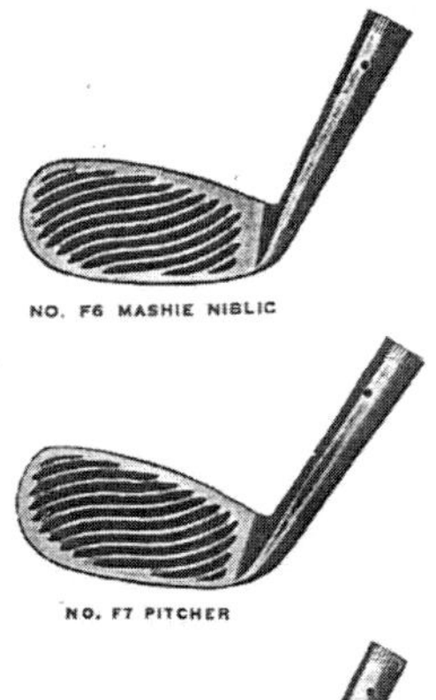

During the 'deep groove' club era, Spalding brought out three different styles of Kro-Flite back spin irons. The most commonly found are those with straight grooves. The 'Waterfall Series' clubs had grooves that curved downward at the toe of the face. The most scarce are the Double Waterfall irons with grooves the curve down at the toe and upward at the hosel. The Double Waterfall pattern was patented in 1920, twenty months before deeply grooved golf clubs were outlawed.

NO. F17 PITCHER

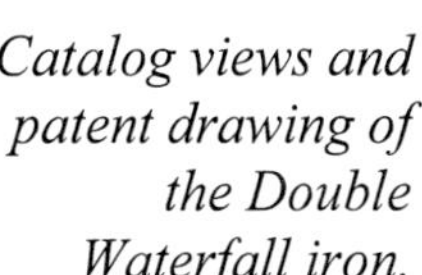

Catalog views and patent drawing of the Double Waterfall iron.

Fig. 3.

Regular and waterfall model F-6 mashie niblicks.

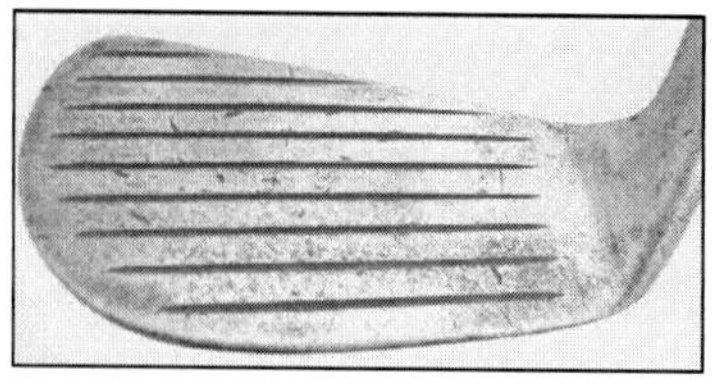

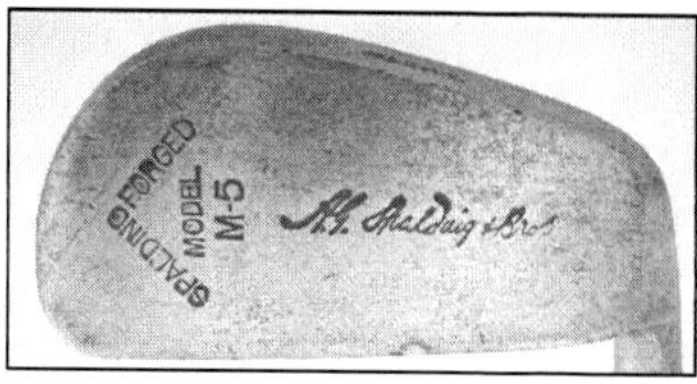

The Spalding Forged series is easily recognizable by its wide grooved on the club face.

peaked crown, Monel and 'baseball' CMs $400
Putter--Model BV, Brown-Vardon style, oval hosel, rounded top to back, dot face $250
Putter--CH (Chicopee) model, iron, center shaft, dot face $250
Putter--CH model, bronze center shaft, dot face $300
Putter--(A) CK model, offset mallet head, 'ball' mark $250
Putter--Crescent series, H model, small steel head, similar to BV model $175
Putter--Dead Strength model, blade, slightly rounded face $125
Putter--HB model, center shaft, dot face $200
Putter--(A) HH model, Schenectady style head $150
Putter--LF model, mallet head, 2 roses CM $250
Putter--LW model, broad sole, 2 roses CM $150
Putter--O 'Olympic' model, pointed toe, curved top edge, square solid steel shaft $600-1,000
Putter--R model, wood Schenectady-type, brass sole plate, wide boat shape $200-350
Putter--(A) RM model, Ray-Mills style head $100
Putter--WT (Walter Travis) model, square wood Schenectady-type head, brass face $250-350
Putter--Travis model, extra-long square wood head, brass face $450
Putter--(A U) American Putter model, Schenectady style, Dysart anvil CM $250
Putting Baffy--Mallet head with large brass backweight .... $ 675

<><>Forged Model series
Cleek--Forged Model, Carruthers hosel, name in script $100
Mashie--Forged Model L9, heavy line face $60
Mashie—Model M-5, widely spaces face grooves $60

Kro-Flite clubs came in several different series. This one was offered through the PGA of America (purchasing) cooperative.

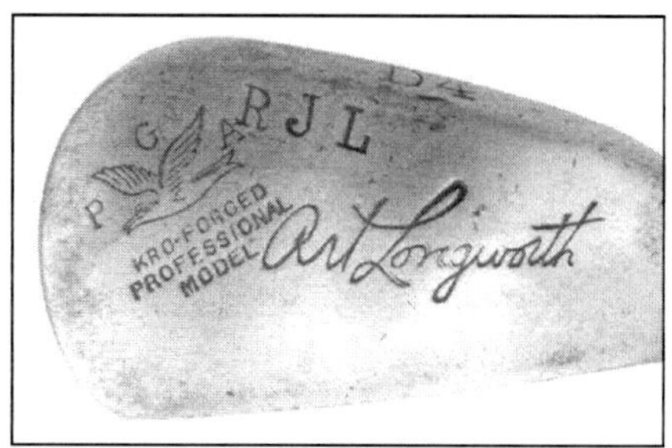

Mashie Iron--(D) Forged Model, ribbed face $100
Mid Iron--(D) Forged Model, ribbed face $100
Niblic--M 9 model, line face $40
Sky Iron--M 8 model, line face $60

<><>Dundee series
Woods--Socket head, plain face .... $50 each
Iron clubs-Dot face .... $35 each
Putter--Iron blade $35

<><>Thistle clubs
Woods--Socket head, "Thistle" italicized .... $40 each
Driver--As above, brown composition head,
wood pin through neck $400
Iron clubs--Line face, "Thistle" italicized between 2
thistle sprig CMs .... $35 each
Putter--Line face, "Thistle" italicized between
2 thistle sprigs CM $35
Mid Iron--Thistle series, made in Australia,
dot face $50
Cleek--Name in block letters, thistle plant CM, circular dot face $50
Mashie--Dot face, small thistle plant CM in name oval $65
Mashie Niblic--Foulis style, small thistle plant CM, concave face $150
Mid Iron--Medal 2, thistle plant CM $40
Putter--Steel blade, Spalding name in block letters,
thistle plant & hammer CMs $50

<><>Symetric Set irons
#1 through 9-Irons--Stainless, trophy CM .... $30 each
#10 (Putter)--Stainless blade, offset head $35

Matched Set--7 or more irons in sequence .... $45 per club

<><>Kro-Flite "F Series"
Driving Iron--F 1, 4-line face $40
Mid Iron--F 2, 4-line face $35
Mid Mashie--F 3, 4-line face, crow CM $40
Mashie Iron--F 4, 4-line face $40
Mashie--F 5, 4-line face, crow CM $35
Mashie--F-5, marked "Junior" $50
Driving Iron--F 1, 4-line face $40
Mashie Niblic--(D) F 6, double waterfall face, crow CM $4,000
Mashie Niblic--(D) F 6, waterfall face, crow CM $400
Mashie Niblic--(D) F 6, corrugated face, crow CM $80
Pitcher--(D) Dedstop Kro-Flite, ribbed face $75
Pitcher--(D) F 7, waterfall face, crow CM $250-400
Pitcher--(D) F 7, corrugated face, crow CM $150
Pitcher--(D) F 17, waterfall face, crow CM $250-500
Sky Iron--F 8, 4-line face, crow CM $75
Niblic--F 9, 4-line face, crow CM $40
Putter--F 10, 4-line face, crow CM $45

<><>Kro-Flite series
Driver--Socket head, flying crow insert $200
Brassie--Socket head, fancy face insert of flying crow $200
Spoon--Socket head, flying crow insert $200
Sky Iron--(D) Dedstop Kro-Flite, ribbed face $150
Sky Iron--K 8, line face $65
Putter--Kro-Flite series, RF model, long hosel $50
Putter--Juvenile, marked J $40

Nos. P1 through P9-Irons--PGA brand (large letters), line face, crow CM .... $35 each
Nos. P10 (Putter)--PGA brand (large letters), thick soled blade, crow CM $40
Putter--9, PGA brand, crow & long golf club CMs, dot face............ $40

Numbered Irons--Stainless, flying crow CM, marked "Pat. Applied For" .... $30 each
Numbered Irons (1-9)--Stainless, dot face, flying crow CM $25

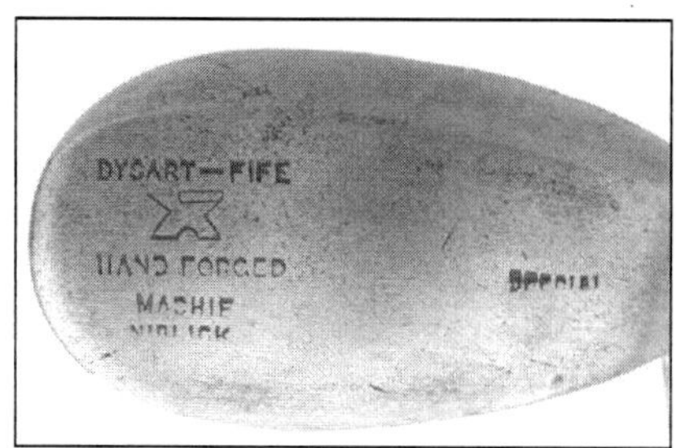

Spalding clubs marked 'Dysart' or bearing that image of the anvil were manufactured by Spalding's plant in Scotland.

#10 (Putter)--Stainless, dot face, flying crow CM $40
#19 or 29-Iron--Stainless, extra-large head, flying crow CM .... $65 each
Matched Set--6 or more clubs in sequence .... $40 per club

#1 through 9-Iron--Stainless, Sweet Spot Irons, dot face, flying crow CM, registration number .... $25 each
#10 (Putter)--Stainless blade, offset head $30
#19 or 29-Iron--Stainless, Sweet Spot Irons, dot face, extra-large head, flying crow CM, registration number .... $45 each
Matched set--6 or 9 clubs in numerical sequence with matching registration numbers .... $50 per club

[Robert T Jones, Jr. iron clubs were produced for almost four decades. Wood shaft clubs were made only in 1932. Jones model clubs with wood grain coated steel shafts are frequently found by collectors. They have minimal value because they are not wood shafted but collectors will continue to seek them simply because of their name association. Collector value............................ $5-15 per club]

#1 through 9-Iron--Stainless, Robert T. Jones, Jr. signature, dot face, registration number .... $100-200 each
Matched Set--6 or 9 clubs in sequence with matching registration numbers .... $250 per club

[Calamity Jane putters were made from 1932 well into the 1960sthere are least six design variations from the several manufacturers that copied Jones's famous putter. The two models shown below are most common models with Kro-Flite markings]
Putter--Calamity Jane model, 3 bands of whipping on shaft, crow CM $150-300

[Calamity Jane steel shaft putter .... $75-150]
Putter—Jones Model, First Flight line, PGA Custom Built $60

<><>Clubs produced in Britain
Cleek--(A S) Model CI, fairway club $250
Driving Iron--Tong brand, tongs CM, line face $100
Iron--Gold Medal series 'push iron', anvil CM $90
Lofter--Tong brand, tongs CM $125
Mashie--Crescent series, hammer CM $60
Mashie--Gold Medal series, anvil CM, roses CM $50
Mashie Niblick—Round head, anvil CM $45
Mashie Niblick—V-back design, V face markings, anvil CM $125
Mid Iron--Large thistle CM, dot face $50
Sammy--Marked "Dysart Fife", weighted back $90
Putter--Anvil CM, iron blade $50
Putter--Anvil CM, deep face iron blade, name in script $125
Putter--Crescent series, iron blade 'ball' CM $75
Putter--(A U) American Putter model, Schenectady style $250
Putter--Parputta model, iron blade,
reverse (hollowed) musselback, anvil CM $300
Putter--Dead Strength model, blade, slightly rounded face $125
Putter--Argyle series, anvil mark, bent neck blade $50
Putter—BR model, round sole, long thin hosel $125
Putter--SR model, round sole, anvil CM $125
Putting Cleek--Tong Brand, iron tongs CM $150
Putting Cleek--Dysart series, iron blade $50
Irons—Argyle series, anvil CM ....$50 each

<><>Spalding Juvenile and Junior clubs
Driver--Name in block letters $35
Brassie--Name in block letters $35
Iron--Dot face, hammer & single rose CMs $40
Mashie--Smooth face, hammer & single rose CMs $40
Mashie--Model C, smooth face, name in arc $45
Niblic--Line face, junior $60
Putter--Hammer & single rose CMs $50
Putter--Kro-Flite series, juvenile, marked J $50

Sparling, George
[Bridgeport, CT]

Putter--Gun metal blade, laminated bamboo shaft $200

Spence & Gourlay*

[St. Andrews]

Iron--Model 1, clover CM, dot face $60

Iron—Club pip CM, celtic style offset $50

Lofter--Small oval head, face scoring in shape of daisy $150

Mashie--Model 12, clover CM, dot face $60

Mashie--Smith-style (anti-shank), made for
Morris & Youds, line face $200

Mashie Niblick--(D) Varsity model, corrugated face $125

Niblick—Maxwell pattern, clover CM $75

Niblick--Heavy medium head, clover CM, dot face $60

Niblick--Dreadnought size head, clover and acorn CMs,
dot face $100

Niblick--Model 10, diamond back, dot face $75

Putter--Dot face, Forgan crown CM $50

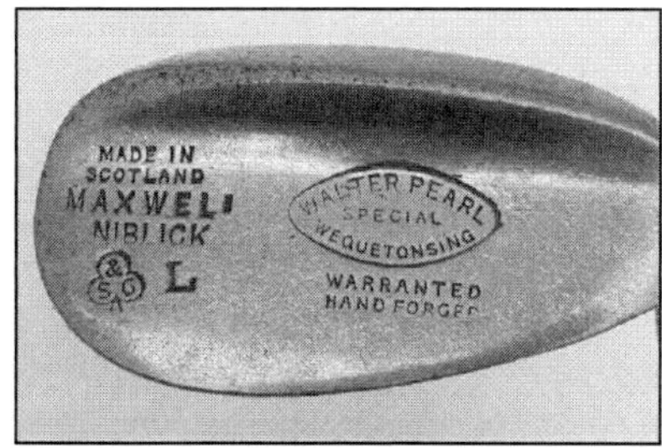

Spence and Gourlay made irons near the harbor in St. Andrews until their forge was purchased by Robert Forgan.

Spence, James*

[St. Andrews; successor to the Spence & Gourlay firm, he sold out to Forgan in 1920]

Mashie--Line face, flagstick CM $50

Mashie Niblick--Oval head, line face, flagstick CM $50

Niblick--Giant model, flagstick CM $125

Numbered Irons--Line face, JS in oval CM $40

Putter--Blackwell model, iron blade $75

Putter--Giraffe model, long thin hosel and blade $125

Putter--Blackwell model, flagstick CM $75

Putter--100 model, dot face, flagstick CM $65

Spittal, David
Driver--(U) Socket head, half metal, half wood shaft $750

'Sport-Mart'
Numbered Irons--Chrome, line face $20

Sports & Games Association, Ltd.
[London]
Iron clubs--Royal Ajax series, line face .... $60 each

'Sports Depot'
[Liverpool e]
Iron clubs--Royal series, stainless, dot face $45

Sportsman's Emporium, The*
[Glasgow & Edinburgh]
Putting Cleek--Long smooth face blade, Gibson star CM $75

Sprague, C.S.
[Boston, MA]
Driver--Socket head, steel plate over face
w/ 4 screws, insert underneath $250
Driver--Socket head, patent Kempshall Pyralin face $300
Cleek—Name in double oval, deep scored diamond face $100
Mashie--Standard series, deep face, line face $60
Mashie--Stewart pipe CM, dot face $65
Putter--(A U) Block shaped head with ball-in-socket
adjustable hosel $2,500
Putter--Stewart bar back model, dash face $125

Stadium Golf Company*

This Sprague cleek has most unusual scoring lines on its face: diagonal and very deep.

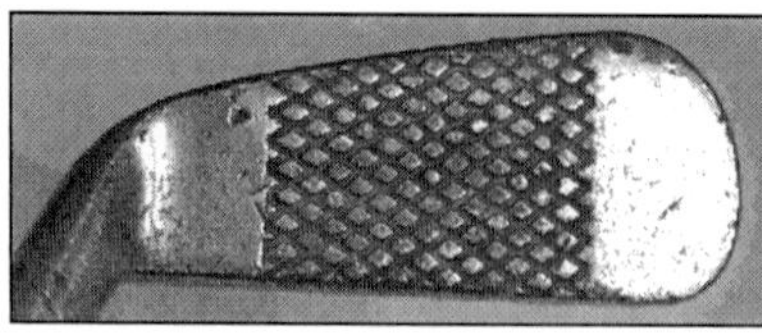

[Bermondsey, London]
Brassie-(B) Loft-em model, concave sole $200
Brassie-Baffy--(B) Dunlewy model, pointed sole $350
Mid Iron--Model 21, stainless, line face, anchor-S CM $50
Mid Iron--(B) Mystic model, round sole, highly
offset hosel $300
Mashie—P6 model, dot face $45
Mashie Niblick--Model 60, dot face $50
Niblick--(B) Dunlewy model, dot face, pointed sole $250
Niblick--Korecta 8 model, anchor-CM, target face $250
Niblick--Model P8, oversize head, line face $80
Scuffler--(B) Rivers-Zambra model
approach putter $150-200
Putter--(B) Per Whit model, round blade, solid back $500
Putter--(B) Korecta model, raised top edge with aiming
notch, line face anchor CM $250
Putter--Model 5, offset blade, square handle, anchor-S CM $60
Putting Cleek--Model 55, steel blade, anchor-S CM $50
Putting Cleek--Model 2, steel blade, anchor-S CM $60
Numbered Irons--The Nacky model ....$50 each

'Standard'
[Model name used on certain Spalding series and B.G.I. series irons]
Cleek--Juvenile smooth face, made by B.G.I. $75

Standard Golf Company*
[Sunderland e; founded by an engineer adept at working in metal, this company strictly produced aluminum clubs. The fame of their creator, Sir William Mills, caused these clubs to be known throughout the world as Mills clubs and they were the one of the first brands to be offered in "matched sets"]

All clubs are made from aluminum and, except for the 1896 Standard model, have a serial number stamped on the crown of the head. Fair-way-type clubs are listed here as 'brassies' although Mills catalogs and advertisements randomly describe them as brassies, spoons or by the names of the iron clubs they emulated.

<><>Drivers, brassies and baffies
Driver--(B) Standard model, 3 wood blocks in face,

This Mills model RL 2 1/2 two-faced duplex club was handy for hitting a left handed shot at a time when little relief was given.

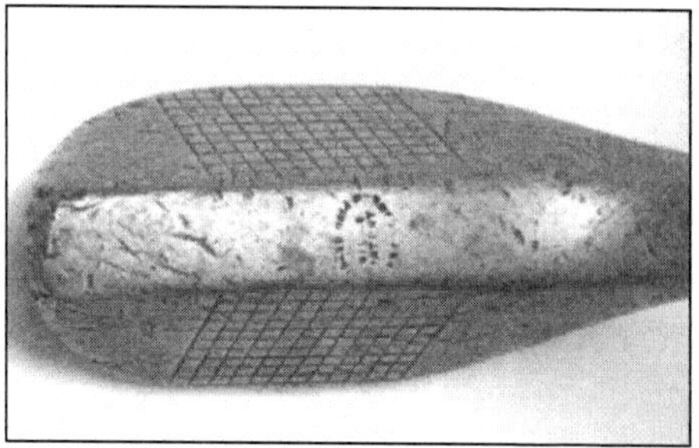

weight markings on crown of head, no serial number $600-800
Driver--DA model, wood face $350
Driver--DB model, wood face $350
Driver--WD model, wood face $300
Brassie--BA model, wood face $350
Brassie--BB model, wood face $350
Brassie--WB model, wood face $300
Brassie Spoon--BGS, wood blocks in back $275
Baffy--BSX, hook face $500
Baffy--BSX2, hook face $450
Baffy--BSZ model $300

<><>BS series semi-long nose clubs
Brassie--BS1 model $350
Brassie--BS2 model, ...$350
Brassie--BSD1 model, ...$200
Brassie--BSD1 1/2 model $225
Brassie--BSD2 model $200
Brassie--BSD2 1/2 model $225
Brassie--BSD3 model $300

<><>CB and MSD series short headed clubs
Brassie--CB1 model $200
Brassie--CB1 1/2 model $200
Brassie--CB2 model $250
Brassie--CB3 1/2 ....$500
Brassie--MSD1 model $100-200
Brassie--MSD1 1/2 model $125-225
Brassie--MSD2 model $125-175
Brassie--MSD2 1/2 model $150-200

The Braid-Mills 1915 model was one of the company's biggest sellers (along with the Ray-Mills model).

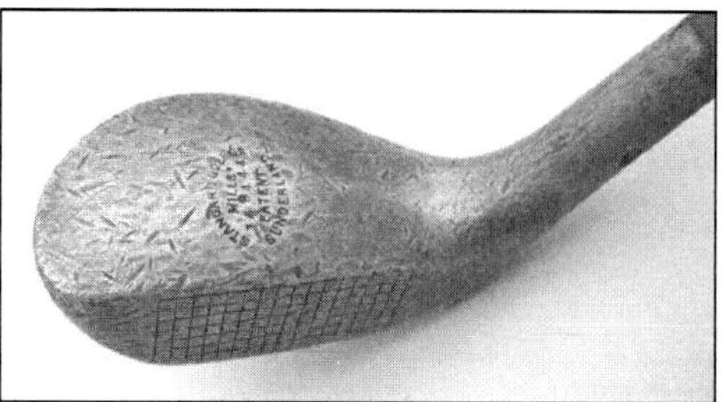

Brassie--MSD3 model $175-250
Brassie--MSD3 1/2 model $300-400
Brassie--MSD4 model $300-400

<><>Miscellaneous clubs
Niblick--NK model $350-500
Duplex Club--RL1 model, 2 sided head $400-600
Duplex Club--RL1 1/2 model, 2 sided head $400-600
Duplex Club--RL2 model, 2 sided head $400-600
Duplex Club--RL2 1/2 model, 2 sided head $400-600

<><>Putters
Putter--AK model, rectangular head $200-300
Putter--(S) Braid-Mills model $100-150
Putter--Braid-Mills-1915 model, mallet head $45-75
Putter--CS model, Schenectady style $175
Putter--CSI model, Schenectady style head $200
Putter--CSA model, Schenectady style head
with rounded top $200
Putter--CSD model, duplex Schenectady style head $500
Putter--CSRA model, Schenectady style head with
right angle shaft $600
Putter--Collins model, Braid-type mallet head $125
Putter--Cotton-Mills model, mallet head $80
Putter--Edgar-Mills model, tiny mallet head $100
Putter--JM model, bent neck, small mallet head $100
Putter--(L) K model $250-400
Putter--(L) KL model, extra long nose $300-500
Putter--(S) KS model $250
Putter--(L) L model $250-400

Putter—(L) Lmodel with leather face insert $500
Putter--MNB model, offset mallet head, truncated back $125
Putter--MNG model, mallet head $75
Putter--Ray-Mills model $45-75
Putter--RRA model, aiming rib $125
Putter--RBB model, top aiming rib $125
Putter--RBB model, 3 rubber aiming dots (2 red, 1 green) on crown $125
Putter--RM model, bent neck $100
Putter--RMG model, gooseneck Ray style $150
Putter--RMR model, aiming groove $100
Putter--RNB model, top aiming rib $100
Putter--RNG model, top aiming groove $100
Putter--RRA model, raised aiming T $100
Putter--RR model, Ray style with raised rib $150
Putter--RSB model, Ray style with slant back $150
Putter--RSR model, top aiming groove and bevel $150
Putter--Rodwell model, large mallet with circular aiming disc $150
Putter--(S) SB model $300
Putter--(S) SS model $200
Putter--WM model, bent neck $100
Putter--(L) X model, Harold Hilton style $150-250
Putter--(L) Y model $175-250
Putter--(S) YS model $175-250
Putter--(L) Z model $200-300
Putter--Mallet model, cylindrical hammer head $1,250
Putter-(L) WF model, wood face insert $1,250
Putter--Steel blade, Birmingham address $125

Steer, J.A.*
[Blackpool]
Brassie--Large head, fiber face insert $75

Stein, Joseph
[Nashua, NH]
Spoon--(U) Wooden cleek, marked 'Pat. Pending' $125

Stephens, Fred
[Liverpool e]
Iron clubs--The Liver model, stork CM, Maxwell pattern,

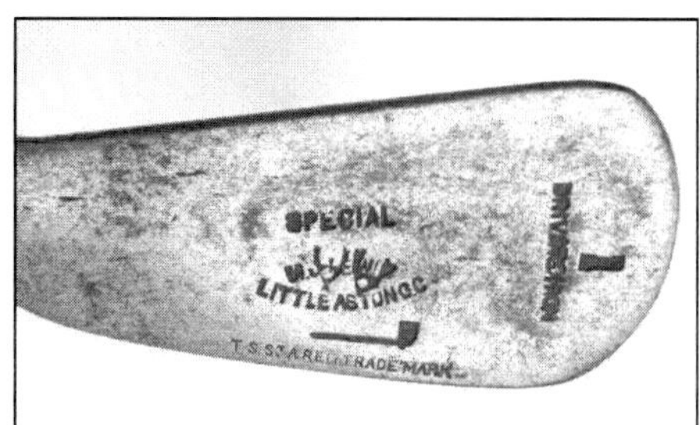

This Tom Stewart 1-iron carries two of Stewart's 'reject' marks (directly above the pipe CM).

stainless, dash face ....$50 each

Stephens, James
[Liverpool e]
Mashie--Huyton brand, stainless, dot face $40

Stewart, Rufus
[Australia]
Niblick--Map of Australia on club back, line face $75

Stewart, Thomas*
[St. Andrews; Stewart was the dean of Scottish iron club makers with a world-wide reputation for excellence. The prime characteristic of all Tom Stewart irons is the pipe cleek mark though a few early ladies and juvenile irons bear a serpent mark]

<><>Pipe CM with no registration legend underneath; also serpent CM
Cleek--Extra long heavy blade, smooth face 4 1/2" hosel $250
Cleek--Smooth face, short blade, serpent CM $125
Cleek--Smooth face, Carruthers hosel $175
Cleek--Smooth face $75
Iron--Smooth face $65
Iron--(B) Fairlie model (anti-shank) $250
Lofting Cleek (Jigger)--Smooth face $125
Lofting Iron--Smooth face $90
Mashie--Smooth face $90
Niblick--Small head, smooth face, serpent CM $400
Niblick--Small head, smooth face, pipe CM $500
Niblick--Medium head, smooth face $50
Putter--Iron blade $50-90

Putter--Long shallow blade, serpent CM $100
Putter--Gun metal blade $125
Putter--Gun metal blade, serpent CM $125
Putter--Iron blade, bent hosel $50-150

<><>Pipe CM with trademark registration legend
Approaching Cleek--Line face, long blade $60
Bobbie--Banana shaped blade with round sole,
line face, pipe CM $90
Cleek--Line or dot face, short Carruthers hosel $100
Cleek--Scored face $50
Driving Mashie--Line face $60
Iron--Smooth face $65
Iron--(B) Fairlie model (anti-shank), scored face $175
Iron--Smooth face, musselback $100
Iron--Dot face $45
Iron--Diamond back, line face $60
Jigger--Smooth face $80
Jigger--Dot face $65
Jigger--Freddie model, dot face $75
Lofting Iron--Dot face $60
Lofting Mashie--Dot face $80
Mashie--Smooth face $75
Mashie--(B) Smith model (anti-shank), line face $200
Mashie--Dot face $45
Mashie--Flange sole, line face $100
Mashie--Vardon model, Vardon autograph, line face $100
Mashie--Maxwell pattern, dash face $75
Mashie--(D) Corrugated face $150
Mashie Iron--Line face $50
Mashie Niblick--Oval head, line face $50

Some of the most sought Stewart irons are from the FO/RTJ model line honoring the two great Amateur and Open Champions.

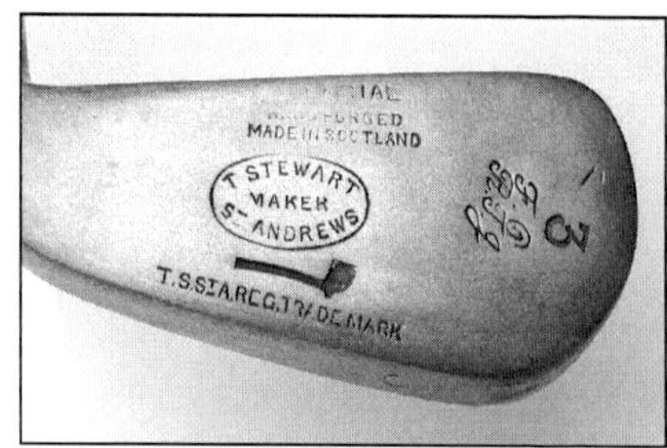

Mashie Niblick--Foulis-type, line face (not concave) $85
Mashie Niblick--(D) Corrugated face $150
Mid Iron--Smooth face $60
Mid Iron--Dot face $45
Mid Mashie--Dot face $60
Mongrel Iron--Rounded head, musselback $100
Mongrel Mashie--Line face $80
Niblick--Giant head, line face $1,500-2,000
Niblick--Medium head, line face $50
Niblick--Large head, line face $75
Pitcher--Oval head, line face $65
Push Iron--Line face $85
Sammy--Dot face $75
Spade Mashie--Deep line face $60
Spade Mashie--(D) Corrugated face $175
1-Iron--Dot face, laminated bamboo shaft $100
1-Iron--Dot face, pipe CM $50
1-Iron—Line face, pipe CM, reject mark $100
2-Iron--Dot face $40
2-Iron--Dot face, 'reject' mark $80
3-Iron--Dot face $40
4-Iron--Dot face $40
#1 through 9-Iron--RTJ model, pipe CM .... $150-250 each
#1 through 9-Iron--RTJ/FO model, pipe CM ....$150-250 each
Putter--(B) Stewart patent, hollow back.. $350
Putter--Bar back model, bent neck style, dash face $150
Putter--Iron blade $50
Putter--Park style bent neck blade $100
Putter--Offset blade, accurate/arrow CM $65-85
Putter--Gun metal blade $75
Putter--Gem style iron head $100
Putter--Concentrated back $90
Putter--Long iron blade, beveled heel and toe $80
Putter--Small iron mallet head $600
Putter--Long shallow blade, flange sole $125
Putter--Sarazen model, blade $100
Putter--'Bassackward' model, hosel bent backward $3,500

[Tom Stewart produced thousands of iron heads for most of the top club makers or maker/professionals of the day. The following list is a gen-

eral guideline for named clubs from these most common makers or series. Sometimes, smooth face irons can be found from these makers although, on 20th century clubs, this only reflects in only marginally higher value. Numbered irons, as opposed to those with names, from the same makers are worth slightly less.]

Anderson & Blyth irons, scored face ....$60 each
D & W Auchterlonie irons, scored face ....$60 each
Tom Auchterlonie irons, scored face ....$60 each
Alex Campbell irons, scored face ....$60 each
Alex Herd irons, line or dot face ....$75 each
Herd & Herd irons ....$60 each
Herd & Yeoman irons, scored face ....$60 each
Jock Hutchison autograph series irons, scored face ....$75 each
Robert T Jones, Jr. autograph series irons .... $600-1,000 each
Willie Kidd irons, scored face ....$60 each
Jack Morris irons, scored face ....$85 each
Tom Morris autograph series irons, scored face .... $50-100 each
Ray, E (Ted) irons, scored face ....$75 each
Ben Sayers irons, scored face .... $50-80 each
Alex Smith irons, scored face ....$60 each
Alex Taylor irons, scored face ....$55 each
Harry Vardon autograph series irons, scored face .... $100-150 each
Tom Vardon irons, scored face ....$100 each
William Yeoman irons, scored face ....$60 each
Jack Youds irons, scored face ....$60 each

Stilton, Robert

Driver--(S) Transitional splice head, fiber insert $300

Stirling & Gibson*

When Mr. Sterling (of Stirling & Gibson) passed away, William Gibson took over the company and renamed it after himself, before moving from Edinburgh to Kinghorn.

[Edinburgh s; forerunner to the firm of William Gibson & Company]
Cleek--Smooth face, short blade $150
Mashie--Smooth face, deep face, name in arc $100
Niblick--Smooth face, medium head $150
Putter--Bent blade style, 2 small stars and Masonic compass CMs $200

Stoddard, W.
Niblick--Splice head $100

Stoddart, W.E.
[Various clubs in New York]
Mashie--Pandy model, 2 flags CM, bottom weighted round sole .. $100
Putter--Stoddart model, reverse musselback, thicker on top, flags CM $125

Stoker, J.
Putter--Triumph model, offset musselback $300

Stokes & Company*
[London]
Putter--Smith model, smooth face $60

Strachan, W.
Spoon--(S) Transitional splice head, leather face insert $400

Strauss Toy Store
[New York]
Iron--Midget size $100

Strath & Beveridge
[New York]
Playclub--(L) Beech head $8,000

Strath, David*
[St. Andrews]
Playclub--(L) Dark stain $4,000-6,000
Spoon--(L) Dark stain $7,500-10,000

Strath, George*+

One of the tidier roller putter designs belonged to H.L. Sutton. His club was made from aluminum.

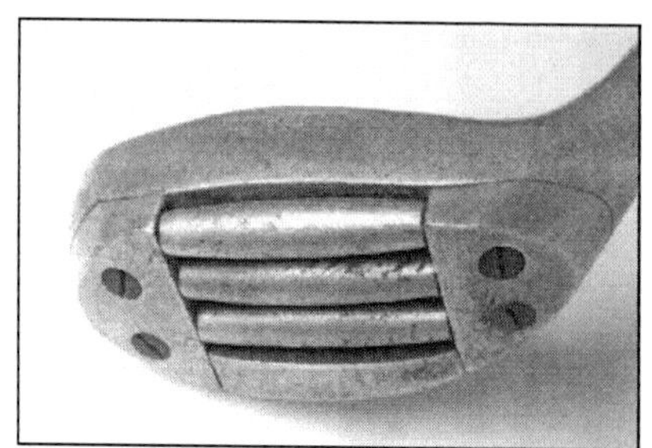

[St. Andrews, Troon s, later US]
Playclub--(L) Beech head $6,000
Driver--(L) Beech head with grassed face $4,000
Driving Iron--Spalding Gold Medal series, smooth face $100
Mashie--Spalding Gold Medal, deep dot face $100
Putter--(L) Beech head $4,000
Putter--Center shaft, crescent shaped head, moon/star CM $1,600

Stream-Line Company+
[St. Louis, MO]
Driver--Melhorn No. 50 model, metal head with sole plate $250
Putter--(A) Melhorn model 10P, rail sole $150

Strong, Herbert
Iron clubs-Line face, arm holding hammer CM .... $45 each

Stuart, J.G.
Driver--Socket head $50

Sunderland Golf Company
[Sunderland e]
Putter--(A) Mills "Mallet" (hammer head) model $1,250

'Supreme'
Mid Iron--Matched, reg'd, chromed $20

'Sure Winner'
[also see Union Golf Company]

Driver--Socket head, stripe top, jockey on running horse CM $60

'Sure-Thing'
Putter--(A) Triangular shaped head $100

Sutton, H.L.
[Rhyl w; Sutton Coldfield e]
Driver--Socket head $75
Putter--(A B) Mallet head with 3 rollers in sole $2,500

Swank, David
Mid Iron--Model 7, musselback, line face $35

Sweny, H.R.+
[Albany, NY]
Driver--(U) Center shafted splice head $2,500-4,000
Driver—Simplex-type, long head $900
Driver--Splice head, heel shafted, marked Sweny Sporting Goods $200
Cleek--Smooth face, name in block letters $150
Iron—Smooth face, name in double oval $250
Niblick—Smooth face, small head $300

Sykes, William*
[Horbury e]
Mid Iron--The Select, Gourlay moon/star CM, dot face $60

H.R. Sweny is best known for the center shaft woods he made and sold but his company also offered irons clubs marked like this.

T

Tait, T.
[Leven s]
Driver--Socket head $100
Mid Iron--Smooth face, Millar thistle CM $65
Putter--Thick blade, thistle CM $75

'Taplow'
[John Wanamaker Co., Philadelphia proprietary model name]
Driver--Socket head $60
Pitcher--(D) Corrugated face, hand CM $125

Taylor Brothers
Jigger--Line face $45
Putter--Convex back, bottom half sculpted out $150
Putter—Stewart pipe CM, bent neck $90

Taylor Company, Alex+
[New York retailer; additional clubs listed under ATCO]
Driver--Autograph model, juvenile socket head $75
Mashie--Ravisloe model, smooth face $60
Mashie Niblick--Atco Brand, dot face $40
Niblic--Model 25, crown CM, large head, flange sole, dash face $50
Named Irons--Alex Taylor model, Stewart pipe CM, scored face .... $50 each

The New York City retail house of Alex Taylor sold many golf clubs including those from their own house brand, like this Alex Taylor autograph driver.

Taylor, Fred
[Oxford e]
Irons—Rite Spot series with 'O' at sweetspot ....$60 each

Taylor, Josh*
[Richmond, Surrey e; J.H. Taylor's younger brother]
Brassie--(B) 'Bombe' model (Confidus patent), crossed sabers CM, bulged sole $400
Irons—Cochrane knot CM ....$50 each
Iron clubs--Mascot model, running greyhound CM ....$60 each

Taylor, J.H.
[see Cann & Taylor]

Taylor, J.W.
[Leeds e and others]
Putter—(A) Mallet with raised aiming bar $80

Taylor, Thomas
[Chicago]
Driver--(U) Streamline shape pointed at back $3,000
Mashie-(U) Comb style sole, line face,
Anderson arrow CM $4,000

Blackheath club maker Angus Teen produced the patent Bar Back Cleek in the mid 1890s.

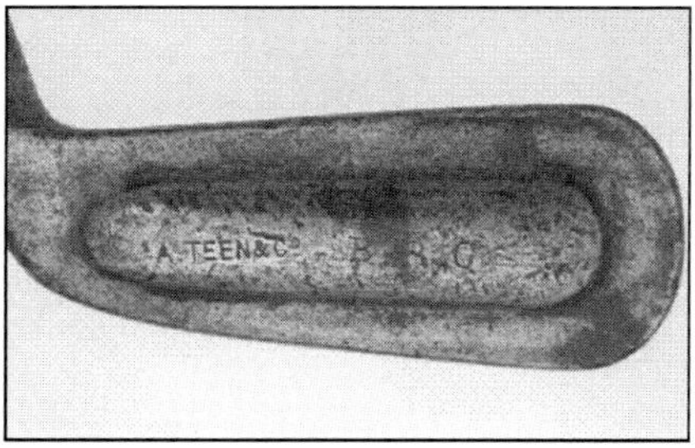

Tedder, Walter*
[Nottingham e]
Driver--Socket head $70

Teen & Company, A.*
[Blackheath, London]
Driver--(B) Claude Johnson patent, round head $2,500

Driver--(S) Angus Teen, Maltese cross CM $1,000
Cleek--Bar back model, horizontal weight along back $1,000
Cleek—Crescent back model $2,500
Iron—Deep smooth face, name in block letters $200
Approaching Putter--Roundback blade made
in nickel bronze alloy $400

'Thistle'
[Clubs named Thistle were produced by many makers. Also see George Bussey, Charles Millar, Spalding, Edward Tryon, J. Winton]

'Thistle Brand'
[Made by Charles Millar]
Brassie--Socket head $75

Thistle Golf Company
[Glasgow; made by Charles Millar]
Spoon--Marked "Baffie", splice head, face insert $450
Putter--Thistle Brand, gun metal blade, thistle CM $75

Thistle Putter Company+

This McDougal T-Square putter had changeable weights housed in the to cavities with black covers.

[New York]
Putter--(A U) McDougal T Square model, mallet head
with aiming T on top $150
Putter--(A U) McDougal T Square model,
removable weights in head $600

Thistle Special
[also see Edward K. Tryon]

Jigger--Smooth face, name in oval $75

Thom, Charles
[Shinnecock Hills, NY]
Driver--Socket head $125
Approach Iron--Dot face, Spalding accurate mark $100

Thompson Valve Company
Named Irons--Thompson Valve Steel, line face $45

Thompson, James
[St. Andrews]
Driver--Socket head, hollow back model $225
Putter--Accurate model, iron blade, bent neck $60

Thompson, J.
Driver--(S) Transitional splice head $350

Thomson, A.
Brassie--Socket head $100

Thomson, Jimmy
Woods--(U) Big Ball model, socket head with patent
extra whippy Limber Shaft .... $300 each

Thornton & Company, Ltd.*
[Edinburgh & Glasgow s and other cities]
Brassie--(S) Beech head, marked for
Willie Davis, Newport $850
Driver--Short splice head $150
Driver--Deep face socket head $125
Brassie--Socket head, line name stamp.. $80
Iron--Stainless, Brodie triangle/BS&A CM $50
Mashie--Stainless, dot face, lion on shield CM $50
Mashie--Wonder series, dot face $40
Niblick--Giant head $1,500
Putter--Wonder series bent neck, dash face $50
Putter--Iron blade, name in block letters $50
Putter—The Champion, shield with cross CM $40
Putter—The Princes, shield with cross CM $40

Tom Thumb putters were used in some of the earliest miniature golf courses.

Tice Golf Company+
[Albany, NY]
Driver--(U) Socket head, laminated hickory shaft $1,250

'Timperly'
Driver--(A B) Baby model, small
Schenectady style head $600
Putter--(A B) Baby model, small Schenectady-type head $200
Putter--(A B) Mallet head, very thick hosel $200

Tingey, Albert*
[St. Andrews; Brancaster and Watford e]
Putter--(S) Beech splice head $1,000
Putter--(S) Socket head $250

Tollifson, Arner C.
[Lake Geneva, WI, et al]
Mashie--Pennant CM, Spalding hammer CM $50
Putter—Duo-flange shape, pennant CM $100

Tolmie, J.
[Great Yarmouth e]
Iron--Smooth face, large head, long blade $300

'Tom Thumb'
Putter--Chromed blade $50

Toogood, Alfred*
[Chingford e, et al]

Brassie--Socket head $60

Toogood, Walter*
[Ilkley e, et al]
Brassie--Splice head $100

Tooley & Sons, A.*
[London and Forest Hill e]
Driver--Small socket head $100
Iron--Forest Brand, Maxwell pattern, stainless, trees CM $75
Iron--(B) Two large hemispherical weights on back of blade $750
Jigger--Smooth concave face, trees CM $85
Mid Iron--Powerful model, line face, trees CM $250
Mashie—Forest brand CM, teardrop shaped grip $250
Putter--(B) Suitall model, Round sole, pointed top edge $300

Trapp, S.
[Wakefield e, et al]
Driver--Socket head, romil face insert $60

Trapp, Tom
[Croydon e, et al]
Spoon--Ideal model, socket head, face insert $60
2-Iron--Dot face, Stewart pipe CM $40

Travers, Jerry+

This mashie from the London firm of A. Tooley & Son is fitted with their patented teardrop shaped grip.

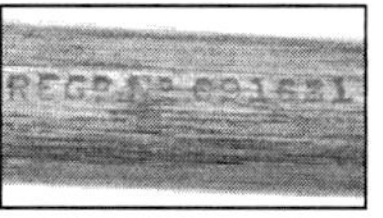

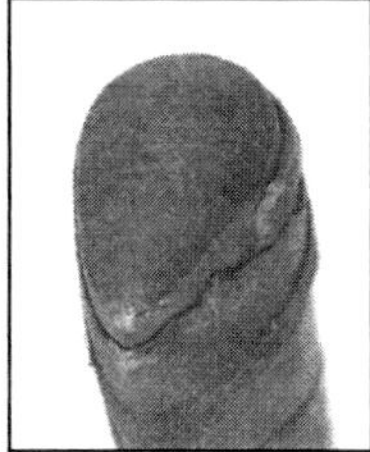

[Amateur winner of US Open, 1915]
Putter--Wood Schenectady style head $175
Putter--(A) Schenectady head, signature & Hartford address on back $200

Travers, T.
[Dublin I, et al]
Brassie--Socket head $60
Spoon--Marked "T T" on splice head, shaft stamp $150
Putter--(B) The Fragile model, wood mallet head , square wood handle $450
Putter--Narrow scare wood head $300

Travis, Walter
[US & British Amateur Champion; designed many clubs most of which were made by Spalding or Wright & Ditson]
Putter--Wood Schenectady-type, brass face plate w/ 5 screws, marked "The Travis" $250
Putter- Extra long wood Schenectady-type, brass face plate w/ 5 screws, marked "The Travis" $450

Tremane-King Co.
Iron clubs—Cayuga series, Burke fleur de lis CM ....$30 each

Tribble, A.
Brassie--Socket head $50

'Truhitol'
[London; brand of Rhys, Spencer & Co.]

Jerry Travers, a US Open and Amateur champion sold this autographed Schenectady type putter after he retired.

Putter--(A) Rectangular head, shafted at heel, sight line on top $275

'Tru-Line'
[Patent Engineering Company, Chicago]
Putter--(U) Removable aiming rod $2,500

'Tru-Put'
[Made by F.H. Ayers]
Putter--(A) Schenectady style with fiber face insert $250

Tryon Company, Edward K.+
[Philadelphia a]
Driver--Splice head, made by J. & D. Clark $250
Driver--Socket head, keystone CM $65
Iron--Smooth face, marked 'Made in Scotland' $100
Iron--Smooth face, oval marks for J & D Clark and Tryon $200
Mashie--The Imperial series, Wilson hammer CM $25
Mashie--M1 model, line face $40
Mashie--Thistle model, line face $40
Putter--Tip-Top model, iron blade, keystone CM $50

Tucker Brothers+
[Brothers Willie and Sam, New York]
Driver--Defiance model, short splice head $200
Driver--Defiance model, short socket head $125

Tucker, William+
[Ardsley and Binghamton, NY; Philadelphia, PA]
Driver--Defiance brand, Ardsley address, splice head $300
Driver--(A S) Metal fairway club $300
Brassie--Defiance brand, splice head $250
Brassie--Defiance brand, socket head $150
Approaching Mashie--Defiance brand, smooth face $125
Driving Cleek--Defiance brand, smooth face $150
Driving Mashie--Defiance brand, smooth face $100
Jigger--Defiance brand, smooth face $150
Lofting Iron--Defiance brand, smooth face $150
Mashie--Defiance brand, Taylor's model, short blade, deep face $150

George Turpie and his brother Harry came from St. Andrews to America to become golf professionals. George used the mark of the clay pipe.

Mashie Iron--Defiance brand, smooth face $125
Mashie Jigger--Line face, name in script $100
Mid Iron--Defiance brand, smooth face $100
Niblick--Defiance brand, smooth face, medium head $150
Putter--Defiance brand, gun metal blade $125
Putter--Defiance brand, gooseneck $150
Putting Cleek--Iron blade $100

Tulloch, J.
[Glasgow]
Driving Iron--Oval name stamp, line face $45
Mashie--Diamond face, Gourlay moon/star CM $50
Putter--Made by D. Anderson, model 100, rounded back $80

Turnbull, Tom
Driver--Splice head $90

Turner, John Henry*
[Abingdon e, et al]
Driver--(B) Centre Balanced model, socket head, dowel plug in toe $150
Driver--Socket head, stripe top $50
Driving Iron--Smith style anti-shank, Sherlock Oxford CM $200
Putter--(B) Combination wood/metal head, metal hosel $450
Putter--(A) Block aluminum head like small Gassiat $200
Iron clubs--(B) Grampian Range series, mountains CM, each club having the name of a Scottish mountain in the range .... $100 each

Turpie, George+
[Edgewater, Chicago, et al]
Jigger—Line face, clay pipe CM (different than Stewart) $80
Mid Iron--Smooth face $60
Mashie--Line face, MacGregor rose CM $45
Mashie Niblick--Dot face, Stewart pipe CM $50

Turpie, Harry+
Mashie--Line face, MacGregor rose CM $50

'Tuxedo'
[Wilson Co. store brand]
Mashie--Stainless, line face $25

Twine, W.T.
Driver--Splice head $100

Tyler, R.G. "Tug"+
[Bradford, PA and Muncie, IN]
Driver--(U) Ball to Ball model, aluminum and wood combination head, wood face plug $125
Driver--(U) Rear Impact model, aluminum/wood combination head $150
Driver--(U) Tyler Wood model, aluminum/wood combination head $150
Driver—(U) Wood/aluminum combination with red fiber face $250
Niblick--(U) Center shafted, round face $3,000
Putter--(U) Wood Schenectady-type, brass face w/ 4 screws $150
Putter--(U) Schenectady-type, wood and aluminum combination head $300

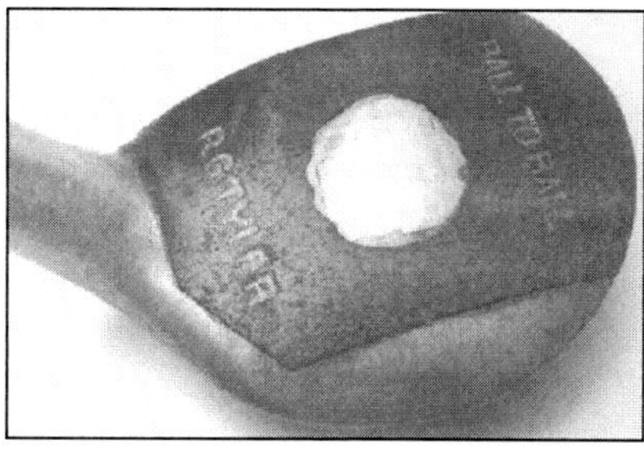

Ralph "Tug" Tyler created several combination wood and aluminum drivers and brassies like this Ball to Ball model with its central weight.

U

U.D.S.
Driver--(A) Ebony Finish model, wood face plugs $250

U.S. Golf Club Manufacturing Company+
[Albany, NY]
Brassie--Model 139 splice head $350
Iron--Smooth face, straight line name stamp, eagle shaft mark $300
Niblick--Oval head, smooth face, shaft stamp $350
Putter--Gun metal blade, name and city in arc $250

U.S. Golf Manufacturing Company+
[Westfield, MA]
Driver--(U) Gold Standard series, combination bamboo, hickory and steel shaft, decal on crown $200
Mid Iron--Holdfast series, line face $50
Mid Iron--Ajax series, patent sewn grip, braided whipping $75
Putter--Reliance series, eagle CM, flange back $60
Putter--Thorobred series, stainless blade, eagle in oval CM $50

Underhill, Gardner F.
[New York]
Putter--(A) Mallet head $75
Putter--Model 20, gun metal blade, name in arc $100

Union Golf Company+
[Nashville, TN]
Driver--Shure Winner brand, stripe top, jockey on horse CM $60
Mid Iron--Shur-Flite series, chromed $40
Niblick--Shure Winner brand, medium size head, jockey on horse CM, dash face $40
Putter--Shur-Putt model, chromed blade $30

Urquhart, R.*
[Edinburgh; Robert Urquhart and his family worked at perfecting adjustable clubs for over 20 years. Several different adjustment mechanisms exist on Urquhart clubs]
Iron--(B) Adjustable club, name in circle on face............$1,200-2,500

As early as 1892 the Urquhart family of Edinburgh was experimenting with adjustable irons, convinced that carrying one club was better than a whole bag full. The ratchet teeth and the release thumb latch in the lower hosel are visible in this photo.

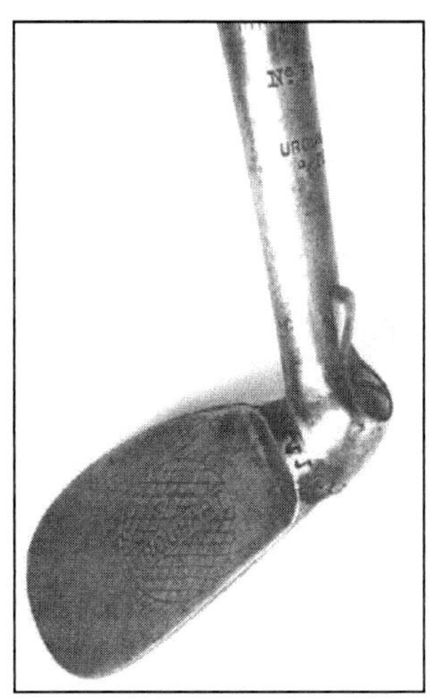

Urquhart ad from a 1906 publication.

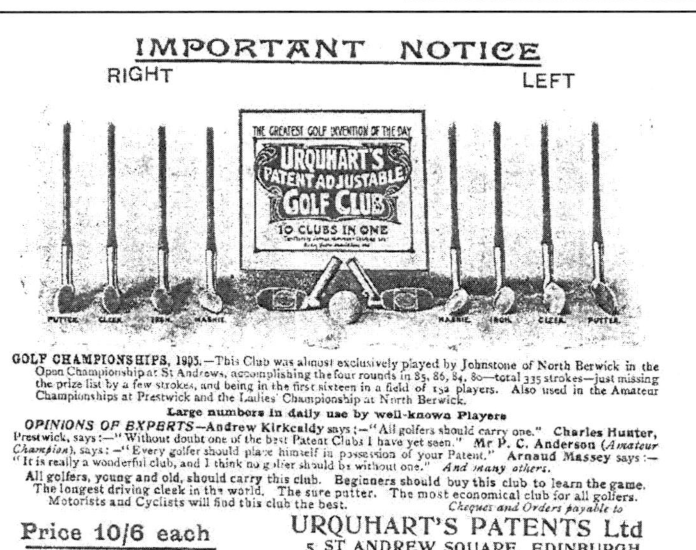

V

V.L. & A.

[Von Lengerke & Antoine, Chicago retailer]

Driver--Stripe top socket head $45
Brassie--Socket head $50
Mashie--Centraject back, name in double oval $45
Mashie--Perfect series, centraject back, dot face $45
Putter--Velanay brand, lion & crown CM $40
Putter--Blade, own brand $40

V.L. & D.

[Von Lengerke & Detmold, New York retailer]

Driver--Yankee Dreadnought model, socket head $80
Approaching Cleek--James Braid model, musselback $80
Iron—Smooth face, simple markings including 349 Fifth Ave. ... $75
Mashie Niblick--Vardon Autograph series,
Stewart pipe CM, line face $75
Niblick--Fairlie model, J.D. Dunn make, Maltese cross CM $200
Pitcher-Gibson star CM, dot face $40

Vaile, P.A.

[New Zealand amateur; wrote the book How to Putt and promoted swan neck clubs]

Driver--(B) Swan neck transitional shaped splice head $650
Brassie--(B) Swan neck socket head $500
Brassie--(B) Swan neck socket head, fancy face insert $550

Tom Stewart made clubs for just about every famous golfer over four decades in St. Andrews. This mashie niblick was made for Harry Vardon.

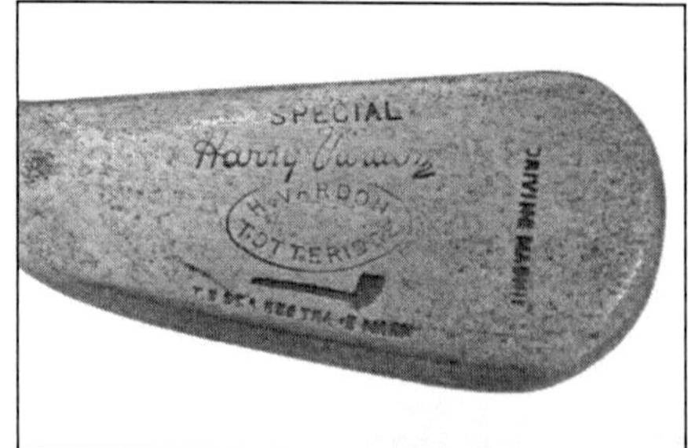

P.A. Vaile designed swan neck irons and woods. This iron was stamped for and sold by F.H. Ayres in London.

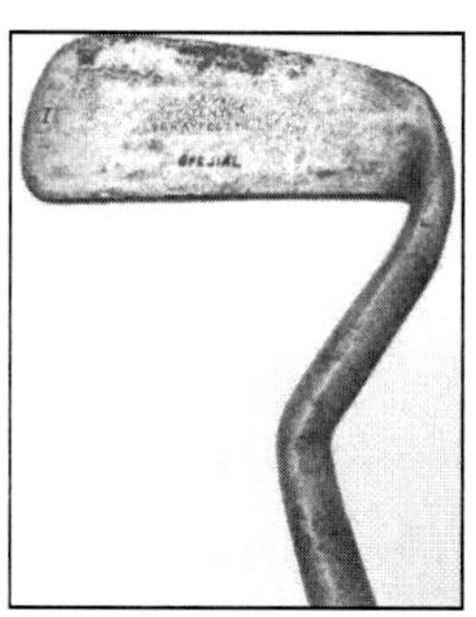

Iron--(B) Swan neck, made by Ayers $600
Putter--(B) Swan neck hosel, gun metal blade $600

Valor Company, The*
[Smethwick e]
Iron--Line face, benchwheel CM $75
Niblick--Fairlie-type (anti-shank), dot face $175

Vardon, Harry*
[Worked several English clubs; he produced clubs in his shops at Ganton, and later Totteridge, but most clubs with his name were made by Burke, Spalding, Wilson or Stewart]
Driver--Short splice head, marked Ganton $350
Driver--Splice head, H. Vardon in big letters $300
Brassie--Small splice head $250
Mashie—Stewart Pipe Brand with Vardon autograph $100
Sammy—Autograph model, made by Ayres, Maltese cross CM $75
Niblick--Small head, smooth face, Anderson arrow CM $300
Named Irons--Harry Vardon autograph,
Stewart pipe CM, scored face ....$100 each

Vardon, Tom*
[Ilkley, Sandwich e; Harry Vardon's brother]
Brassie--Bulger splice head, marked "Ilkley" $350
Brassie--Splice head $150
Mashie--Autograph model, deep line face,
Nicoll hand CM $75
Named Irons--Tom Vardon autograph model,
Stewart pipe CM scored face ....$75 each

One of the early American brands was produced by the Overman Wheel Company. "The Victor" brand clubs were sold in turn of the century Sears Roebuck catalogs.

'Velometer'
[Made by Martin's Velometer Golf Clubs]*
Driver--(B) Socket head, slightly pointed $200-300

Venters, Jack
[Shinnecock Hills, NY]
Brassie--Splice head $400

Vickers, Limited*
[Sheffield e]
Jigger--Stainless, line face, VK CM $50
Mid Iron--Model 19, stainless, VK CM $40
Mashie--Model 6, stainless, VK CM $40
Mashie--Model 6 B, KK CM $40
Mashie--Model 23, rustless, flange sole, dot face $40
Niblick--Model 28, stainless, VK CM $50
Niblick--Mammoth-type, dot face $1,500
Spade Mashie--Stainless, VK CM $45
Putter--Model 20, stainless blade with thickened sweet spot $75
Putter--Model 14, stainless blade, VK CM $55
Putter--Model 15, stainless straight blade, VK CM $50
Putter--Invicta model 20, gem style, VK CM $100

Victor+
[Chicopee and Boston, MA]
Iron--Concentric back, smooth face $125
Mashie--Smooth face, name in circle $125
Putter--Iron blade $100

Victor-O.W.C.+

[also see Overman Wheel Co.]
Cleek--Smooth face, round sole $150
Iron—Smooth face, long blade $200
Niblick--Gun metal, small head, smooth face $2,200
Putter--Gun metal blade $200

'Vim'
Driving Iron--Greenfield series, line face, name in script $25
Spade Mashie--Chrome, name in script $25
Putter--Thick blade, name in script $30

Vories, I.H.
Iron--Adjustable iron with 3 selectable hitting faces $2,500

Vulcan Golf Company+
[Portsmouth, OH]
Driver--Model V-10, stripe top, socket head, face insert $45
Driver--Socket head, green/white face insert $80
Driver--Model V-12, socket head, fancy face insert $60
Driving Iron--Stainless, line face $35
Jigger--Nipper model, long hosel $100
Jigger--"Chipper" 4 Loft $75
Mashie--Pirate series, stainless, line face $30
Mashie--Septem 5, stainless. Line face $30
Niblick--Septem 7, line face $30
Putter--Septem 8, stainless blade $50
Putter--Model 8, long thin blade and hosel $150
Putter--V-V model, 6" hosel $150
Putter--Burma model, sunset CM, dot face blade $35
Putter--Marked "Junior" in script $35

This Vulcan model V-V putter had the long blade and long, pencil thin hosel.

W W P
[see Wilson Co.]

W W S
[Wilson Western Sports; the name of the Thomas Wilson Company after 1931. See Wilson Co.]

'W.S. Flite'
Niblick--Eagle CM, line face $40

Waggott, Thomas*
[Edinburgh s, et al]
Driver--(S) Splice head, dark stain $1,000
Driver--Short splice head $150

'Wales'
Putter--Line face, chromed blade $20

Walgreen Company
[Chicago]
Numbered Irons--Chromed head, line face .... $20 each

Walker, Cyril
Driver—Spalding socket head, name in oval (Page D) $85
Spoon--MacGregor model A733 .... $100
Niblick—Spalding, name in circle $150

Walker, George
Driver--Stripe top socket head $45

Walker, J.
Playclub--Thick head, golden finish $5,000
Putter--(L) Beech head, dark color $4,000

Walker, Thomas

Driver--(S) Bulger splice head $400
Long Spoon--(S) Well dished face $900

Wallace, S.B.
Driver—(B) Bullet model, streamline design, tiny oval sole plate . $250
2-Iron--Talisman model, large spade pip CM, line face $30

Wallis & Fulford
[Brough e]
Driver--(B) Double V splice(2-axis) $750

Wallis, Willie
[Brough e]
Niblick--Star Maxwell model, Gibson star CM,
diamond/dot face $50
Putter--Small steel mallet head (like Donaldson Bunny
with no inserts) $150

Wanamaker Company, John D.
[New York-Philadelphia retailer]
Driver--Taplow model, socket head $50
Brassie--Socket head, made by D. & W. Auchterlonie $60
Irons--Stewart pipe CM ....$45 each

Watt, James
[North Berwick s]
Driving Iron--Line face, Winton diamond CM $40

Watt, Tom
[*Timperley e]*
Driver—Large V shaped stripe top stain design (Page D) $125
Putter—Magic model, weight ridge along back $75

Tom Watt marked this putter with the fact he was a "Scottish Internationalist," meaning he played in the Scotland vs. England matches.

Watt, William*
[Perth, Edinburgh s, et al]
Spoon--Socket head, face insert $45
Mashie Niblick--Bobbie model, D&W Brodie CM $50

'Waverly'
[Vulcan Golf brand name]
Iron clubs--Line face ....$25 each

Way, W.H. (Bert)+
[Cleveland, OH]
Driver--Splice transitional head $250
Cleek--Smooth face, short blade, Condie rose CM $80
Niblick--Medium head, smooth face, Carruthers hosel $125

Way, Ernest
[Detroit, MI]
Mashie--Line face, Burke scales CM $45
Niblick—Anvil CM, for PG Mfg Co. $250

Way & Ross
[Alec Ross & Ernest Way, Detroit, MI]
Mashie--Mussel back, dot face $100

Webb, W.H.*
[Frinton-on-Sea e]
Driver--(B) Own model one-piece $1,800
Niblick--(B) Fairlie model, Nicoll hand CM, line face $200

Weir, A.N.*
[Aberdeen s]
Driver--Socket head $60
Driver--(B) Short splice head, offset neck $300
Brassie--Short splice head $150
Putter--(A S) Marked Aberdeen $100

Wellington-Stone Company+
[Chicago; clubs were part of a golf motif smoking stand called the Par-

lor Putter]
Putter--Parlor Putter, line face, made without grip $200

'Westward Ho!'
Mashie--Line face, marked 'Made in England" $40

'Joyce Wethered'
[The English ladies champion; an amateur, she allowed her name to be put on clubs after retirement from active competition]
Numbered Irons--Autograph series ....$80 each

Whitcomb, E.R.
4-Iron--Dot face, Stewart pipe CM $35

White, Jack*
[Sunningdale e, et al; Open Champion 1904]
Driver--Stripe top, socket head, name in script $75-125
Driver--(B) Sit-Rite model, concave sole, socket head $150
Driver—Small ivorine aiming inlay on top of crown, socket head . $200
Iron--Own Model, sun CM $45
Iron--Autograph model, stainless, Palakona (bamboo) shaft $95
Iron—(B) Non-skid model, raised dots on face $600
Mid Iron--K 2, sun CM, stainless $45
Putter--(B) Civic model, flange sole, holes drilled
through face, Gibson star CM $400-600
Niblick—Broad sole, like sand wedge $200
Putter--Boat shaped blade, pointed toe, convex face $250
Putter--The Sunningdale model, musselback-type
weighted sole, 7" thin hosel, sun CM $200
Putter--Super model, marked for Longniddry shop,
W on face $125

Robert White was one of the last old style cleek makers and he trained Tom Stewart and Robert Condie.

Numbered Irons--Stainless, flange sole, Gibson star CM ....$50 each

White, Robert*
[St. Andrews; blacksmith and pioneer iron club maker]
Cleek--Smooth face $200-600
Iron--Smooth face $200-500
Lofter--Short blade, smooth face $200-500
Lofter--Long blade $300-800
Mashie--Smooth face $200-800
Niblick--Small head $350-1,200
Niblick--Medium head $250-600
Putter--long iron blade $300-500

White, Robert+
[Scottish immigrant working in Cincinnati, OH and several Chicago suburbs; head of P.G. Mfg. Co.; a founder of the American P.G.A. and early developer in the Myrtle Beach, SC area]
Driving Iron--Dot face, name in diamond CM,
marked Ravisloe CC $85
Mashie--Smooth face, anvil CM $60
Mashie--Smooth face, marked Cincinnati $80
Mid Iron--Dot face, anvil CM, Homewood, IL $60

Whiting, Albert
[Folkstone]
Spoon--(B) Wooden-iron model, socket head $200

Whiting, S.
Driver--Socket head $50

A different Robert White left St. Andrews, came to America and was first president of the PGA. His first professional assignment was in Cincinnati.

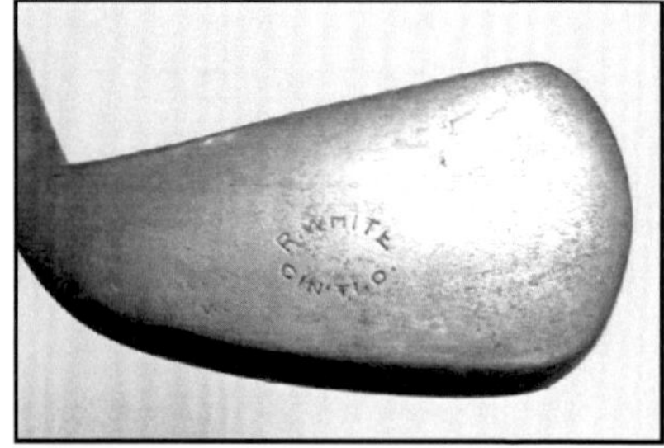

Robert Wilson was another of the old style blacksmith cleek makers of St. Andrews working in the last quarter of the 19th century.

Whittet, William
[Falkirk s]
Driver--(B) Dovetail/splice head $500

Williams Company, J.H.+
[Brooklyn, NY; maker of many iron heads for early U.S. club manufacturers. Their CM was a small W in diamond stamped into the hosel]
Jigger—Shallow face, Williams circular mark $150
Mashie--Smooth face, Williams name stamped in circle $200
Putter--"Metropolitan", straight blade small W in diamond CM .. $150

Williamson, Tom*
[Nottingham s]
Brassie--Splice head $175
Iron clubs--Smooth face, Stewart pipe CM ....$75 each
Putter--Offset blade, Stadium anchor CM $60

'Wills'
Putter--(U) Overspin model, gun metal, deep face blade, horizontal weight bar on back $300

Wilson Company, Harold A.+
[Toronto, ONT; sporting goods importer and retailer; also see Hawco]
Iron--Smooth face, Forgan plume CM, Hawco mark in circle $200
Mashie Niblick--Ace model 35, dash face $50
Numbered Irons—The Acme, chromed heads ....$30 each

Wilson, James*
[St. Andrews; Hugh Philp's assistant for 7 years, he ran his own shop from 1852-1866]

R.B. (Robert Black Wilson) made clubs and served at several early American clubs including Shinnecock Hills.

Playclub--(L) Beech head $7,500-15,000

Wilson, Robert*
[St. Andrews; one of the earliest cleek makers in the home of golf]
Cleek--Smooth slightly concave face $400-800
Iron--Smooth face $300-700
Lofter--Smooth face $300-700
Lofter--Concave face $500-900
Niblick--Small head, concave $800-2,000
Putting Cleek--Long iron blade $400-800

Wilson, R.B.*+
[St. Andrews and US; pro and club maker to several English, American and German clubs. Most clubs also marked "O K Special"]
Driver--Small splice head $250
Driver--Transitional splice head, leather face $250-450
Brassie--Transitional splice head, leather face $250-450
Cleek--Smooth face long blade, "OK Special" $100
Cleek--Guttie face insert, Stewart pipe CM $2,000
Iron--Smooth face, Condie single fern CM $250
Mashie--The Haskell model, spring-face type face plate
backed with gutta percha $1,250
Mashie--Wide toe head, smooth face $200
Mashie--Smooth face $90
Mashie Cleek--Smooth face, short blade $150
Niblick--Small heavy head, smooth face $350
Putter--Marked 'Rex Iron,' long shallow blade $250
Putter--Short iron blade, deep face $150
Putter--(B) 1000 model, iron blade, square hole cut in face $750
Putter--(B) A 1 model, blade with no hosel $800

Putter--Gun metal blade $80
Putter--Accurate model, offset blade $75
Putter--Oval convex faced blade $500
Putter--Raised face (after Skinner), diamond face $250

Wilson, R.G.
[S. Croydon e, et al]
Driver--Splice head, red face insert, aluminum
backweights $250
Brassie--Socket head $50
Mashie Niblick--Long blade, line face $60

Wilson Company, Thomas E.+
[Chicago]
<><>Early series and individual clubs
Driver--Name in straight line, socket head $60
Cleek—11, Pinehurst series, wavy lines on face $125
Mashie--Line face, thick blade, large W' CM $40
Mashie--(D) Baxpin model 1M, corrugated face $150
Mashie--(D) Baxpin model 2A, corrugated face $150
Mashie--Jock Hutchison autograph, line face $75
Mashie--(D) Wonder model, baxpin corrugated face $150
Mashie--Open Hearth series, hammer CM, flange sole, line face $40
Mashie--Carnoustie series with large W CM, line face $40
Mashie—Diamond back with medallion face marking $75
Mashie--Wilsonian series, midget model $125
Mashie Niblick--Tom Bendelow autograph $75
Mashie Niblick--(D) Baxpin model 1M, corrugated face $150
Mashie Niblick--(D) Baxpin model 2A, corrugated face $150

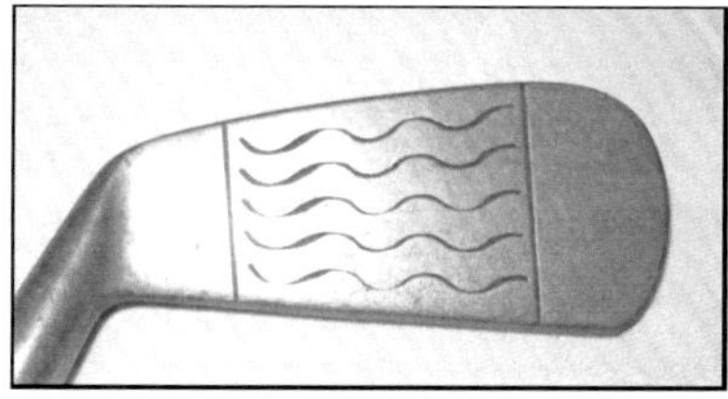

The special "Pinehurst" model 11 cleek had an unusual face of wavy grooves.

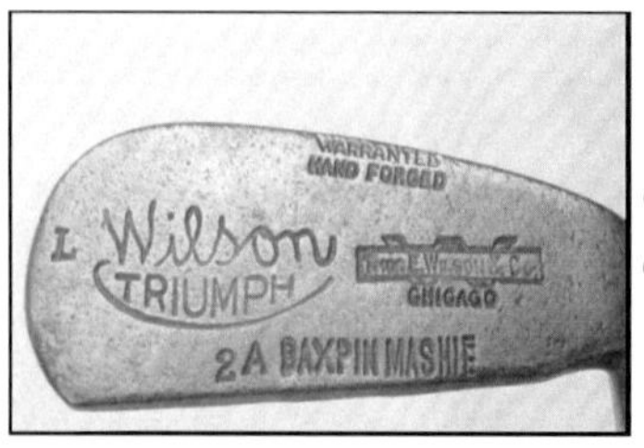

The Wilson Triumph line of clubs included this Baxpin deep groove mashie.

Mashie Niblick--(D) Baxpin model 2A1/2, ribangled face $175
Mid Iron--Ashland Mfg. Co., line face, monogram CM $60
Mongrel Iron—Plumbob CM $90
Putter--Special 6 model, flange sole $60
Putter--Amby-dex model, two-sided, wood head $350
Putter--James Braid model 9, offset blade $45
Putter--(A) Success model, mallet head $85
Putter--(A) Mallet, Wilson in small script $75
Putter--Kelly Club model $50
Putter--Juvenile, straight line name $35
Putter--(A) McNamara 3-way model, mallet head,
three aiming lines on crown $100
Putter--(A) Schenectady with patent date on back,
large hollow W CM $175
Putter--Wilsonian series, gun metal blade, lined ball face $100
Putter--XTA model, Sarazen autograph, extra long thin hosel $175
Putter--Model 2, extra long hosel $150

◇◇Sets of clubs
Aim Rite series, irons .... $30 each
Blue Ribbon series irons, stainless, line face .... $30 each
Carnoustie series woods .... $35 each
Carnoustie series irons .... $25 each
Archie Compston, champion series .... $60 each
Crest Inter-related series irons, stainless .... $50 each
Cup Defender series irons, line face .... $25 each
Derby series irons .... $30 each
Dixie series woods or irons .... $25 each
Fairview series irons .... $60 each
Johnny Farrell autograph National Open series, chromium .... $50 each
Johnny Farrell model irons, stainless .... $40 each
Lady Lucky Stroke eries irons, line face .... $25 each

The Wilson plumb-bob mark is relatively scarce. Finding it on this mongrel iron makes the club even more collectible.

Lincoln Park series clubs ....$25 each
Linkhurst series irons, stainless, line face ....$25 each
Mac Smith series woods, fancy alum. backweight (Page C) .. $90 each
Ogg-mented, stainless, weighted toe ....$40 each
Open Hearth series irons, hammer CM ....$25 each
Pinehurst series irons ....$50 each
Plus Success series woods, socket head ....$35 each
Plus Success series irons (named) ....$35 each
Plus Success series irons (numbered) ....$30 each
Range series irons, stainless ....$25 each
Red Ribbon series irons, stainless, line face ....$30 each
Gene Sarazen series woods, splice head ....$200 each
Gene Sarazen series woods, plain or stripe top ....$50 each
Gene Sarazen series irons, stainless, line face ....$45 each
Gene Sarazen 6-9 series clubs, juvenile size ....$30 each
Gene Sarazen 11-13 series clubs, juvenile size ....$25 each
Sharpshooter series woods, socket head ....$30 each
Skokie series irons, stainless, line face ....$30 each
Streak series irons, stainless ....$25 each
Super Stroke series irons, chromed ....$30 each
Super Stroke series, Everbrite steel ....$50 each
Taplow series woods or irons ....$25 each
Ted Ray Seventy-Two series woods ....$50 each
Ted Ray Seventy-Two series irons, stainless or chromed ....$40 each
Triumph series irons ....$35 each
Harry Vardon Seventy-Two series woods, green grip ....$60 each
Harry Vardon Seventy-Two series irons, green grip ....$50 each
Vogue Set Irons--Green leather grips, line face ....$30 each
Vogue Set--4 irons (2,5,7,9) and putter $225
WWP irons, open face-beveled toe series, stainless,
dot face, WWP in circle CM ....$35 each
George Walker series woods ....$30 each

Several club makers produced copies of J.H. Taylor's putter after his 1894 Open win. Willie Wilson was the first to produce the copy.

Walker Cup series woods, ivory inlay on crown ....$85 each
Walker Cup series woods, plain crown, face inserts ....$45 each
Walker Cup series irons, rainbow face grooves ....$125 each
Walker Cup series irons, dot face ....$35 each
Western Star series irons, dot face ....$45 each
Wilson Midget series clubs, toddler size ....$50 each
The Wilsonian series woods, socket head ....$35 each
The Wilsonian series irons, line or dot face ....$25 each
Wilsonian Junior series clubs, juvenile size .... $30 each

Wilson, William*
[St. Andrews; blacksmith and early maker of iron heads]
Cleek--Long blade, smooth face $200-600
Iron--Long blade, deep face $200-500
Lofter--Long blade $200-500
Lofter--(B) Anti-shank style, smooth face $650
Mashie--Thick heavy blade, St. Andrew CM $300-400
Niblick--Small head $600-1,500
Putter—(B) Taylor's Putter, bent blade, St Andrew CM $250
Putter--Iron blade $150-250
Putter--Gun metal blade, straight line name stamp $150-250

Club makers R.B. Wilson, Andra' Kirkaldy and Geordie Lorimer joined forces for only a year or two to make clubs together.

The Winchester Company, best known for firearms, sold clubs made for it by Wilson, Burke, William Gibson and others.

Putter--Gun Metal blade, St. Andrew CM $300
Putter--Iron blade, 'St. Andrew' CM $200

Wilson, William Christie*
[Hereford e]
Iron clubs--Solwin model, rising sun CM, line face $75

Wilson, Kirkaldy & Lorimer
[St. Andrews]
Iron clubs-Name in circle with O.K. Special, cross face $100

Winchester Arms Company+
[New York arms and hardware company selling its own branded clubs obtained from several makers]
Driver--Jock Hutchison model, fiber face insert $160
Driver--Model 6375, socket head $125
Driver--Model 6358, socket head, insert $150
Driving Iron--Model 6590, Vardon series, Monel, dash/line face $100
Mashie—Made by Wilson, Ranger series, flange sole $100
Mashie--Model 6611 (Burke), flange sole. Dot face $100
Mashie--Pickwick series model 6617 (Burke), dash face $75
Mashie--Model 6716 (Burke), dot face, ronded back,
Burke thistle CM $100
Mashie--Model 61, St. Andrew Golf Co. stag CM $125
Mashie--(D) Corrugated face $275
Mashie--Jock Hutchison model, made by Wilson, dot face $85
Mashie--Model 6601, monel. Line face $100
Mashie Niblick--Model 6637, Monel, line face $100
Mashie Niblick--Model 61, made by St. Andrew Golf Co.,
Stag CM $125

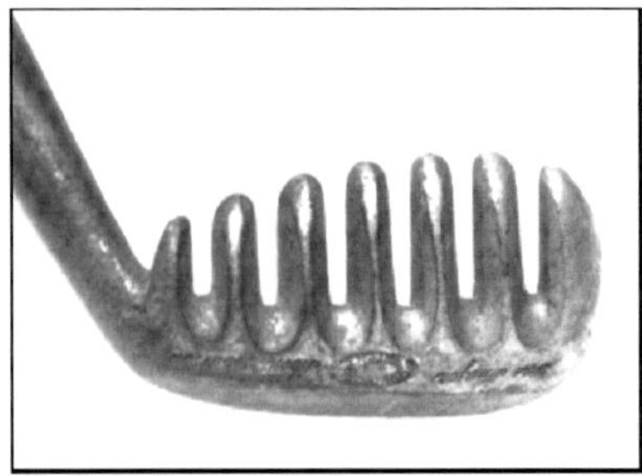

James Winton was the manufacturer of the Brown Patent irons (now called Rake Irons because of their rakelike form).

Mashie Niblick--Jock Hutchison autograph $125
Mid Iron--Brae Burn, round sole $75
Niblick--(D) Ribbed face, Gibson star CM $175
Niblick--Model 6718 (Burke), Monel $150
Rotary Iron--(D) Made by Burke for Winchester $400
Putter--Brae Burn, blade $75
Putter--Pickwick series, blade, dot face $85
Putter--Model 6632, gun metal, flange sole $250
Putter--Model 6662 (Burke model 69), wide sole
thistle CM $125
Putter--Model 6650, Jock Hutchison autograph series,
Monel, Burke thistle CM $120
Putter--(A) Model 6671, 1915 Braid-Mills, stamped
for Winchester $200
Putter--(U) P.A. Vaile model, double bent neck,
dash face, Burke thistle CM $350
Putter--Model 6660, Brown-Vardon style $250
Putter--Mills AK model, marked Winchester $250

Winckworth-Scott, E.H.
[see Lillywhite's]
Putter--(B) Winckworth-Scott model, autograph name stamp,
square solid steel shaft $750

Winders, N.
Brassie--Socket head $45

Winfield Special
Putter--Iron blade $40

Wingate, S.
Brassie--Socket head $45

Winton, James
[Montrose s]
Brassie-Short splice head, face insert $200
Brassie--Socket head $90
Lofter--Smooth face $70
Putter--(S) Transitional splice head $250

<><>Brown patent series irons
Cleek--(B) Horizontally slotted face $2,000-3,500
Driving Mashie--(B) Horizontally slotted face $2,000-3,000
Mashie--(B) Horizontally slotted face $2,000-4,000
Mashie--(B) Thistle model, vertically slotted face $2,000-4,000
Mashie Niblick--(B) The General model,
vertically slotted face $2,000-4,500
Mashie Niblick--(B) The Major model,
vertically slotted face $2,000-4,000
Mashie Niblick--(B) Roger Brown model, vertical
slots in top edge and sole $3,000-5,000
Mid Iron--(B) Horizontally slotted face $2,000-4,000
Niblick--(B) The Major model, vertically
slotted face $2,000-4,000
Putter--(B) Straight neck, horizontally slotted face $2,000-4,000
Putter--(B) Bent neck, horizontally slotted face $2,000-4,000

Winton Company, W.M.*
[Montrose & London, used the diamond cleek mark]
Driver--Socket head, stripe top $80
Brassie--Socket head, stripe top $80
Cleek—Model 27, round back $50
Cleek--Model 86, "Bogie" groove in bottom center of back $80
Cleek--Model 97, dot face $50
Driving Iron--Model 1, line face $45
Driving Iron--Model 4, dot face $45
Driving Iron--Model 26, standard blade $50
Driving iron—Model 164, groove in back bottom edge $75
Iron--Model A5, Harry Vardon series, standard blade $75
Iron—Model 83, thumb groove in back $75

Jigger--Model 5, dot face $50
Jigger--Ted Ray own model, line face $50
Jigger--Totteridge-Vardon model, line face, diamond CM $50
Jigger--The Jumper model, shallow face, pointed toe, line face $100
Mashie--Model 1, line face $40
Mashie--Model 4, dot face $40
Mashie--Model 20, flange sole, line face $50
Mashie--Model 41, dot face $45
Mashie--Model 42, Smith model (anti-shank) $175
Mashie--Model 43, slightly rounded back $45
Mashie--Model 82, groove in bottom center of back $90
Mashie--Model 92, Ted Ray own, line face $75
Mashie--Model 143, standard blade $50
Mashie--Model AM, line face $40
Mashie—The Backspin, weighted sole, line face $75
Mashie—The Kemmy, line face, pointed toe $200
Mashie--The Cert model, concave face $80
Mashie--(D) The Cert model, ribbed face $150
Mashie--Model C5-Vardon, musselback, line face $85
Mashie Niblick--Model B4, thick blade $50
Mashie Niblick--Model M18, standard blade $50
Mashie Niblick--Model P4, dot face $50
Mashie Niblick--(B) Smith model (anti-shank), dot face $150
Mashie Niblick--(D) The Cert model, corrugated face $150
Mashie Niblick--Model Z, stainless, diamond CM $60
Mid Iron--Model 3, line face $40
Mid Iron--Model 5, dot face $40
Mid Iron--Model 66, line face $40
Mid Iron--Model 72, dot face $40

W.M. Winton made this extra long blade putter for Tom Brewer, a pro in the SE London area.

Mid Iron--Model 83, groove in bottom center of back $90
Mid Iron--Model 89, slightly concave dot face $50
Mid Iron--Model H, straight back $40
Mid Iron--Model P3, centraject back $60
Mid Iron--Alex Herd own model $60
Niblick--Model 7, large head $50
Niblick--Model 12, dot face $50
Niblick--Model 17, dreadnought head, line face $50
Niblick--Model 24, Fairlie model (anti-shank) $100
Niblick--Model 77, dot face $50
Niblick--Model 106, dot face $50
Niblick--Ted Ray own model, diamond back, pointed toe $85
Niblick--Giant model, super large head, dotface $1,500
Niblick--The Last Word model, ex-large head, dot face ...$1,500-1,800
Niblick--Win-On model, smooth face sand iron $100
Niblick--Bogie model, cavity back, smooth face $250
Sammy--Line face, shallow blade $65
Sammy Niblick--Line face $85
Spade Mashie--Model 6, line face $50
Putter—(A) Typical mallet head, checkered face $60
Putter--Model 11, bent neck $60
Putter--Model 33, 2 level back $75
Putter--Model 35, long face $50
Putter--Model 64, dot face $50
Putter-Model 103, blade $50
Putter--Model A6-Vardon, iron blade $60
Putter--Model A7-Vardon, iron blade $60
Putter--Model M, gem style $80
Putter-Long blade head, shallow face $50
Putter--The Spieler model $90
Putter--Calamity Jane model, stainless, replica C.1960s $75
Putter--Harris model, long teardrop hosel $25
Putter--Square wood head, weight in toe $250
Putter--Miracle model, splice wood head, brass sole, lead face $250
Putter--Mascot model, oval hosel, dot face blade, pointed toe $250
Putting Cleek--Model 22, iron blade $50
Irons--The Spieler series, notched hosel joint .... $60 each

A late model Winton aluminum mallet putter in the style of the popular Mills clubs.

Wisden & Company, J.*
[London sporting goods house]
Mashie--Royal series, smooth face $75
Putter--Gun metal blade $125
Putter--(A) Royal series, mallet head $125
Putter--Wisden's Royal model, bent blade style, 2 lions CM $100

'Wood-Wand'
Putter--Iron blade $35

Woolley, Ted
6-Iron--Wilson Red Ribbon model, stainless, dot face $35

Worthington Company+
[Elyria, OH; largely a ball manufacturer, also produced clubs]
Driver--Socket head, W. Anderson autograph $225
Driver--Socket head, made by Worthington Mfg. Co. $150
Putter--Iron blade $60

Wright & Ditson Company+
[Boston, MA sporting goods manufacturer and retailer]
Driver--Model A, socket head, deep face $50
Driver--Model AV, circular ivorine face, 5 plugs $100
Driver--Model C, narrow head, plain face $60
Driver--Model F, small head, plain face $50
Driver--Model HV, circular ivorine face, 5 plugs $100
Driver--Model IV, circular ivorine face, 5 plugs $100
Driver--Model M, small head, plain face $50
Driver--Model N, socket head, plain face $50
Driver--Model O, ivory 2-screw face insert $150

Driver--Model P, plain face $50
Driver--(U) Model R, Rigden brass backweight $75
Driver--Model RD, plain face $60
Driver--(U) Model RJ, Rigden backweight,
3 dowel plugs in face $250
Driver--(U) Model RN, Rigden brass backweight $75
Driver--(U) Model RNC, brass one piece sole
plate/backweight $100
Driver--(U) Model RNJ, Rigden backweight,
3 dowel plugs in face $250
Driver--Model X, socket head, plain face $50
Driver--Model XBE, socket head, ivorine insert
with 9 plugs $125
Driver--Model 1, socket head, steel face $150
Driver--Model 1, socket head, plain face $60
Driver--Model 2, socket head, plain face $60
Driver--Model 3, socket head, plain face $60
Driver--Model 6, socket head, plain face $60
Driver--Model 7, socket head, plain face $60
Driver--Model 53C, socket head, black fiber
insert with 5 plugs $75
Driver--Model 53C, socket head, ivorine face insert $90
Driver--Model 56C, splice head, brass backweight $100
Driver--Dreadnought model, large socket head, plain face $100
Driver--Model 71, socket head, plain face $50
Driver--Socket head, Bamfar laminated bamboo shaft $150
Driver--(A) Square wood plug in back $200
Driver--Splice head, name in block letters $150
Driver--(B) One piece, leather face insert $1,500-2,000
Brassie--Model A, plain face $50
Brassie--Model AV, circular ivorine face, 5 plugs $100
Brassie--Model C, narrow head, plain face $60
Brassie--(U) EM model, triple splice head $400
Brassie--Model F, plain face $50
Brassie--Model H, plain face $50
Brassie--Model HV, circular ivorine face, 5 plugs $100
Brassie--Model IV, circular ivorine face, 5 plugs $100
Brassie--Model N, socket head, plain face $50
Brassie--Model O, ivory 2-screw face insert $150
Brassie--Model P, plain face $50

Brassie--(U) Model RN, Rigden brass backweight $75
Brassie--(U) Model RNC, brass one piece sole plate/ backweight $100
Brassie--(U) Model RNJ, Rigden backweight, 3 dowel plugs in face $225
Brassie--Model X, socket head, plain face $50
Brassie--Model XBE, socket head, ivorine insert with 9 plugs $100
Brassie--Model 1, socket head, plain face $50
Brassie--Model 2, socket head, plain face $50
Brassie--Model 3, socket head, plain face $50
Brassie--Model 6, socket head, plain face $50
Brassie--Model 7, socket head, plain face $50
Brassie--Model 73, socket head, plain face $50
Brassie--Dreadnought model, large socket head, plain face $125
Brassie--Model 53C, socket head, black fiber insert with 5 plugs $75
Brassie--Model 53C, socket head, ivorine face insert $90
Brassie--Model 56C, splice head, brass backweight $140
Brassie--(A) Square brass plugs in back $200
Brassie--(U) Skooter model, brass sole edge plate $250
Spoon--(A S) Long head, checkered face $250
Spoon--Model CS, socket head, plain face $60
Spoon--Model LS, long face $60
Spoon--Model 6, socket head, fiber face $60
Spoon--(U) Model 52C, fiber face insert, 5 plugs $80
Baffy Spoon--Model RS, long face $75
Wood Cleek--Model WC, long narrow socket head $150
Approaching Cleek--Dysart Fife model, made in Scotland, musselback, anvil CM $75
Approaching Cleek--Model 9, straight name stamp, smooth face $75
Cleek--(U) Cran model, wood face $700-900
Cleek--(U) Spring face model $700-900
Cleek—Horseshoe CM, smooth face $400
Niblick--Name in arc at toe, small head, smooth face, hosel knurling $650
Iron--Model 5, straight name stamp, smooth face $75
Iron--Model Y-5, youth club $35
Mashie--(U) Spring face model $750-1,000

Some early Wright & Ditson clubs were simply marked in script like this iron.

Mashie--(B) Vertical slotted face ('rake iron' type), open on bottom, Roger patent $8,000
Mashie--Junior model, stainless, dot face $25
Mid Iron--(U) Spring face model $750-1,000
Mid Iron--Kro-Flite model, line face $30
Mid Iron--Kro-Flite F 2 model, bottom half of face line scored $40
Mid Iron--Kro-Flite model, marked "Wright & Ditson, Licensees" $50
Niblic--Smooth face, concave face, small head $600
Niblic--Flange sole, dot face, lion CM $75
Mid Iron--Kro-Flite model 29, marked "Wright & Ditson, Licensees," oversize head $75
Pitcher--Kro-Flite F 7, ribbed face $100
Putter--T-shaped pendulum style head $1,200
Putter--(A) BM model, mallet head $75
Putter--Spring face model $1,000-1,200
Putter--(A) HH Model, Schenectady style $150
Putter--Travis model, square wood head, brass face $300
Putter--Rainbow model, dot face $50
Putter--(A U) Schenectady, marked in double circle

A.H. Findlay was a Scotsman who came to America in the 1880s and went to work at Wright & Ditson in 1898. This socket head driver dates from c. 1910.

Wright & Ditson outside, BGI inside $300
Putter--Model 10, wood Schenectady style, brass face $200
Putter--Model LW, oval hosel, broad flange sole $100
Putter--Model C94, oval hosel, round sole, blade $75
Putter--ARF model, long hosel, offset blade $50
Putter--Model CH (Chicopee), ... $200
Putter--Model HB, oval hosel, hollow back $200
Putter--(A) Model NH, Schenectady style with
ridge on top $150
Putter--(A) Model MR, mallet head after Ray model $75
Putter--Model RL, wood mallet head, large brass
backweight $200
Putter--Fownes model, wood mallet head with heel,
paddle handle long face $500
Putter--George Wright Autograph, stainless blade $50
Putter--Super gooseneck, gun metal $250

<><>Early clubs with script stamp
Driver--Splice head, bulger face $200
Cleek--Selected model, smooth face $100
Iron--Smooth face $100
Niblic--Smooth concave face $500
Putter--Gun metal blade $100
Putter--(A,S) $250

<><>A.H. Findlay series
Driver--Short splice head $175
Driver--Socket head $75
Driver--(A) $225
Brassie--(A) $225
Brassie--Stem shaped neck on short socket club head $350
Cleek--Smooth face $75
Mashie--Smooth face $75
Mid Iron--Smooth face $75
Niblic--Smooth face, medium head $125
Niblick--Fairlie-type (anti-shank) smooth face $225
Putter--Thick, T-shaped gun metal head $1,200
Putter--Wood Schenectady style $250

<><>St. Andrews series (earlier clubs have no CM, later clubs have

The mark of the arm holding a shot glass was for the "One Shot" series.

hammer & roses CMs)
Driver--Socket head $40
Brassie--Socket head $40
Cleek--Line face $35
Driving Iron--Line face $35
Driving Mashie--Dot face $35
Jigger--Dash face $45
Mashie--Dot face, hammer & roses CMs $25
Mashie--St. Andrews, convex dot-dash face $200
Mashie Iron--Dot face $35
Mashie Niblic--Dash face $35
Mashie Niblic--Hammer & roses CMs, dot face $25
Mid Iron--Dot face, hammer & roses CMs $25
Niblick--Dot face $35
Niblick--Hammer & roses CMs, dot face $25
Putter--Blade, dot face $40
Putter--Gooseneck blade $50
Putter--Blade, hammer & roses CMs, dot face $30
Putting Cleek--Long blade $50

<><>Juvenile clubs
Driver--Socket head $30
Brassie--Socket head $30
Cleek--Smooth face $35
Mashie--Smooth face $30
Mid Iron--Smooth face $30
Putter--Blade $35

<><>One Shot series (arm holding shot glass CM)
Approach Cleek--Model 8, musselback, dot face $60

Bee Line series clubs were made with three or four different bee designs, this being the most commonly found.

Approach Iron--Model 1, circular dot face $60
Cleek--Model 2, line face $45
Cleek--Model 3, convex back, circular dot face $60
Cleek--Model 4, Carruthers hosel, dot face $60
Cleek--Model 6, diamond/dot face $50
Cleek--Model 7, smooth face $60
Cleek--Model G9, gooseneck, beveled sole, dash face $45
Driving Iron--Model WDI, line face $50
Driving Iron--Model 1, smooth face $60
Driving Iron--Model 2, circular dot face $60
Driving Mashie--Model 1, dot face $50
Jigger--Model 1, dot face $50
Jigger--Model G4, gooseneck, dash face $50
Lofting Mashie--Model 6, diamond/dot face $50
Lofting Mashie--Model 10, dash/dot face $50
Mashie--Model 2, short head $45
Mashie--Model 3, short hosel, circular dot face $60
Mashie--Model 7, Taylor's model, deep face $60
Mashie--Model 8, diamond/dot face $45
Mashie--Model 10, convex face with lines $100
Mashie--Model G11, gooseneck, beveled sole, dash face $45
Mashie—Flange sole, dot face $50
Mashie--(D) Dedstop DS6, corrugated face $125
Mashie Iron--Model 1, dot face $45
Mashie Iron--Model 2, circular dot face $60
Mashie Iron--Model 3, line face $45
Mashie Jigger--Model 3, long narrow blade $50
Mashie Niblic--(U) Model 3, Foulis model, concave face $150
Mashie Niblic--Model 6, deep face, line face $45
Mashie Niblic--(D) Model C51, corrugated face $125

Mashie Niblic--(D) Model C92, slotted face $125
Mashie Niblic--Model C51, circular dot face $60
Mashie Niblic--Model G11, gooseneck, beveled sole,
dash face $45
Mashie Niblic--Model M, dot face $45
Mid Iron--Model WM, line face $45
Mid Iron--Model 2, smooth face $50
Mid Iron--Model 3, short head $45
Mid Iron--Model 5, diamond back, diamond/dot face $60
Mid Iron--Model 6, dot face $45
Mid Iron--Model 7, diamond/dot face $45
Niblic--Model 4, random dot face $60
Niblic--Model 6, smooth face $60
Niblic--Model 9, cross/dash face $50
Niblic--Model G5, gooseneck, dash face $50
Niblic--(D) Model C98, corrugated face $150
Niblic--Model M, dot face $45
Push Iron--Model G8, gooseneck, beveled sole, dash face $45
Sammy--Model WY, smooth face $60
Putter--Straight face, iron blade, dot face $50
Putter--Flange sole, dot face $60
Putter--Gem style, dot face $100
Putter--Model 1, gooseneck $50
Putter--Model 2, gooseneck $50
Putter--Model 5, half gooseneck $50
Putter--Model 9, Maxwell pattern, cross/dash face $60
Putter--(A) Model BM, mallet head after Braid-Mills $60
Putter--Model BV, shallow face, rounded back $250
Putter--Model F, narrow blade, line face $50
Putter--Model H. heavy offset head, diamond face $60
Putter--(A) Model RM, Ray style $70

This style of horseshoe shaped mark is the oldest of the Wright & Ditson marks and is very scarce. Names of cities other than Boston can also be found.

Putting Cleek--Model 8, circular dot face $60

◇◇Bee Line series
Driving Iron--B 1, line face $35
Jigger--B 8, line face, bee CM $60
Mashie--B 5, line face, bee CM $35
Mashie Iron--B 4, line face, bee CM $35
Mashie Niblic--B 6, line face, bee CM $35
Mashie Niblic--(D) B 6, double waterfall face $3,500
Mid Iron--B 2, line face $35
Mid Mashie--B 3, line face $35
Niblic--B 9, line face, bee CM $35
Pitcher--B 7, line face, bee CM $40
Pitcher--(D) B 7, grooved face $150
Pitcher--(D) B 17, waterfall face, bee CM $300-400
Pitcher--(D) B 17, double waterfall face $3,500
Putter--B 10, line face, bee CM $40
Putter--B 15, line face, bee CM $50

◇◇Rainbow series
Iron lubs—Graduated Irons, rainbow and bucket CM ....$40 each

Wynne, Philip*
[Chingford, London, et al]
Driver--Socket head $75
Spade Mashie--Line face, pipe CM $45

This Baxpin Mashie was sold under the Wilson Triumph brand name by Thomas E. Wilson.

The J.H. Williams Co. forged many iron heads for B.G.I., Spalding and MacGregor. They made a few marked with their own trademark.

Y

Yeoman, William+
[Chicago]
Brassie--Short splice head $150
Driver--Splice head, marked "Formerly Herd & Yeoman" $250
Named Irons--William Yeoman model, Stewart pipe CM,
scored face .... $60 each
Numbered Irons--William Yeoman model,
Stewart pipe CM, scored face .... $50 each
Numbered Irons--Stewart RTJ/FO model, line face .... $250 each

Yonkers Sporting Goods Co.
[New York City]
Niblick--Dash face $65

Youds, J.*
[Chislehurst and Hoylake e]
Driver--Short splice head $125
Driver--Socket head, face insert $60
Mashie--(B) Smith model (anti-shank), Stewart pipe CM $175
Named Irons--J. Youds model, Stewart pipe CM scored face ..$60 each
Putter--(A B) Mallet head, lead face $300

Young Company, L.A.+
[Detroit, MI; sole manufacturer of Walter Hagen brand golf clubs from 1926 onward. Also see Hagen, Walter]
Sand Iron--(U) Walter Hagen model, stainless, concave face, flange sole $350-500

Z

Zappe, S.A.
[Springfield, OH]
Driver--Socket head $75

'Zozo'
Putter—Gun metal mallet head with steel face, made by J Anderson, Anstruther $200

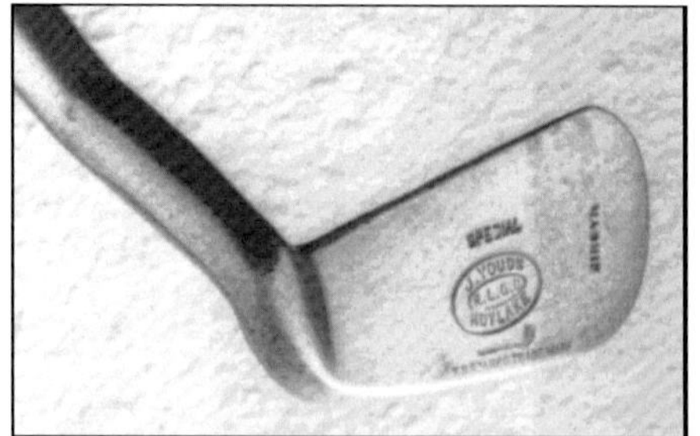

Jack Youds worked at Hoylake for many years. This Stewart forged Smith patent anti-shank mashie is marked for Royal Liverpool.

Modern Wood Shafted Putters

The following clubs made with wood shafts were produced a decade or more after the discontinuance of the general use of hickory shafts in golf clubs. These specialty putters have become collectible in recent years and are not included with the original wood shafted club entries because of their more modern manufacture dates.

There are also a large number of 'replica' and 'souvenir' putters with wood shafts in circulation. Many of these are made in Scotland and none are included here because they are considered more novelty than clubs for serious golf play. (Special thanks to Tom Stewart for his help with this list).

Auchterlonie, Laurie (D & W Auchterlonie*)
[St. Andrews, Scotland]
Putter—Classic blade in polished steel $35

Auchterlonie, Tom*
[St. Andrews, Scotland]
Putter—Classic blade in polished steel $40

Austads
[Sioux Falls, SD]
Putter—Woodie model, wood head mallet $45

Burberry
[London, England]
Putter—Old style semi-long nose $75

Billyclub Co., The
[Shreveport, LA]
Putter—Classic flange head (like 8802) with maple shaft $40

Bronty
Putter—Autograph model, classic blade $35
Putter—Gem style blade $35

Burton

Putter—Calamity Jane, brass blade, man shooting gun mark $20

Callaway

[Carlsbad, CA]

Putter—Hickory Stick, "The Purist",
mallet with brass sole and weight port $75

Putter—Hickory Stick, Billet series, black Anser type head $75

Putter—Hickory Stick, Billet series, Bobby Jones
brass flange blade $60-75

Putter—Hickory Stick, Billet series, Bobby Jones
black flange blade $60-75

Putter—Hickory Stick, Little Poison I, flange heel shaft blade $65

Putter—Hickory Stick, Little Poison II, flange center shaft blade $65

Putter—Hickory Stick, Little Poison III,
flange center shaft blade, no offset $65

Cleveland Golf

Putter—Schenectady replica, aluminum mallet $50

Putter—Calamity Jane replica $100

Chicago

Putter—CNC, milled Anser type head $25

Competitive Edge Golf

Putter—The Scottish Gem, gem style blade $30

Confidence

Putter—Intilt, classic blade $30

'Craftsman'

See MacGregor or Goldsmith

Crisman, Otey

[Selma, AL; Founded in 1946, Otey Crisman Jr. and his son, Otey III have made clubs, primarily putters under their own name as well as for a number of other companies, notably, First Flight, Scoggins, and King, all of which are stamped with the "Otey Crisman" mark in script. COLT Golf Co., N.Y. putters were made by Otey Crisman but without cleek mark attribution. Best known for his hickory shafted

putters, most models were also offered in a variety of shafts inc. steel, aluminum, bamboo or fiberglass]
Dates generally run as follows:

- *1946-1964 Clubs stamped both "Selma, Al." and the letter "C" surrounded by the letter "O" on the hitting face.*
- *1964-1977 "Selma, Al" stamp dropped but O.C. in face remains.*
- *1977 to Present - O.C. in face dropped.*

◇◇Non-"Selma" marked clubs.
Putter--(A) FLM-1, mallet head, brass insert for First Flight $25
Putter--AH, made for Scoggins $20
Putter--31H, George DeLuca Memorial Pro-Am $30
Putter--38G, brass blade, fiberglass shaft) $25
Putter--Otey Original, 40th Anniv. Ltd. Ed.(1986) $100
Putter--Model 55,Colt Golf $55
Putter--(A) 82H, Colt Golf, mallet head $55

◇◇"Selma" stamped clubs
Sand Wedge--Model 99 .... $45
Putter--(A) 12H, mallet head $30
Putter--15H, brass blade $30
Putter--(A) 18HB, mallet head, brass face insert $30
Putter--23X, brass blade, bamboo shaft $45
Putter--34H, stainless steel blade $30
Putter--Silver Touch model, nickel silver blade $40
Putter--(A) 70B, mallet, brass face insert $30
Putter--NN1, brass blade $30
Putter--Bell S model, similar to Ping (rings like a bell) $45
Putter--(A) Croc H, croquet style head $200
Putter--(A) 111H, "bassackwards" $175

◇◇Modern Era
Putter—Bullseye shape head, First Flite model $25
Putter—Brass blade, First Flite model $25
Putter—FS2, mallet head $35
Putter—Cash In style blade $30

Dinaire
[Buffalo, NY]
Putter—Square wood center shaft head $15

Dunlop
Putter—Dow Finsterwald model, mallet head $30

Dudley, Ed
Putter—Penny Head Mallet,
US penny set in crown over sweet spot $50

F & F
[Roslyn, NY]
Putter—Model E888, brass blade $25

Fernquist & Johnson
[Colma, CA]
Putter—Tony Lema Golden Gate model, brass flange blade $50
Putter—Heel shafted flange blade $40
Putter—P-1
Putter—P-2 P models are Acura Brand
Putter—P-3 All P model mallet heads made from "Tenzaloy"
Putter—P-4 with bronze face .... $45 each
Putter—P-5
Putter—P-6

Goldsmith+
[Cincinnati, OH]
Putter—Craftsman, bronze blade, long square hosel 'Bench Made' ... $40

Golf Design
Putter—"Rolls In" model, brass blade $15
Putter—Black flange blade, Anser style $25
Putter—Reliable two, Ducks Unlimited, flange blade $30
Putter—Reliable, aluminum & brass mallet, putting man mark $30

Gradidge
[London]
Putter--Bobby Locke autograph model,
stag head CM $75

Haas, Freddie
Putter—H26, aluminum & brass mallet $35

Putter—H29U, mallet $35

Hawaiian Lightning

[Honolulu, HI]

Putter—Flanged blade, Ironmaster style $30

Hill Company, Tom

[Salem, OR]

Putters—15 traditional head shapes available ....$25-30 each

Hillerich & Bradsby ("H & B"; "PowerBilt")+

[Louisville, KY]

Putter—Miller Barber model, aluminum & brass mallet $40
Putter—Alum & brass mallet (like, and made by Otey Crisman) . $40
Putter—H-50, from 1940s, aluminum mallet $40
Putter—45HB, bullseye type blade $25
Putter—P-42W blade $30
Putter—Citation blade $35
Putter—The Dewdrop, aluminum mallet head $35
Putter—Invincible (1939) offset steel blade $35

Hogan, Ben

[Ft. Worth, TX]

<><>Macdougall-Carnoustie series putters
Model P-200, brass blade $100
Model P-202, semi mallet $100
Model P-204, thick blade $100
Model P-206, mallet $100
Model P-208, streamliner $100
Model P-210, adjustable weight mallet $100

Hunter, Mac

Putter—"Auld Blade", traditional blade $20

Johnson, Frank

[Portland, OR]

Putter—Continental model, aluminum mallet $40
Putter—"Original Combo," wood and aluminum mallet $40
Putter—Lloyd Mangrum, aluminum mallet for GolfCraft $35

L Cast, The
Putter—Ironmaster type head $25

MacGregor+
[Dayton, OH; other cities later]
Putter--Model 102GH, Mity Mite, Bob Toski
autograph, bronze w/ heel & toe chromed $45
Putter—Model 102GH brass back mallet $30-50
Putter—Yardsmore wood mallet (reproduction, edition of 500) $175-200
Putter—Craftsman, bronze blade, long square hosel 'Bench Made' ... $40

Master Wand
Putter—Bullseye type head in wood, wood grip $30

Matzie
Putter—Velvet Touch, heel shafted, flange blade $35
Putter—Velvet Touch, aluminum mallet with brass face $35
Putter—Velvet Touch #15 .... $35
Putter—Velvet Touch, 95H, classic brass blade $30
Putter—Velvet Touch, El Toro model, Cash In style blade $30

Morris, Tom (Shop)*
[St. Andrews, Scotland]
Putter—Steel blade $35
Putter—Model 61
Putter—Model 62 Four putters whose model numbers designate
Putter—Model 64 the years in which Tom won the Open ...... $50 each
Putter—Model 67

Nicklaus, Jack (made by Swilken)
[Columbus, OH]
Putter—Replica of Condie/Winton/Acton Calamity Jane
presention club for 1976 Memorial Tournament,
signature on shaft $500-750

Nicoll, George*
[Leven, Scotland]
Putter--Gem model, chromed finish, modern hand mark $35
Putter--White heather model, blade $30
Putter--Splice wood head, perforated leather grip $30

Northwestern Golf+
[Chicago]
Putter--Forward Thrust model, shaft with offset
bend 6" above hosel $25
Putter—Model 1000, Forward Thrust Johnny Revolta autograph,
24K gold plated mallet $30
Putter—Model 1000 mallet $25
Putter—Model 4300, blade $25
Putter—Model 700, octagonal wood shaft $25

Orvis Co., Charles F.
[Manchester, VT]
Putter—Model 33, bronze center shaft rocker $50
Putter—Model 37, bronze goose neck blade $50
Putter –Model 70, aluminum goose neck mallet $50
Putter—Model 99, aluminum center shaft mallet $50

P.G.A.+
Putter—Velvet Touch, blade $35

Pedersen+
[Mt. Vernon, NY]
Putter—Center shaft brass flange blade $35

Poppe, E.R.
Putter—Model 201, mallet head, brass face plate $40

Richter, Ben
Putter—"Old Timer" mallet head $45

Rosasco Bros. (made by Northwestern)
Putter—Uniwood 70, wood and brass mallet $25

Sayers, Ben*
[North Berwick, Scotland]
Putter—"Old Nick" steel blade with pointed toe,
made for Jack Nicklaus, then placed into production $45
Putter—Benny model, post war version, grooves in sole of blade $45

Sears (made by H & B)
Putter—Doug Ford model, flange blade, marked Levelume $35

Smith, Ted
Putter—Model 8 .... $35
Putter—Aluminum mallet, weights in sole $40
Putter—Blade putter $30
Putter—Model 22, head like Ironmaster $40

Spalding+
[Chicopee Falls, MA]
Putter--Blue Chip model, flanged blade $50-56
[the Blue Chip also was made in a steel shaft model]
Putter--Calamity Jane, cartoon lettering $45-75
Putter--Calamity Jane model, anvil CM, markings
painted colors $50-75
Putter--Calamity Jane model, Winton/Condie replica $50
Putter--Chicopee model-1960s replica $100
Putter—Deadline mallet $30

Super Max II
Putter—Flange brass blade $20

Sutters Mill
Putter—Heel shafted flange blade $25

Thompson, Stan
Putter—Gasser model, offset blade $35

Throughway Putters
Putter—Model 555, center shaft mallet $30

U.S. Royal
[Toledo, OH]
Putter—Model 5130, low profile offset blade $25

"Wee" Scot Golf Co, Inc.
[Montgomery, AL]
Putters—15 different shaped heads in most traditional patterns,
available w/ wood shafts .... $35 each

Weetman, Harry
Putter—Blade with "58" on face,
former British Ryder Cup player and captain $40-60

Wilson, Thomas E.+
[Chicago]
Putter—Mark Harris model, classic blade $35
Putter—TNT model, classic blade (1940s) $35
Putter—Ray Mills aluminum mallet (1940s) $35
Putter--Perfect Balance model, iron blade with brass face $45
Putter--283 model, standard blade, Gene Sarazen autograph $75
Putter—The Sinker, brass blade (1941) $35

Wood Wand
Putter—Wood and brass mallet, wood grip $35
Putter—Flange brass blade, wood grip $35

Pete Georgiady's

Playing golf at the National Hickory Championship

ABOUT PETE GEORGIADY

Pete is, without doubt, the most scholarly collector I have yet come upon. He has an unabated love for British golf, especially the formative years in Scotland. In addition to obtaining two degrees from Miami University in Oxford, Ohio he attended law school at Dundee University in Scotland. It was there his interest in golf collecting actually began.

He was befriended by an elderly resident of the city who, after recognizing Pete's love for the game, gave him his first wood shafted golf club, a 1915 Braid-Mills aluminum mallet head putter. Pete laughs as he says, "I thought it was valuable beyond all consideration because it was old and unusual. I came to find out that it was very common." His father gave him two more wood shafted clubs the following Christmas, and thus the malady of golf collecting had claimed another victim. He started scouting around Salvation Army stores and thrift shops to "collect anything and everything with wood shafts. My love for Scotland made me especially interested in clubs of Scottish origin."

Pete quickly developed a burning desire to know who made the various clubs he acquired. The thing that sets him apart from most collectors is the voluminous research he does. He has spent countless hours pouring over golf handbooks, trade publications, patent journals and advertisements. Over the years he has undertaken and successfully completed some extensive research projects including those on deep groove irons and aluminum headed clubs. Pete has also identified more than 1000 different cleek marks. As he got more and more into this process he wanted to learn all he could about the club makers. On trips to Scotland he spent much time with the late Eric Auchterlonie from whom he learned so much about early Scottish club makers. Pete's Compendium of British Club Makers is the authoritative work on the subject and before his death, Eric wrote the foreword for that volume.

During the rare hours that Pete is not involved in golf research, golf collecting or golf writing, he is probably checking internet reports of his beloved Manchester United Football Club. He is an avid fan of English and Scottish Premier League soccer. His son Bryan has inherited his father's love of golf and has begun his own collection with a special interested in Old Tom Morris. Pete also enjoys playing golf and antiquing with his lovely wife Kay. Their home is a pleasant mixture of antique items and golf memorabilia.

For me, one incident accurately reflects Pete's expertise on golf history. At a recent Annual Meeting of the Golf Collectors Society, the after dinner speaker cancelled at the last moment. The Committee turned to Pete and, with little notice, he gave n informative and entertaining speech. He is able to combine an encyclopedic knowledge of old golf clubs with a modest personality and an effusive sense of humor. I have learned more about the history of the game of golf from Pete than any other person and perhaps that is the highest compliment of all.

Dan Bagdade
West Bloomfield, Michigan

Resources

If you are interested in collecting golf clubs (and other items and meeting other collectors)...

GCS — The Golf Collectors Society
PO Box 2386
Florence, OR 97439
www.golfcollectors.com

BGCS — The British Golf Collectors Society
Hamish Ewan, Membership Secretary
20 Druim Ave.
Inverness IV2 4LG, Scotland
www.britgolfcollectors.wyenet.co.uk

If you have an interest in playing golf with hickory shaft clubs...

SoHG — The Society of Hickory Golfers
Roger Hill, Membership Chairman
2875 Cascade Springs Dr. SE
Grand Rapids, MI 49546
www.hickorygolfers.org

NHC — The National Hickory Championship
PO Box 981
Kernersville, NC 27285
www.nationalhickory.com

If you're interested in seeing old golf clubs in a museum setting...

USGA — The Museum of the United States Golf Assn.
77 Liberty Corner Rd.
Far Hills, NJ 07931
www.usga.org

WGHoF — The World Golf Hall of Fame
I-95, exit 323 International Golf Parkway
St. Augustine, FL 32092
www.wghof.com

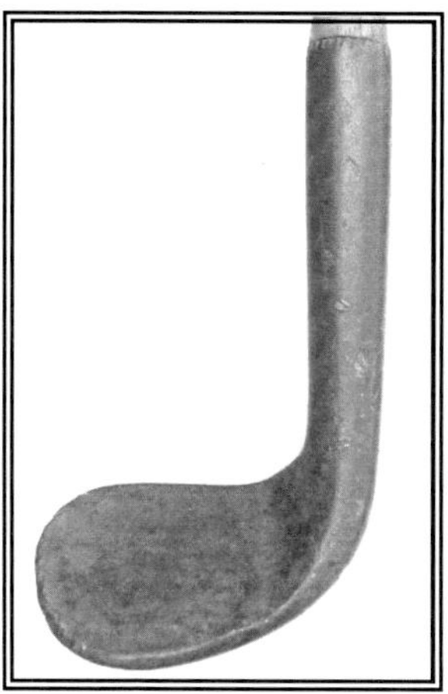

A small headed niblick or rut iron from the 1880s made by F & A Carrick, Musselburgh. The only mark on the club is the small Carrick cross.
(page 84)